RED RISING
RED ECLIPSE

Edited by
Geremie R. Barmé

with
Jeremy Goldkorn

Carolyn Cartier and Gloria Davies

CHINA STORY YEARBOOK 2012

Australian Centre on China in the World
中华全球研究中心 / 中華全球研究中心

ANU College of Asia & the Pacific
Canberra, Australia

Note on Visual Material
All images in this publication have been fully accredited. As this is a non-commercial publication, certain images have been used under a Creative Commons license. These images have been sourced from *flickr*, and the owner of each original picture is acknowledged and indicated in the source information.

ISBN 978-0-9873655-0-7

First published in August 2012
THIS BOOK IS NOT FOR SALE

Published by:
Australian Centre on China in the World
The Australian National University

Edited, typeset and illustrated by Markuz Wernli Design Works
Printed by Blue Star Print Canberra, Australia

The Australian Centre on China in the World is an initiative of the Commonwealth Government of Australia and The Australian National University

CONTENTS

China Story Yearbook 2012

INTRODUCTION

RED RISING

Geremie R. Barmé

A Year of the Dragon

A dragon at the Nine-dragon Wall in Beihai Park, Beijing.
Photo: Geremie R. Barmé

The start of 2012 ushered in another Year of the Dragon according to the twelve-year cycle of the traditional Chinese lunar calendar. It also marked a time of pre-ordained political change – over the following year and a half, the leaders of China's Communist Party and civilian government would hand over power to the next generation.

A son born in a Dragon Year can be a blessing. 'May the son become a dragon' (a success) is an ancient benediction: this birth year is associated with enterprise, intelligence and daring. Yet China's political leaders know all too well that Dragon Years are also fraught with hidden dangers: ambition can easily be frustrated and the best laid plans can go awry. The Dragon Year of 1964-1965 saw the first stirrings of Mao Zedong's Cultural Revolution in the form of the Socialist Education Movement in the countryside. The next cycle in 1976-1977 witnessed natural disaster, political upheaval, Mao's death and the unravelling of his revolutionary enterprise, while the economic and cultural ferment of 1988-1989 called forth a nationwide protest movement culminating in its suppression by massive state violence on 4 June 1989.

Initially, observers both inside and outside China presumed that the years 2012-2013 would see an orderly transition of power and the untroubled retirement of a generation of party-state leaders, from Communist Party General Secretary Hu Jintao and State Premier Wen Jiabao downwards. Even within China's Communist Party, however, there were already signs of discontent – over corruption, social anomie and the perceived stagnation of the economy and the political system.

The year 2011 had seen a rise in protest against underlying systemic problems. It started out with police clampdowns on protests inspired by the Arab Spring. In the middle of the year, a disaster involving the country's much celebrated new high-speed rail system at Wenzhou, near Shanghai, killed dozens of people; the accident raised serious questions about the accelerated rate of construction and frenetic change in the country. The year ended with villagers in the southern province of Guangdong revolting en masse against the collusion between local party bosses and unscrupulous developers that had resulted in brutish land-grabs. Increased surveillance of the Internet, which played an ever-increasing and unpredictable role in these unsettled times, was also a sign of official anxiety that social unrest could escalate into violence and trigger wide-scale rebellion.

Meanwhile, continued ethnic tensions in China's west – Xinjiang and Tibet – led to waves of protest and repression. In its immediate region, China had been increasingly aggressive in pressing its territorial claims over the South China Sea. Since 2009, bellicose statements by several army leaders had alerted the international community to the new realities they faced with a country that was mov-

The Beijing Olympics

At the auspicious hour of 8:08 pm on the eighth day of the eighth month of 2008 (8 August), the XXIXth Olympiad began in Beijing with an opening ceremony extravaganza directed by the filmmaker Zhang Yimou. Beijing had become only the third Asian city to host the Olympics.

It was the hottest month of the year, but thanks to the shutting down of industry, a strict system of traffic management and even 'rainmaking' cloud-seeding to clean the air, the city's usually stifling summer smog-haze was kept at bay. Still, human rights activists, particularly concerned with the recent crackdown in Tibet, held their noses. Regardless, the international community supported China's hosting the summer games thanks in no small part to US$44 billion in expenditure, the construction of twelve large sporting facilities, a restructuring of the city's transportation system, an extensive program to relocate polluting industries, a multiyear propaganda blitz and 'civilizing' campaigns aimed at improving civic behaviour.

The Games enjoyed unprecedented popularity, breaking records for TV audience numbers. The Chinese national team won a record fifty-one gold medals and the US swimmer Michael Phelps won eight gold medals – the most ever won by an athlete in one Olympics. The overall result was deemed a resounding success by the Chinese government, the majority of participants and most media observers.

The positive impact of the Games can still be seen in Beijing today. Plastic shopping bags still have to be purchased and are no longer given away by supermarkets, new subway lines have opened up and older ones extended and public transport is more convenient than ever. That said, air pollution is more noxious than ever and the giant Bird's Nest stadium where the opening and closing ceremonies were held in 2008 looms on the north central axis of the city, costing more money to run than it can generate in income.

Still, China's self-image was burnished by the Games, and the smooth management of the event is held up by the official media as one of the country's greatest recent national achievements.

ing away from a former policy of 'hiding its light' and biding its time (*tao guang yang hui* 韬光养晦) to one of asserting its influence on the world stage. Some commentators have chided China condescendingly as demonstrating 'adolescent behaviour'. Others saw China's precipitous rise to regional and global stature from 2008 onwards as thrusting the current political leadership into an international role for which it was ill-prepared given the decades of self-imposed isolationism under Mao and the eclectic approaches to 'opening up' under Deng and since. Moreover, the unhappy legacies of the past – the bullying conduct of the West and Japan in the colonial era as well as the post-World War II international dominance of the United States and its concomitant hostility to China – together with the fractured interests of the countries of Asia and the Pacific and Japan's economic sluggishness also contributed to China's assertiveness.

Fireworks at the Beijing National Stadium – the 'Bird's Nest' – on the night of the Opening Ceremony of the XXIXth Olympiad, 8 August 2008.
Photo: Lois Conner

Tour of the South (*nanxun* 南巡)

During the seventeenth and eighteenth centuries, the Kangxi and Qianlong emperors of the Qing Dynasty whose rule represented the greatest Prosperous Age (*shengshi* 盛世) in Chinese history, revived the ancient practice of the imperial tour of inspection, or 'imperial progress'. 'Tours of the South' became major events in imperial administration.

Mao Zedong frequently 'toured the south', spending much of his time away from Beijing. In 1992, Deng Xiaoping undertook what was officially described using the imperial-era term *nanxun*, travelling to Shanghai and Guangdong province. The tour signalled to the nation his commitment to economic reform and market-driven prosperity. Remarks he made during the tour contributed directly to a new stage of the country's economic opening up and market reform.

International leaders welcomed Chinese capital to help stabilize European financial institutions in the ongoing financial crisis of the Eurozone. Several business commentators lauded the Beijing model as a success story about state capitalism married to authoritarian politics. In China, there was growing discontent and alarm over corruption and official brutishness. Some see systemic change – a liberalization of the one-party political system – as a possible way ahead; others on the left are critical of an authoritarian market economy in league with global capital. As the contributors to this volume show, in the years between 2008 and 2012 there are Chinese citizens who regard a return to socialist values, Mao-era egalitarianism and a strong populist one-party state as the solution to China's mounting social crises. Others believe that the political and media reforms promised at the hopeful start of the country's transition to a market economy thirty years ago remain the vital remedy. Still others note that following the successful 2008 Beijing Olympics, China has witnessed the reassertion of the party-state (that is, Communist Party control over the civil governmental bureaucracy, the one inseparable from the other) in major aspects of national life.

The result is a series of contentions over the national narrative required to articulate the next stage of economic reform and the country's modern transformation. 'Collective vision' is an integral part of political rhetoric under the Communist Party. In practice, we find in recent years the divided agendas of a cautious, fearful and time-serving bureaucracy with a vested interest in maintaining the status quo.

An Overlooked Anniversary

The China Pavilion, 2010 Shanghai Expo.
Photo: Geremie R. Barmé

At the start of 2012 there were muted commemorations of the 1992 Tour of the South (*nanxun* 南巡) that Deng Xiaoping, the celebrated 'grand engineer' of China's open door policies, undertook after economic reform stalled in the wake of the Beijing Massacre of 3-4 June 1989. The massacre had brought an end to the 'chaos' of nationwide student-led demonstrations in favour of freedom of expression and government accountability. It had also thrown into doubt the reformist agenda of Deng and his allies; for a time, economic conservatives and ideological neo-Maoists held sway and along with a clampdown on all forms of public protest, further economic liberalization was sidelined. Deng realized that China was in danger of going the way of the Soviet Union and that if the welfare and prosperity of the majority of China's people was neglected, as it had been with disastrous consequences under Mao Zedong, his own attempts to bring the country into the global market economy and to play a major role in world affairs would be thwarted.

In early 1992, during what was ostensibly a family holiday, Deng Xiaoping toured the southern cities where economic liberalization and market economies had been allowed. He warned his fellow Party members that they could not afford the luxury of continued ideological wrangling over whether economic reform and engagement with the international economy was by nature 'socialist' or 'capitalist'. Development, he declared, was an inescapable necessity; ideological and systemic stagnation were the enemies of future prosperity. His words (and behind-the-scenes politicking) ignited a wave of change in China that has since awed the world. His efforts were formally recognized at the Party's Fourteenth Congress in October 1992, setting an economic course for the country that was maintained for the next two decades.

Red Boomers

The red boomers, or 'princelings' (*taizi dang* 太子党), typified by the deposed Chongqing Party Secretary Bo Xilai and president-in-waiting Xi Jinping, are the generation of men and women born either at the war-era Communist capital of Yan'an in Shaanxi in north-west China in the 1940s, or around the founding years of the People's Republic. For decades the progeny of Party leaders at all levels have been active both politically and economically. Through alliances, marriage and various coalitions of interest they form a complex socio-political strata in the Chinese world.

In February 2012, Premier Wen Jiabao made his own southern trip and in Guangdong he invoked the memory of Deng's Tour of the South by pointedly repeating his predecessor's calls for continued reform in China. Quoting Deng he said: 'Opening-up and reform should be implemented unswervingly, or there will only be a dead end.' Nonetheless, the twentieth anniversary of Deng's original tour passed with scant celebration in Beijing. It was a sign, perhaps that, faced with myriad other problems, the country had lost its enthusiasm and will for further, necessary change. Some critics declared that Chinese 'crony capitalism' and 'vested interests' – long evident in the country, and identified in their nascent form by the protesters of 1989 as a major threat to the country's future – were frustrating reform of the state sector. 'The state', they warned, 'was on the march and private enterprise was in retreat.'

In 1992, Deng and his supporters in the army pushed for a new agenda of accelerated development in which they sidelined attempts by left-leaning and even Maoist ideologues to slow down the pace of market reforms. Twenty years later, in 2011-2012, left-leaning thinking was again a feature of political infighting. For neo-Maoists and a range of left sympathizers, both inside and outside the Party and army, the status quo was evidence that traitors were pursuing their own economic agenda at the behest of international capitalism and that they were selling out the country to Western (that is, US) interests.

It is against this backdrop that the change of Party and state leadership would take place in 2012-2013. Moreover, this time around, and for the first time in the history of the People's Republic, true heirs of the dragon, that is the progeny of the founding party rulers of modern China, were jockeying for key command jobs in the Party's highest decision-making bodies.

Red Boomers

A group called the 'revolutionary successors', that is children of the Communist leaders born in the 1940s up to the time of the founding of the new state in 1949, first made a play for power in the early months of the Cultural Revolution of 1966. As high-school students initially favoured by Mao for their ideological fervour, they enjoyed privileged access to state information due to their parents' positions in the Party hierarchy. This led them to believe they would play a leading role in shaping the nation's future, or as the phrase has it, directing China's 'rivers and mountains' (*jiangshan* 江山). These ambitious high-born adolescents helped create the idealistic and iconoclastic Red Guard movement that gained notoriety for violence. The support they received from Mao was short-lived. They were soon cast aside for their links to Party leadership figures when the old guard itself became the target of Mao's plan for 'continuous revolution'. Over the 'vested interests' of the Party's leading bureaucrats and their progeny, Mao advanced a new and unaffiliated cadre of activists that for nearly a decade steered the country on a radical path.

The now displaced revolutionary successors joined countless other former Red Guards in a forced march to the countryside and factories for re-education by the labouring masses. They have bided their time for nearly fifty years, establishing political powerbases and commercial empires throughout the country from the smallest locality to the largest urban megalopolis.

The two revolutionary successors to gain the greatest international name recognition in the transition years were Xi Jinping, son of the general Xi Zhongxun (1913-2002) who helped oversee early economic reform in China's south, and Bo Xilai, whose father was Bo Yibo (1908-2007), a party planner extraordinaire. Both men were tipped for power, Xi as General Secretary of the Communist Party and President of China, and Bo for possible entry into the Standing Committee of the Party's ruling Politburo. Their individual machinations – a vast and intricate power play involving in-coming as well as out-going leaders – were pursued under the cover of consensual politics.

Poster for *The Xinhai Revolution*, a 2011 film produced to commemorate the centenary of the rebellion that ended China's dynastic political system.
Photo: Geremie R. Barmé

Besides Xi and Bo, other members of this group of 'red boomers' have also agitated to be recognized as the rightful heirs of the revolution. Among them, many like Bo have flaunted a leftist stance and attempted to act as a loyal opposition to the mercantilist policies of a party they feel had lost its moral and revolutionary moorings. These leaders and others had been jockeying for key posts in the new line up for the Politburo and State Council for years.

What could be dubbed the Chinese party-state's electoral cycle actually began in the lead-up to the Olympic year of 2008. Numerous events provoked the hyper-nationalism of that time, most notably, the March 2008 uprising in Tibetan China and the debacle of the Olympic Torch Relay the international progress of which was dogged by human rights protesters. The resulting fervour was in part directed by Xi Jinping in Beijing, in patriotic defence of state action against Tibetan protesters and rights activists. Bo Xilai, meanwhile, was championing mass media cosmetic socialism – 'red culture' – in the province-size autonomous city of Chongqing in the country's south-west which he ran as Party Secretary. Other signs of this disquieting shift were China's harsh demeanour and hard line at the November 2009 Copenhagen talks on climate change followed not long after by the intimidating behaviour on display in relation to territorial disputes with the country's neighbours in the South China Sea.

Just as the power transition began in February 2012, the mysterious death of an Englishman in Chongqing and the attempt of Bo Xilai's police chief and right-hand man, Wang Lijun, to seek refuge in the US Consulate in Chengdu threw Bo Xilai's carefully-laid plans for ascension into chaos. Then, in March, with his wife under suspicion for the Englishman's murder and his police chief allegedly having revealed all manner of malfeasance related to Bo Xilai's rule in Chongqing, Bo himself was removed from his post and disappeared from sight. For years commentators had presumed there would be a relatively unruffled leadership handover in China. Suddenly the world gained a glimpse of the fractious nature of the country's politics, and the ideas and interests that motivate it. For some weeks after Bo's downfall, the leftist ideology of the Mao era that he had revived in his bid for power continued to be volubly defended by many Party members, army leaders and intellectuals.

One day before the sensational news of Bo Xilai's fall was announced, Premier Wen Jiabao spoke at what would be his last press conference as the head of China's government. Twice Wen referred to the 1981 Communist Party decision on 'certain historical questions'. That document provided the ideological rationale for China's post-1978 economic reforms. A carefully worded text, it formally negated the socio-economic policies that had underpinned the Mao era, including the Great Leap Forward and the Cultural Revolution. Wen referred to the 1981 decision in the following way:

> I want to say a few words at this point, since the founding of the People's Republic of China, under the leadership of the Party and the government, our country's modernisation drive has made great achievements. Yet at the same time, we've also taken detours and have learnt hard lessons. Since the Third Plenum of the Eleventh Party Central Committee [in December 1978], in particular since the central authorities took the decision on the correct handling of relevant historical issues, we have established the line of thinking and that we should free our minds and seek truth from facts and we have formulated the basic guidelines of our Party. In particular, we've taken the major decision of conducting reform and opening up in China, a decision that's crucial for China's future and destiny.
>
> What has happened shows that any practice that we take must be based on the experience and lessons we've gained from history and it must serve the people's interests. The practice that we take must be able to stand the test of history and I believe the people fully recognize this point and I have full confidence in our future.

Over a year before Bo Xilai was put under investigation for breaching Party discipline, there were signs that ideological contestation and a concomitant power struggle were well under way. The last major public power struggle within the Chinese Communist Party (CCP) occurred in 1989, and in recent times commentators on China have pondered the possible forms that jostling for position within the top Party echelon might take in the current iteration of China's brand of one-party consensual authoritarianism. Such educated guesses, known as Zhongnanhai-ology, remain at best an imaginative art. It is all but impossible to track effectively the backroom dealings, the power plays and the political feints involved in what is a byzantine process. Nonetheless, the media provide some indication of the nature of intra-party tussles.

Regardless of who rises or falls during 2012-2013, the Chinese Communist Party's nomenclatura, whether they have a family pedigree or not, face a profound dilemma: how do the contending individuals, factions and groups allow this extraordinary nation to flourish locally and globally while dealing with parochial or vested interests and the exigencies of situations requiring immediate solution? How does the Party maintain stable rule and legitimate succession despite having reneged on seventy years of promises to introduce democracy, basic freedoms and oversight of its power? These problems are not unique to China but they are particularly acute at present. China has a political system conceived at the time of the Russian Revolution nearly a century ago. It is a system not open to public debate and despite the appearance of bureaucratic order and functionality, its operations often recall its underground, conspiratorial and mafia-like origins.

China's labyrinthine politics in which personal alliances and loyalties are tangled with regional alignments and commercial interests complicate the present regime's aspiration to high professionalism and reasoned idealism. These competing impulses, together with the simple survival instincts needed for success in leadership contests, demand a multi-dimensional approach for any deeper analysis.

China's prominence in the Asia and Pacific region as well as its increased role on the international stage mean that many aspects of Chinese reality now attract global media coverage. These include: the behaviour of the government both at home and abroad, the country's rapidly changing urban and rural landscape, the ideas that enliven public and elite debate, influential religious beliefs in Chinese society today and the government's response to them, the Internet and censorship, the current situation and future prospects of the rule of law and human rights, and many other issues besides.

The China Story

The song-and-dance extravaganza staged on 8 August 2008 for the Opening Ceremony of the Beijing Olympics offered an enthralling account of China's great traditions and its aspirations. It was just after that opening ceremony that I was invited on 9 August 2008 by the then Australian Prime Minister Kevin Rudd to join him in conversation with a number of Chinese officials and individuals. They included a leading Party propagandist who emphasized how the events of 2008 brought home the importance for China to tell the world its own story – what he called *Zhongguode gushi* 中国的故事 that is 'The China Story'.

As is so often the case with such encounters, this senior bureaucrat was interested in 'using the foreign to serve China'. Indeed, he enjoined us in the language of friendship diplomacy to act as a bridge between China and the world. Having spent my professional career as an historian attempting to understand, translate and relate 'Chinese stories' and not to convey to others a monolithic 'China Story', I remarked that it was the plurality of Chinese stories, be they in the People's Republic or globally, that form the natural bridge to an understanding of China today.

Telling national stories has been part of the creation of nation-states since the nineteenth century, and many history projects have been devised as part of or, at least, under the umbrella of creating a foundational narrative for the political purpose of nation-building. The China Story, as part of the official Chinese narrative, has in recent years served as propaganda for continued one-party rule in a highly unequal society.

If we wish to be critically engaged with China, we must understand the official discourse and its historical and ideological underpinnings. We need to be alert to the highly orchestrated nature of the official 'Chinese world view' and to discern the gulf between it and the larger Chinese realities, possibilities and uncertainties that it seeks to obscure. To the extent that the government compels the media to endorse party-state programs and pronouncements, the information approved for publication often reflects something of what I have called 'China's Flat Earth'.

Approaching The China Story as scholars and educators requires us to bring an empathetic understanding to the task. We must pursue facts with sensitivity to people's often-raw emotional reactions to the received history and the political uses made of that history. We should also heed differences and similarities between the values inherent in The China Story and those enshrined in the stories we tell of ourselves, our society and our nation. We also should be alert to the ways in which the official national 'China Story' is used to legitimate countless local Chinese stories, ways of leveraging, negotiating and bypassing in provincial China the strictures of Beijing. The approach that frames the writings of this volume, one based on what I call a New Sinology (*Hou Hanxue* 后汉学), resonates with Clive James's observation of a form of humanistic inquiry that is distinguished by 'its hunger, its scope, its vitality and its inner light – an inner light produced by all the aspects of life illuminating one another, in a honeycomb of understanding.'

The *China Story Yearbook*

China Story Yearbook is a project initiated by the Australian Centre on China in the World (CIW) at The Australian National University (ANU). It is part of a broad project aimed at understanding The China Story, both as portrayed by official China, and from various other perspectives. Our Centre on China in the World is a Commonwealth Government-ANU initiative that was announced by then Australian Prime Minister, the Hon. Kevin Rudd MP, in April 2010 on the occasion of the Seventieth George E. Morrison Lecture at ANU. The Centre was created to allow for a more holistic approach to the study of contemporary China: one that considers the forces, personalities and ideas at work in China when attempting to understand any major aspect of its socio-political or cultural reality. The Australian Centre on China in the World encourages such an approach by supporting humanities-led research that engages actively with the social sciences. The resulting admix has, we believe, both public policy relevance and value for the engaged public.

This first volume of the Centre's *China Story Yearbook* takes as its theme the colour red, and the title *Red Rising, Red Eclipse*. We believe that the red of Party control, of state enterprises, of reformulated Party ideology and culture, the red dominion of the party-state over the individual and the red successors who have been moving onto centre stage are a particular feature of the political transition period that began furtively in 2008. In the years 2009 to 2012, the colour red featured also in the major celebrations of the Chinese state and the Communist Party – the commemoration of the sixtieth anniversary of the

George E. Morrison

George Ernest Morrison (1862-1920) was an adventurous Australian traveller who arrived in Beijing in 1897 as China correspondent for *The Times* of London. He later served as an advisor to the Chinese government following the Xinhai Revolution of 1911 and the establishment of the Republic of China. He was an *engagé* writer and avid collector of books whose library formed the basis of the renowned Toyo Bunko in Tokyo. The major shopping thoroughfare in central Beijing, Wangfujing, was during most of the Chinese Republic (1912-1949) known as 'Morrison Street' in honour of its famous inhabitant.

In 1932, the inaugural 'George Ernest Morrison Lecture in Ethnology' was delivered in the new Australian capital city of Canberra; the annual lecture series continues to be held at The Australia National University (see: http://chinainstitute.anu.edu.au/morrison/).

Building the Wangfujing Mall on what was once known as 'Morrison Street' in 1998. The reconstruction of Wangfujing entailed the demolition of George E. Morrison's house.
Photo: Lois Conner

founding of the People's Republic of China on the 1 October National Day of 2009, which was marked by a grand parade in the heart of the Chinese capital, just as the marking of the ninetieth year since the foundation in July 1921 of the Chinese Communist Party led to months of media-saturated celebration in 2011. The red symbolism of politics, society and culture will remain a fixture of the Chinese world for some time to come, but the fall of Bo Xilai in early 2012 and the seeming lack of viable long-term solutions to China's socio-political problems also cast a shadow over the country's contentious red traditions.

Long ago, Mao Zedong warned that after his death careerists and opportunists would attempt to use the Party's ideology to justify a return to what he called the 'bourgeois dictatorship'. These traitors to the revolution would, he said, 'wave the red flag to oppose the red flag' (*da hongqi fan hongqi* 打红旗反红旗). In recent years China's 'new left' (an ill-defined coalition of mostly armchair Marxists, academics and proto-patriots) and neo-Maoists have criticized the economic reforms for doing just that, and they have supported those populists who would raise once more a red banner to forge a path for China's future. For them the Asia-Pacific century should be led by a return to the red past. Others argue that only by reforming the political party that Mao helped create and by establishing a modern polity that better reflects the will of the majority of Chinese can the nation enjoy a global status and future worthy of its size and promise.

The specialists whose work features in *Red Rising, Red Eclipse* are members of or associated with the Australian Centre on China in the World. They survey China's regional posture, urban change, social ativism and law, economics, the Internet, history and thought. Their contributions cover the years 2009-2011, updated to mid 2012 and offer an informed perspective on recent developments in China and what these may mean for the future. *Red Rising, Red Eclipse* provides a context for understanding the underlying and ongoing issues of modern China, issues that will resonate far beyond the Dragon Year of 2012–2013.

China Story Yearbook is produced by the Australian Centre in the World in collaboration with the Danwei Media Group in Beijing, a research organization that has been collecting and collating Internet and media information in and on China for CIW and this project since 2010. The chapters are arranged thematically and they are interspersed with information windows that highlight particular words, issues, ideas, statistics, people and events. Shorter essays, or 'interstices', provide updates on relations between the polities on either side of the Taiwan Straits, on disturbances in Tibetan China and Xinjiang, as well as top ten lists and highlights of Chinese achievements. A list of People and Personalities and a Chronology at the end of the volume provide an easy reference for words, peoples and events featured in the body of the text. Footnotes and the CIW-Danwei Archive of source materials are available online at: www.TheChinaStory.org

Acknowledgements

The editorial group that has overseen this project led by Geremie R. Barmé consists of Jeremy Goldkorn, Carolyn Cartier and Gloria Davies. Jeremy and his colleagues at Danwei Media in Beijing – Eric Mu, Joel Martinsen, Freedom Zeng, Barry van Wyk and Nicholas Richards – provided updates of Chinese- and English-language material relevant to the project, as well as helping to compile much of the information used in the additional windows in chapters and interstitial essays. Mark Harrison agreed to write on cross-strait relations and Chris Buckley offered a series of comments on the Chongqing and Guangdong models. Robbie Barnett and David Brophy read over the material on ethnic China and Lois Conner kindly provided us with the cover image. Multimedia Services, ANU College of Asia and the Pacific created the maps in Chapter 2 and we are particularly grateful to Linda Jaivin for her extensive and painstaking editorial work on the final draft of the manuscript, as well as to Glen Rose for copy-editing the final text. Markuz Wernli created the elegant visual and typographical style of the book.

Chapter Motifs

Each chapter in this book is introduced by a pictorial motif. They are:

Introduction: the head of a dragon, inspired by dragon boat at the Yihe Yuan Summer Palace in Beijing.

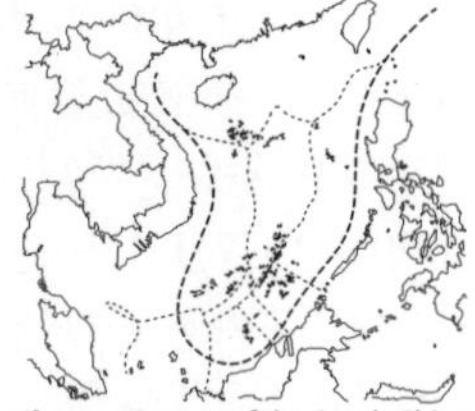

Chapter 1: map of the South China Sea.

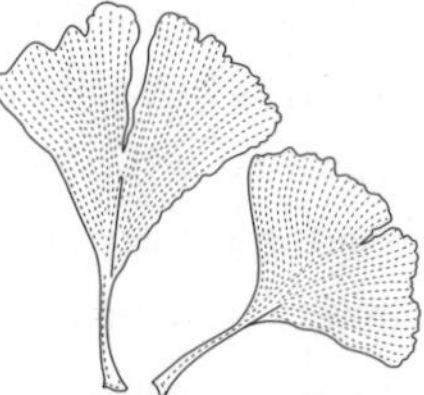

Chapter 2: the leaf of a gingko tree, a reference to the mass planting of gingkos during Bo Xilai's tenure as Party Secretary of Chongqing.

Chapter 3: a crab with three watches. The 'river crab' (*hexie* 河蟹) is a mocking reference to 'harmonising' (*hexie* 和谐) or Chinese government censorship on the Internet. The three watches (*san ge biao* 三个表) is a pun on the 'three represents' (*sange daibiao* 三个代表) Jiang Zemin-era Party theoretical formulation of the year 2000 that declared: 'the Party must always represent the requirements of the development of China's advanced productive forces, the orientation of the development of China's advanced culture, and the fundamental interests of the overwhelming majority of the people in China.'

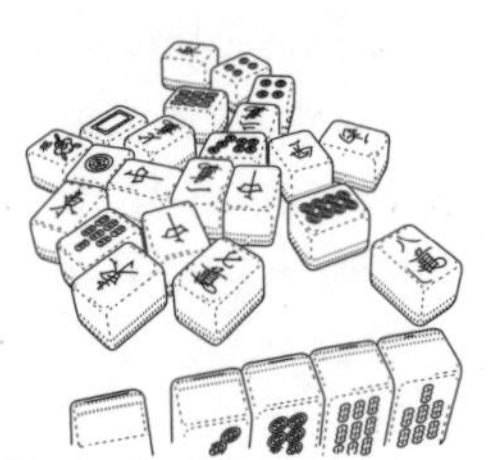

Chapter 4: mahjong tiles.

Chapter 5: a jasmine flower, which was banned in China for some months due to the 2011 Jasmine Revolution in the Middle East.

Chapter 6: a caricature of the modern-day pseudo-sage Li Yi, pictured in a gourd, a traditional Taoist symbol related to alchemy.

Chapter 7: a map of of China's high-speed train system.

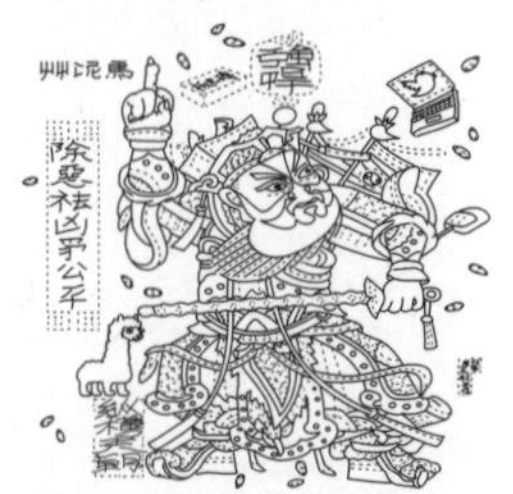

Chapter 8: a temple door god as reinterpreted by Ai Weiwei's studio.

Chapter 9: a temple door god as reinterpreted by Ai Weiwei's studio.

Chapter 10: *huabiao*, the leitmotif of this volume.

The Cover Image

Huabiao 华表 are sculpted marble pillars. Such pillars are entwined by a carved dragon, pierced by a decorative wing-like cloud and topped by a crouching animal. They traditionally feature at entrances to palace buildings, imperial ancestral temples and along processional paths. The stylized cloud represents what in ancient times was called the Board of Criticism and Protest, or the 'wood of direct speech' (*feibang zhi mu* 诽谤之木). These boards were affixed to pillars situated outside the palace or court so that common people could write complaints about their rulers on them. Subsequently, even in their highly abstracted form, the pillars were supposed to symbolize the right of the people to speak out against official injustice and to demand conscientious government. Tiananmen Gate in central Beijing is flanked by *huabiao*.

A *huabiao* painted by an unknown artist on a wall in Beijing.
Photo: Lois Conner

Bo Xilai, during his tenure as Mayor of Dalian, Liaoning province (1993-2000), ordered the construction of a *huabiao* twice as large as those in front of Tiananmen. Critics commented that the appearance of a mammoth *huabiao* in the city's Xinghai Square was an early sign of Bo's 'imperial presumption'.

1

1

CHINA'S FOREIGN POLICY AGGRESSIVENESS

Brendan Taylor

THIS CHAPTER analyses the 'aggressive turn' in Chinese foreign policy during the 2010–2011 period, including examples and sometimes competing explanations. It also surveys international reactions to shifts in Chinese policy, including a backlash from other countries in Asia. While most of these seem keen to maintain equidistance between China and the United States, the sharp and public debate that China's foreign policy provoked in Australia illustrates the policy dilemmas that an increasingly assertive China will inevitably generate.

今年中菲禮樂灘衝突事件簿

時間	地點	事件
3月2日	禮樂灘海域	兩艘中國海軍巡邏船阻止正在作業的一艘菲律賓石油勘測船, 菲兩架軍機一度升空
5月11日	禮樂灘海域	兩架懷疑來自中國的戰機與菲律賓軍機對峙空域
10月18日	禮樂灘海域	菲巡邏艦誤撞中國漁船, 菲國防部道歉

Map and timeline of incidents between Chinese and Philippine vessels in the South China Sea in late 2011 and early 2012.
Source: the nationalist and military affairs website Tiexue.net (aka 'Ironblood Forum')

The most puzzling and perturbing aspect of Chinese foreign policy during the 2010-2011 period was its growing aggressiveness. Over the previous decade, Beijing had made considerable diplomatic inroads in Asia. This was particularly evident in Southeast Asia, where some analysts went so far as to suggest that China was carving out a 'sphere of influence' through its kinder, more nuanced 'new' diplomatic approach. A flurry of books and articles emerged pointing to the growth in Chinese 'soft power'. Yet within a relatively short period of time, all of this work appears to have been undone. Scholarly and journalistic accounts alike now rarely refer to Beijing's 'softer side', pointing instead to the dangers of an 'assertive China' and to an emerging Cold War between Beijing and Washington.

China's Assertive Turn

The rise of any great power tends to generate apprehension and a heightened sense of instability in the international community. By the mid-1990s, such fears were already beginning to intensify with respect to China. This was reflected by the emergence of a cottage industry of writings discussing the 'hegemon on the horizon' and the prospect of a 'coming conflict with China'. The so-called 'China threat' of the 1990s was multi-faceted, stemming from a variety of disparate concerns including Beijing's human rights practices, its growing economic power and military might, and its exercise of the latter with respect to a number of security flashpoints such as disputed territories in the South China Sea and the Taiwan Strait.

Peaceful Rise and Peaceful Development
(*heping jueqi* 和平崛起; *heping fazhan* 和平发展)
Zheng Bijian, the former Vice-president of the Central Party School, is often given the credit for popularizing the term 'peaceful rise'. Speaking at the 2003 Bo'ao Forum for Asia, a forum for world leaders modelled on the Davos event and held in China's Hainan province, Zheng said China should be: 'integrated into economic globalization yet not overly reliant on foreign countries; achieve modernization not through military expansion like Western powers did, or through industrialization at the cost of damaging the environment.' Zheng further noted that China should make a bigger contribution to the development of all humanity (paraphrasing a line from Mao Zedong).

The phrase 'peaceful rise' soon found favor with China's leaders and became common in official speeches, until it was later modified into a more politically sensitive 'peaceful development' – 'development' apparently a more benevolent and less aggressive sounding word than 'rise'.

A previous use of the word 'peaceful' to describe changing China – the 'peaceful evolution' strategy of John Foster Dulles – was firmly rejected by Mao Zedong in Hangzhou in 1959 and again by Deng Xiaoping following 4 June 1989. Both claimed that 'peaceful evolution' was part of a US-led global conspiracy to see communism replaced by a liberal, bicameral democracy that would inevitably turn China into a mere economic vassaldom of the West.

On the surface at least, by the late 1990s China had gone a long way toward alleviating these concerns. Beijing introduced a 'new security concept' which sought to dispel the adversarial mentality that was a dominant feature of the Cold War paradigm that had held sway from the 1950s until the late 1980s. At the same time, the People's Republic of China became increasingly engaged with multilateral organizations – particularly in the Asia-Pacific region – where previously it had harboured deep suspicions regarding the underlying motivations of such groupings. China's diplomacy became increasingly nuanced and sophisticated, as demonstrated most visibly in the astuteness of its diplomatic appointments. In the early 2000s, China introduced foreign policy concepts formulated in terms of a 'peaceful rise' and 'peaceful development', reinforcing the sense that benign intentions underpinned China's (re)emergence on the world stage.

Even as recently as 2008-2009, against the backdrop of Sino-US cooperation in the context of the emerging global financial crisis, optimism surrounding the rise of China allowed eminent American figures such as Zbigniew Brzezinski and Henry Kissinger to entertain the prospect of a 'G2' arrangement between the world's two dominant powers – the US and China – to address the world's most pressing security challenges. By late January 2010, however, this sense of optimism was rapidly evaporating. Reacting to the decision of the Obama administration to approve the sale of Black Hawk helicopters and *PAC-3* missiles to Taiwan – a relatively inconsequential package in practical and historical terms – the Chinese suspended military exchanges with the US and threatened to impose sanctions against American companies involved in arms sales to Taiwan.

Beijing's opposition to US arms sales to Taiwan was not unexpected (and neither surprising nor unprecedented). Chinese policy-makers have criticized previous announcements, such as in April 2001 when the new George W. Bush administration pledged that America would do 'whatever it took' to help Taiwan defend itself in the event of an attack from the mainland and the following day unveiled an arguably more provocative package. Yet, most analysts concur that Beijing's January 2010 response was far more strident. In the following months, this rhetorical bellicosity extended to a range of other issues that have long dogged Sino-US relations. These include extensive hacking of the Internet company Google that allegedly originated in Chinese universities and the valuation of the Chinese currency, the Renminbi. Then, following US President Barack Obama's meeting with the Dalai Lama in late February 2010, an editorial in the official *People's Daily* asserted that: 'a significant fact he can never change is that the Tibet issue is China's internal affair and a powerful China has become a significant force in the world political structure.' While China had long rebuked foreign leaders for meeting with the Dalai Lama, a man they regarded not as the head of a government-in-exile, but rather as a traitor and a dangerous 'splittist', the tenor of the official response to the February meeting contained a new warning.

China has become equally assertive in other key bilateral relationships, especially in the case of Japan. Indeed, perhaps the clearest example of the new tenor of Beijing's foreign policy occurred in September 2010, when a Chinese fishing vessel collided with a Japanese Coast Guard vessel, leading Tokyo to detain the captain of the offending boat. The incident provoked anti-Japanese demonstrations in China – and vice versa – while

The Fishing Vessel Incident, September 2010
The Nanjing Massacre Controversy, February 2012

Sino-Japanese relations have experienced periods of tension since imperial Japan's colonization of large parts of China from the early twentieth-century and particularly as a result of what China calls the 'Anti-Japanese War' (7 July 1937 – 2 September 1945). After the fall of the Republican Chinese capital of Nanjing on 13 December 1937, some 300,000 people are said to have been killed in a frenzy of mass murder and rape carried out by Japanese troops: the 'Nanjing Massacre'.

Both Japanese and Chinese scholars and officials have long accused the other side of falsifying history: China blames Japan for not apologizing sincerely enough for war atrocities, while some in Japan argue that Chinese governments have always exaggerated the death toll in Nanjing. The depiction of the war in Japanese highschool textbooks has been a focus of contention since the 1980s. Over the years, visits by senior Japanese politicians to the Yasukuni Shrine, a memorial to Japan's war dead in Tokyo that houses the remains of soldiers and military figures whom China (and other countries) consider war criminals, have provoked Chinese sensitivities. Former Prime Minister Koizumi Junichiro's decision to make an annual pilgrimage to the shrine during his tenure from 2001 to 2006 sparked outrage in the Chinese media, anti-Japanese demonstrations in Beijing and Shanghai, and inspired some of the earliest outpourings of online nationalist rage from what are now called China's 'angry youth' (*fen qing* 愤青).

In September 2010, a Chinese fishing trawler and a Japanese Coast Guard vessel collided in disputed waters. The Japanese Coast Guard detained the trawler's captain. A Japanese court ruled that he had broken maritime laws and was liable for damage to the Japanese patrol vessel. The Chinese government denounced the detention as illegal and suspended high-level diplomatic exchanges with Japan. Small-scale anti-Japanese protests broke out in various Chinese cities. After seventeen days in Japanese custody the captain was released. He returned to China on a chartered plane sent by Beijing and welcomed home in the media as a hero.

In February 2012, Kawamura Takashi, the mayor of Nagoya, made a comment in which he denied that the Nanjing Massacre had taken place. As a result, the Nanjing authorities suspended its city's sister-city relations with Nagoya and there was another outburst of patriotic fury on the Chinese Internet and in the media.

Beijing responded by demanding the captain's immediate release and allegedly blocking the export of rare earth metals (an abundance of which are mined in China) to Japan. Even following the captain's release Beijing continued to demand compensation from Tokyo.

China's 'assertive turn' also manifested itself with respect to two of the region's major flashpoints. On the Korean Peninsula, Beijing's responses to North Korea's sinking of the South Korean Navy corvette *Cheonan* in March 2010 and shelling of Yeonpyeong Island in November of the same year sharply departed from the spirit of Sino-American cooperation on security issues on the Korean Peninsula from 2003-2010. Following the sinking of

A Xinhua News Agency rendering of an imaginary future development on Yongxing Island 永兴岛 (also known as Woody Island and Đảo Phú Lâm) in the South China Sea.
Source: Xinhua News Agency

the *Cheonan*, Beijing waited more than a month before offering condolences to Seoul. The delay generated widespread resentment amongst the South Korean public. Beijing also stymied efforts to resolve either the Cheonan or the Yeonpyeong Island crises through the agency of the United Nations and doggedly refused to criticize Pyongyang's provocations. Chinese policymakers vociferously protested US carrier deployments to the region in the aftermath of the two crises, insisting that US-South Korea military exercises should not be held in the Yellow Sea. Washington and Seoul chose to ignore Beijing's objections and the exercises went ahead, largely without incident.

China's greater stridency was even more apparent with respect to the South China Sea. A key 'tipping point' came when, in March 2009, five Chinese vessels performed aggressive manoeuvres against a US surveillance ship – the USNS *Impeccable* – in the waters of the South China Sea. Washington had previously remained largely neutral with respect to South China

China and North Korea

In 1950, 500,000 Chinese troops marched into the Korean Peninsula as a 'volunteer army' fighting in support of the communist-led Democratic People's Republic of Korea (DPRK) against the forces of the Republic of Korea and their American allies. Three years of fighting led to a stalemate and split the peninsula in two.

A decade after the cessation of overt hostilities (no peace accord has ever been signed), on 11 July 1961 China and the DPRK signed the Sino-North Korean Mutual Aid and Cooperation Friendship Treaty. The agreement announced mutual exchanges in trade and defence, among other areas; it has subsequently been renewed every twenty years. The current treaty is valid until 11 July 2021.

Trade with China has become essential for the North Korean economy, and China is known as one of the regime's only substantial friends. Yet Beijing has limited influence over the North Korean leadership and there is increasing evidence that China is tiring of the North's erratic behavior, particularly regarding their drive for nuclear weapons, not to mention their dynastic politics.

Sea issues, but this incident piqued its interest and Secretary of State Hillary Clinton subsequently referred to the matter as being of US 'national interest' at a July 2010 gathering of the ASEAN Regional Forum (ARF). The Chinese Foreign Minister responded by conveying Beijing's strong opposition to any efforts to 'internationalise' the issue. Subsequently, China's approach to the South China Sea has become more assertive not only in word but also in deed. It has conducted an increasing number and range of military exercises – both naval and air – there and added to its maritime patrols in the region, something that has led to a rise in the number of clashes with Philippine and Vietnamese vessels.

Beijing's claims with respect to the South China Sea has strained what had become increasingly friendly and close ties with many if not most governments in Southeast Asia. At the November 2011 meeting of the ASEAN-led East Asia Summit (EAS) in Indonesia, ASEAN leaders (with strong US backing) insisted that this issue be placed on the agenda over Beijing's objections. Chinese Premier Wen Jiabao was forced to discuss the South China Sea and broader related questions of maritime security with seventeen other Asian leaders.

Western analysts tend to attribute the increasingly strident nature of Beijing's diplomacy to the growth in Chinese economic and strategic weight and the sense of national hubris that this has instilled. For scholars such as the 'realist' John Mearsheimer, Chinese assertiveness is largely unsurprising: rising powers generally seek to gain power at the expense of others to further their ultimate goal of becoming the dominant actor in the international system. This explanation also notes that China's growing foreign policy assertiveness since 2010 coincides with a perception that US power is in decline. This perception stems from America's role in the global financial crisis as well as its protracted military commitments in Iraq and Afghanistan. These wars have proven costly, both financially and in terms of their impact upon international perceptions of the US. Some commentators suggest that under such circumstances any accommodatory gestures on the part of the US toward a rising China are interpreted by Beijing as an indication of incipient Western weakness. Concomitant perceptions of Japanese decline – the other historical great power of East Asia – further reinforce this sense of Chinese hubris.

A second line of reasoning – one more popular amongst Chinese analysts – explains Beijing's newfound assertiveness as a direct response to external pressure and provocations. This line of argument posits that, rather than throwing its growing economic and strategic weight around, China is merely 'pushing back' against a succession of US actions such as the January 2010 US arms sales to Taiwan, Obama's decision to meet with the Dalai Lama in February 2010, Washington's overt expressions of support for Google and continuing American pressure on China to revalue its currency. Reflecting this school of thought, a February 2010 article carried in the government-run English-language *China Daily* observed that: 'looking at each of Obama's decisions at face value, his policies do not differ from those of his predecessors. But his timing – one blow quickly followed by another – has infuriated China's leaders. The importance of saving face in Chinese culture is well known.'

A third school of thinking attributes China's 'assertive turn' to the influence of domestic politics. There are several variations on this theme. One suggests that Chinese assertiveness is a temporary phenomenon that reflects the jostling for power among elites in the lead up to the 2012-2013 leadership transition. According to this view, Beijing's behavior with regard to its foreign policy posture is cyclical in nature and will likely be modulated once the leadership transition has been completed. A second variation, however, characterizes China's stance as reflecting a 'secular shift' in Beijing's foreign policy approach. This shift is seen to stem from the increased number of bureaucratic actors in the Chinese foreign policy process – some of whom benefit directly from tensions in the US-China relationship and through the maintenance of close ties with pariah states such as Iran and North Korea. It also owes something to the proliferation of Internet and other media platforms by which Chinese citizens can criticize their leadership on nationalist grounds. China's leaders are sensitive to the prospect described by Thomas Christensen wherein 'nationalist pundits and bloggers in China find allies in high places' to push mutually compatible agendas.

China's growing assertiveness has major benefits for Washington. As Carl Thayer observes, for example, 'recent Chinese military assertiveness in the Western Pacific and the South China Sea provides a stimulus for stepped up US-Vietnam military cooperation. Both countries share an interest in preventing China or any other country from dominating seaborne trade routes and enforcing territorial claims through coercion.' It has given

China and Myanmar

In the last decade, China has invested heavily in Myanmar and provided some political support for what has until recently long been a pariah regime. China has bought Burmese oil and is considering developing a deep-water port on its coast that could service the trans-shipment of goods to Yunnan and elsewhere in south-western China. Burma, as it then called itself was the first non-communist country to recognize the People's Republic of China, establishing diplomatic ties with Beijing in 1950. Trade between the two countries is now worth over US$1.4 billion per annum.

During the 1950s and 60s, Burma remained neutral in regard to matters concerning China. During the Cultural Revolution period (1964-78) relations soured when Chinese communities were expelled from Burma.

Relations improved when Deng Xiaoping came to power and withdrew support for the Communist Party of Burma. Cross-border trading soon opened and military support from China poured in. In 1988, after the government brutally crushed pro-democracy protests, the international community turned away from Burma, giving Chinese influence free rein.

In September 2011, following popular protests by Burmese, work was halted on a Chinese-funded dam construction project at Myitsone. Since then, the release of the opposition leader Aung San Suu Kyi from house arrest, elections, and thawing relations with Washington have contributed to changing the dynamics of Myanmar's relationship with China.

a similar boost to US cooperation with a number of other countries including Australia, India, Indonesia, Japan, the Philippines and South Korea, and the Obama administration has made a conscious effort to re-engage with this part of the world, particularly the Southeast Asian sub-region.

Yet it would be a mistake to jump to the conclusion that many of these Asian governments are abandoning altogether their relatively longstanding 'hedging' strategies of maintaining a degree of diplomatic and policy equidistance between the US and China and gravitating unequivocally into America's orbit. In the case of India, although some American analysts advocate deepening strategic ties between Washington and New Delhi in a way that would be of similar geopolitical significance to the normalization of US-China relations during the 1970s, India continues to exhibit a strong preference for strategic independence in foreign relations. Reflecting this, a headline carried on the front page of the influential *Hindustan Times* in November 2011 read: 'Assertive India Takes on China, US in Global Game'. The article discussed ongoing tensions between China and India over the latter's oil and gas exploration efforts in the South China Sea, while highlighting a recent meeting between the Indian Prime Minister Manmohan Singh and the Chinese Premier Wen Jiabao in which the two leaders pledged to develop 'the best of relations' and agreed that the '21st century belongs to Asia'.

Other Asian governments have also equivocated in the face of China's foreign policy stance. South Korea is fond of metaphorically characterizing itself as a 'shrimp between two whales'. It has made it clear that it does not want to be dragged into a conflict involving the US and China. While South Korea's alliance with the US has strengthened since the election of President Lee Myung-bak in December 2007, Seoul has also initiated an annual South Korea-China-Japan trilateral summit which, significantly, excludes the US. South Korea also held its first 'strategic defence dialogue' with China in July 2011, during which Beijing and Seoul pledged to deepen their bilateral military exchanges and cooperation, not only in relation to Korean Peninsula security issues but also in the areas of peacekeeping, disaster relief, humanitarian aid and anti-piracy.

Tanks on Jianguomen Avenue on their way to join the military parade marking the sixtieth anniversary of the founding of the People's Republic of China, 1 October 2009.
Photo: Jeremy Goldkorn

Yet questions are being raised as to the sustainability of such equidistant postures over the medium-to-longer term, particularly during an era where China is becoming increasingly assertive, and in an atmosphere of heightened tensions between Beijing and Washington. As Robert Kaplan noted in an oft-cited article about growing tensions over the South China Sea: 'Asia cannot continue to change economically without changing politically and strategically; a Chinese economic behemoth naturally will not be content with American military primacy in Asia.' Kaplan was referring specifically to a heated Australian foreign policy debate regarding appropriate responses to the rise of an increasingly powerful and assertive China. This debate has attracted a somewhat disproportionate level of international attention given Australia's relatively small size. As Brad Glosserman has observed, the Australian debate: 'deserve[s] more attention for this discussion is or will be taking place in capitals throughout the region, although there is little chance it will be as public or as sharp. Australia is the canary in the Asian security coal mine.'

Australia's China Debate: a warning to the world?

Australia itself has been a focus of China's foreign policy assertiveness. Australia's most intense experience of this occurred in 2009 – a year that then-Australian Ambassador to China Geoff Raby characterized as the '*annus horribilis* of Sino-Australian relations'. Beijing's response to the Australian Defence White Paper of May 2009, for instance, was reportedly one of 'fury': a senior Australian defence official and the lead author of the document, Mike Pezzullo, was reportedly told by Chinese officials to water down its references to China or 'suffer the consequences'. Two months later, China lambasted the Australian government for ignoring pressure from Beijing and granting a visa to the Uyghur human rights advocate Rebiya Kadeer so that she could attend the Melbourne International Film Festival. More recently, responding to Obama's November 2011 announcement while on a visit to Australia that up to 2,500 US marines would be deployed to Darwin, for instance, an article carried in the semi-official *Global Times* indicated that governments lining up alongside the US would suffer economic reprisals. Reports also appeared in the Australian media suggesting that Beijing had 'demanded' answers to its concerns related to the planned deployment of marines and associated military equipment in Darwin.

Australia's own 'China debate' was sparked in September 2010 by the publication of *Power Shift: Australia's Future between Washington and Beijing*, a *Quarterly Essay* written by the Australian academic and former senior defence official Hugh White, discussing how Australia should respond – diplomatically and strategically – to the rise of China. White began the essay with the observation that the US-led security order that Australia had enjoyed for the better part of four decades was challenged by China's rise. He argued that any new order that replaces it will be a far more contested and potentially far less peaceful one. China will seek increased influence commensurate with its growing power, an outcome that the US will seek to prevent because it would involve treating China as an equal. White made the case that most Australians were oblivious to this looming challenge, mistakenly believing that Canberra can continue to enjoy the luxury of not having to choose between its leading trading partner (China) and its leading strategic ally (the US). White advocates that Australian policy-makers should abandon this sense of complacency and initiate a diplomatic campaign designed to persuade Beijing and Washington to construct a great power 'Concert of Asia' that would also include India and Japan and that would be modelled upon the Concert of Europe of the nineteenth century.

White's essay provoked a visceral reaction from some quarters. *The Australian* newspaper's foreign policy editor Greg Sheridan described it as the 'stupidest strategic document ever prepared in Australian history.' Much of the criticism directed at White's important contribution was not quite so polemical, however, and can be divided into four basic arguments:

- that White had overestimated the sustainability of China's growing power through underestimating the significant raft of domestic challenges which Beijing must deal with at the same time;
- that White had erroneously underestimated the durability of US primacy in the Asia-Pacific and that his predictions of American decline were exaggerated;
- that White had overlooked the role that other regional powers – namely India, Japan, South Korea and Vietnam – can play in countering China's growing power and, hence, in constituting regional order; and, finally,

Australia and China

The interests of great powers will be most closely engaged in Asia and the Pacific. In the absence of a conscious effort on the part of all, ours could become a more strategically contested region. We can assert that both Australia and China will maintain an ongoing interest in stability, and that political cooperation will serve the needs of both countries. Unlike other aspects of the relationship, political relations and international cooperation are areas that are most clearly dominated by the two governments. In the international political arena the extent and nature of cooperation between Australia and China will be determined on a political level. Overall, both governments are highly likely to continue to seek to develop a deeper, sustainable and increasingly mature relationship. But on occasion different views and different interests will come into sharp contrast.

—from *Australia and China: A Report on the Australia-China Bilateral Relationship*, co-written by the Australian Centre on China in the World and The China Institutes of Contemporary International Relations, Canberra: CIW, ANU, 2012, p.46.

- that White's policy prescriptions were unduly Euro-centric in nature and thus of dubious application to the highly variegated and diverse Asian region.

Australia's 'China debate' was given further impetus in early 2011 when Ross Babbage of the Kokoda Foundation launched his confrontational report *Australia's Strategic Edge in 2030*. Babbage started from the premise that Canberra ought to respond to the challenge of China's rise by adopting a strategy focused on the direct defence of Australia. Such a strategy would mimic elements of China's 'asymmetric warfare' approach by developing the capacity to offset and deter China's capacity to operate in Australia's air and maritime approaches. Babbage argued that Australia could achieve such an outcome by acquiring capabilities – including nuclear-powered submarines, arsenal ships armed with cruise missiles, and special forces designed for long range missions – that would provide Canberra with the capacity to metaphorically 'rip an arm off' China in the case of conflict. Babbage ultimately conceded that conflict between the US and China is not inevitable, however, and for this reason he also advocated that Canberra should continue to engage strongly and positively with China and its neighbours.

As with White, Babbage's paper has been subjected to four different lines of criticism:

- that it is unduly provocative and risky. It could even prompt a nuclear-armed China to take pre-emptive action against Australia;
- that Babbage severely overestimates the strength of a Chinese military that possesses equipment vastly inferior to that of the US, and that has yet to be tested in modern conflict. It will likely remain unable to project its power over vast distances for some time yet;
- that Babbage grossly overestimates the damage that Australia – a so-called 'middle power' at best – could inflict upon a great power such as China; and, finally,

- that Babbage overestimates the financial capacity of Canberra to fund his preferred policy prescriptions, not least in an environment where an ageing population and degrading infrastructure will likely place increasing strains upon the Australian defence budget.

Three features of Australia's ongoing 'China debate' seem particularly worth mentioning in terms of their broader international relevance. The first is the extent to which Australian perceptions of China's rise have entered the public consciousness and the degree to which they have shifted during the 2010-2011 period. Prior to the release of White's essay, the issues were being debated but largely in academic and government circles. That has now changed and China's rise is being discussed more broadly. Segments of the Australian population are gradually developing a more nuanced understanding of its ramifications.

China and India

China and India are the two most populous and rapidly developing nations on the planet. They share a strong relationship, but there is mutual distrust and many points of contention.

Border disputes that were the cause of a war in 1962 as well as border skirmishes in 1967 and 1987 remain unresolved. The possibility of further conflict still exists since China lays claim to areas of Indian territory, although increased trade has strengthened relations. China's strong ties with and support of India's rival, Pakistan, are another sore point.

India has not recognized China's status as a market economy. China's rise has led to talk of a 'China threat' from some Indian officials and widespread and negative discussion of China in the Indian media and Internet. Indian nationalist sentiment is strong, and news stories are often sensationalized to cast China in an unfavourable light. India, by contrast, rarely inspires lively discussion on the Chinese Internet or in the media, although prejudices regarding India are common.

Power Shift

As its power approaches America's, we can be sure that Beijing will not settle for less than a place among equals in a collective leadership for Asia. It would rather risk greater disorder than accept that it has no more influence than it was accorded in 1972. The question, then, is whether the other great powers are prepared to concede that much. In particular, will America be prepared to sit down with China as an equal?

—from Hugh White, *Power Shift: Australia's Future between Washington and Beijing*, Quarterly Essay 39, 2010, p.24.

Recent polling suggests that while continuing to offer strong support for the American alliance a growing number of Australians realize that this strategic relationship could compromise their country's all important trading relationship with China. A substantial seventy-four percent of the Australian public feels that Australia should not become involved on the side of America in any future conflict over Taiwan. Contrary to earlier characterizations of the region's future as a *Pax Americana* and an 'Asia-Pacific Century', Australian politicians have begun employing such alternative descriptors as a *Pax Pacifica* and the 'Asian Century'. Consistent with this, subjects normally regarded as articles of faith in Australian foreign policy – such as the US alliance and Australia's middle power status – are now also openly discussed and debated, often provoking quite passionate reactions. As the former Australian Foreign Minister Gareth Evans has observed, these are 'uncomfortable' topics for Australians to talk about. That such a perceptual shift could occur relatively swiftly in a 'hard case' such as Australia – a country steadfastly wedded over a long period of time

A propaganda billboard in Baoji city, Shaanxi province.
The slogan reads: 'The people build the people's air defences; the people's air defences are for the people'.
Photo: Geremie R. Barmé

to its alliance with the United States – suggests the likelihood of similar deviations occurring elsewhere as the practical ramifications of China's rise come into sharper relief.

Second, the debate has attracted considerable attention beyond Australia's shores, particularly in China and the US. As noted previously, prominent American analysts such as Kaplan and Glosserman, for instance, have each made explicit mention of White's *Quarterly Essay* in their work. I was also particularly struck when visiting Beijing in November 2010 by the degree of familiarity exhibited by Chinese scholars and policy analysts – and even students – with the arguments advanced in White's 'Power Shift' thesis. Less comforting was the fact that many of these scholars and analysts appeared to rely heavily on the Australian media and blog sites such as The Interpreter, produced by the Sydney-based Lowy Institute for International Policy, as the primary and in many cases the only sources of information regarding Australian perspectives on China's rise. One certainly does wonder and worry about how Beijing interprets it when an individual as prominent as Babbage – who served as one of three experts on the external review panel for Australia's 2009 Defence White Paper – is quoted in these outlets proposing that Australia should develop 'the capability to stir serious internal disruptions and even revolts in the event that the Chinese leadership threatened Australia's vital interests.'

Finally, the lack of engagement thus far by Chinese Studies and other regional specialists in Australia's 'China debate' has been one of its most disappointing and worrying features. The one notable exception here is an excellent paper written by Scott Dewar, an advisor to former Australian

The South China Sea

The South China Sea channels a third of the world's shipping and is rich with islands, fisheries, oil and gas deposits. It is also one the most disputed areas in Southeast Asia and has the most potential for armed conflict.

China, Taiwan, Vietnam, the Philippines, Indonesia, Malaysia and Brunei have made overlapping territorial claims to these waters, as well as to some of the islands and rocky outcrops in them such as the Paracels and the Spratly Islands. Small naval confrontations and skirmishes between official vessels and fishing boats of various nations are common.

In late 2011 and early 2012, US President Obama was widely interpreted to have made an 'Asian pivot', referring to his government's renewed emphasis on the Asia Pacific and military and diplomatic ties with Vietnam and other south-east Asian countries.

Prime Minister Kevin Rudd, who wrote under the auspices of the Australian Centre on China in the World (CIW) while on a six-month secondment at The Australian National University. Dewar concluded his paper by saying:

> Since the end of the Cold War, Australians have had little or no reason to consider great power politics. America has been pre-eminent. Systemic financial instability and terrorism have been a focus of international cooperation. The situation has now changed. The recent threats to our national wellbeing have not evaporated, but they are now part of a complex strategic landscape that includes great power politics focused on our region.
>
> Hugh White is right to ask how we will deal with this new situation. The great power politics that will take place in our region over the next two decades will be a crucial determinant of our future. We need to engage with the great powers to ensure that our interests are registered. But it is not in our interest to be the proposers of a radical shift in the geopolitics of our region. In the short term it would not work; in the long term it could well backfire.
>
> What we need is a nuanced and incremental approach to our foreign policy that adapts our settings to changing circumstances and does not overly constrain our ability to respond to future events. To support the development of such a policy approach, a deep debate about the future of our region is essential. White's essay has made a provocative contribution to start that process. This paper, too, aims to join that discussion.

Beyond Dewar's important contribution, however, most if not all of Australia's leading China specialists are working either in government or at universities, and it seems fair to conclude that neither setting produces the strongest of professional incentives to engage in public debate. Hence, while the absence of area studies specialists (that is those with an expertise in the study of Asia and the Pacific) from Australia's China debate is understandable, it is also unfortunate and potentially somewhat risky. For if the failure of International Relations scholars and strategic analysts to predict the ending of the Cold War taught us anything, it is of the importance of being able to open up the 'black box' of foreign policy-making processes – as Graham Allison famously put it in his classic study of the Cuban Missile crisis – to understand the domestic drivers that invariably condition these processes. Fine as the strategic analysts currently engaged in Australia's China debate unquestionably are, they each – unlike Chinese Studies specialists – have a tendency to still largely treat China as a unitary actor. They thus tend to underestimate – whether consciously or inadvertently – the centrally important influence of domestic politics, social change and cultural perceptions in framing and shaping Chinese foreign policy. Looking forward to 2013, finding ways to better encourage China scholars everywhere to engage in the debate – bringing to it much-needed texture and nuance – is a major and absolutely critical challenge. Outside the US, this is not something which is thus far occurring as systematically as it could and should be, though the present volume as well as the CIW-CICIR (Australian Centre on China in the World and The China Institutes of Contemporary International Relations) *Australia and China, A Joint Report on the Bilateral Relationship*, launched in Beijing in February 2012, are both contributions along these lines.

US Marines in Darwin

During his first visit to Australia in November 2011, US President Barack Obama and his Australian counterpart Prime Minister Julia Gillard formally announced an enhancement of US-Australia defence cooperation. The centrepiece would be the deployment on a rotational basis of US marines to the northern Australian city of Darwin. There would also be increased US Air Force access to bases in northern Australia and US Navy access to a Royal Australian Navy base (HMAS *Stirling*) in Perth, Western Australia. The deployment of US marines to Darwin commenced in April 2012, with the arrival of approximately 200 US personnel. It is envisaged that this figure will grow to 2,500 within the next five to six years. During their six-month rotation, US marines will spend two to three months based in Darwin and the remainder in cooperative engagement with US security partners in the Asia-Pacific region.

In May 2012, Chinese officials expressed their displeasure with what they categorized as a 'Cold War era' strategic move by the US and Australia to Bob Carr, the Australian Foreign Minister, during his first official visit to the Chinese capital.

During a visit to Beijing by the Australian Defence Minister, Stephen Smith, in early June 2012, the Chinese authorities questioned whether Australia was trying to have a 'a foot on two boats' (*jiao ta liang tiao chuan* 脚踏两条船) when it came to its relations with China and the US.

Conclusions

By 2012, there were some early signs of moderation in China's foreign policy approach. Beijing's response to the Obama administration's September 2011 announcement that the US would upgrade Taiwan's fleet of F-16 A/B fighters was relatively muted, for example. Chinese and American policy-makers also reportedly consulted closely in their responses to the death of North Korean leader Kim Jong-Il in December 2011, which had the potential to destabilize the Korean Peninsula. Modest diplomatic inroads were also made regarding the South China Sea, including the agreement in July 2011 between China and ASEAN on a set of guidelines for implementing the 2002 *Declaration of Conduct of Parties in the South China Sea* and a separate October 2011 agreement between China and Vietnam on principles for settling maritime disputes.

环球时报
GLOBAL TIMES
中国膏药 羚锐打造
外交谈判仍在等结果 中国增派一艘海监船
菲战舰撤出南海对峙
世界焦虑等待朝鲜发卫星

Front page of *The Global Times*, 13 April 2012, with a headline reading 'Philippine warship backs down from South Sea conflict'.
Source: *Global Times*

An optimistic analysis of these developments suggests that Chinese policy-makers, having recognized the negative impact of the strident rhetoric of recent years, and the damage that Beijing's assertive turn has done to China's international image, have been seeking to repair that damage. An alternative interpretation posits that Chinese foreign policy is more conducive to positive change when confronted with strength and resolve, rather than with weakness, and that the shifts now occurring in Beijing's foreign policy posture are a product of the resolute and unified approach of the international community in the face of China's growing assertiveness. A third, more cautious interpretation suggests that it is far too early to say what these apparent shifts in Chinese foreign policy portend and that they can only be viewed as tactical at best. According to this latter perspective, firm conclusions cannot be drawn on the future trajectory of Chinese foreign policy until after the 2012-2013 leadership transition.

The 2010 to mid 2012 period has been an intriguing one so far as Chinese foreign policy is concerned. The dramatic manner in which Beijing has essentially undone the impressive diplomatic gains it had made in Asia over the space of a decade is most puzzling. Repairing that damage and regaining lost ground through winning back the trust of regional governments is likely to take a considerable amount of time. If such moderation does not ultimately eventuate, however, the Australian policy debate which has played out during the 2010-2012 period offers useful and important insights into the tensions and dilemmas that an increasingly assertive China is likely to pose for policy-makers everywhere.

2

2

SYMBOLIC CITIES AND THE 'CAKE DEBATE'

Carolyn Cartier and Luigi Tomba

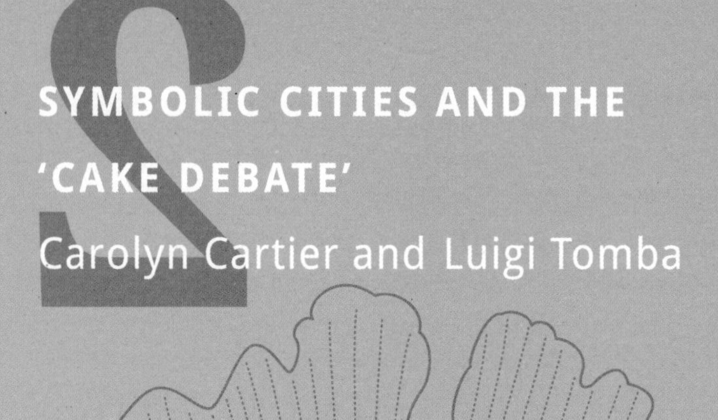

CITIES PROVIDE the most spectacular evidence of China's transformation. New urban landscapes punctuated by landmark skyscrapers proclaim the country's rapid development and modernisation. Since 1978, over 500 new cities have been built and constructing them has been a major social and political achievement as well as a major driver of economic growth. The process has also dispossessed millions of rural landholders without due or sufficient compensation, resulting in tens of thousands of protests in recent years. In historic cities, displacement of long-established residents and the replacement of socialist-era housing and factories by sleek office buildings and shopping malls also demonstrate the changing economic functions of the city and throw up new social and economic issues. Moreover, the design and development of cities is a highly competitive process. Key Communist Party officials stake their careers on the 'quality' of urban development in the cities in which they govern. They do so not only as a matter of governance but also to manipulate the symbolic significance of the cities in their charge for the sake of their own political advancement, as a kind of personal exercise in 'branding'.

Two cities were at the forefront of debates over national directions in social and economic development in China during 2010-2012: Chongqing in west China and Guangzhou on the south coast. Both cities are centres of massive conurbations and urbanizing regions – large and growing metropolitan areas comprising groups of cities with complex governments and diversified economies that serve major planning and development goals. Guangzhou is the provincial capital of Guangdong province and the regional capital of the Pearl River Delta region, which led China's opening to the world economy in the 1980s based on export manufacturing and

Map 1: **Guangzhou, Guangdong Province**
Source: Multimedia Services, ANU College of Asia & the Pacific

capital inflows from adjacent Hong Kong. [Map 1] Chongqing is China's newest major city and at the forefront of the current national focus to develop the vast inland region of western China. [Map 2] The prominence of these two cities in national development has been driven by extensive 'image engineering', a process that focuses on their supposedly outstanding characteristics. This is done to attract domestic and international capital, bolster the loyalty and civic pride of their residents, and promote their relatively leading roles in national economic development.

These two cities potentially define different national trajectories. Guangzhou (formerly known in English as Canton) is an historic trading city that boasts an early liberal tradition. It is a city that, in recent decades, has been a place where local officials have been innovators both economically and in the area of politics. Its local media, led by the South-

The Chongqing Model and the Guangdong Model

The Chongqing Model and the Guangdong Model are terms that have been popularized in the media and occasionally in official communications. They refer to two political-economic approaches variously promoted by Bo Xilai during his tenure as Party Secretary of the city of Chongqing (2007-2012), and by Wang Yang, Party Secretary of Guangdong province since 2007. Chongqing is China's biggest urban administrative district with a population of nearly thirty million, while Guangdong is home to about eighty million people and is China's richest province as measured by GDP.

The Guangdong Model promotes a more liberal interpretation of the market economy, especially for private enterprise, and prioritizes economic growth. The Chongqing Model, by contrast, emphasizes a renewed role for the state in urban and economic planning, including improving the urban environment, addressing social and economic inequalities, and aggressively supporting government-backed industrial enterprises.

In February 2012, a long-standing grievance between the government and residents of the village of Wukan in Guangdong was successfully settled with an apparently democratic election of new village officials. Some commentators saw this as a victory for the Guangdong Model, and a possible sign that liberal ideas and political reform may still have a future within the Communist Party.

The Chongqing Model was closely associated with Bo Xilai's highly visible 'Sing Red, Strike Black' (*changhong dahei* 唱红打黑) campaign: vigorous communist propaganda reminiscent of the Mao era, and a sustained crackdown on 'black societies' or organized crime. Various advocates of broad social justice, including leftists, neo-Maoists such as the Utopia group (whose popular website was silenced by state censorship), and many citizens of Chongqing (if some media reports are to be believed), continued to support the Chongqing Model. Bo's ouster as Party Secretary in mid March 2012 cast doubt on the viability of a Chongqing Model.

ern Media Group, has a national reputation for quality reporting and investigative journalism. In contrast, Chongqing represents an entirely different set of characteristics that relate to the history of Sichuan province, from which it was administratively severed to become a provincial-level municipality (like Beijing and Shanghai) in 1997. Like Chengdu, the provincial capital of Sichuan province, Chongqing is part of the Chinese heartland and a major center of Mao-era defence industries. During 2010-

Map 2: **Chongqing**
Source: Multimedia Services, ANU College of Asia & the Pacific

2011, Chongqing's national image continued to draw boldly on its 'red' past – 'red culture', 'red politics' and the socialist organisation of production – to present a neo-socialist vision of urban modernity. Before he was sensationally removed in March 2012, Bo Xilai, the Party Secretary of Chongqing, had built the image of the city on the color-coded twin campaign, 'Sing Red, Strike Black' (*changhong dahei* 唱红打黑). This included literal singing, including mass choral renditions of popular Maoist-era patriotic and political songs, as well as the study of 'red classics' (films, books and stories about the country's revolutionary past). 'Strike Black' referred to a far-reaching police campaign aimed at tackling the city's notorious organised crime.

Gingko trees on the streets of Chongqing.
Source: *Chongqing Morning Post*, 2 December 2009

Turning Red Chongqing Green

The removal of Bo Xilai from his position as Party Secretary of Chongqing in March 2012 saw the national media hastily declare the end of the 'Chongqing Model'. Yet both the idea and the reality of the model had always been more complex than the media coverage suggested. The idea of the Chongqing Model as a set of economic and policy conditions emerged as a symbolic discourse employed by the Chongqing government in association with writings produced by scholars affiliated with New Left political interests. The use of the word 'model' in China historically connotes good and correct government. In fact, some social and economic policies associated with the model were not unique to Chongqing and had been established in Chongqing before Bo took office, by central government plans; these included the low-cost housing program and the extension of household registration (*hukou* 户口) permits to migrant workers from rural areas.

In 2010, Chongqing announced plans to build ten million low-income rental and subsidised apartments, followed in 2011 by a plan to build enough public rental housing to accommodate two million more low and middle income people, or thirty to forty percent of urban residents, to be allocated by a lottery in response to demand. Both schemes are part of the national plan, first announced in 2007, to implement affordable housing funds in the four provincial-level municipalities and major cities in fifteen provinces. The housing schemes complemented household registration reform to encourage rural-urban integration as a basis for energizing the consumer economy. The multi-national manufacturer Foxconn – a Taiwan company that has in recent years weathered highly publicized labor disputes in its Pearl River Delta factories – predictably endorsed Chongqing for its commitment to treating migrants like other urban residents, providing them access to housing, local healthcare and schools.

A city logo promoted on Chongqing municipal government websites during Bo Xilai's rule.
Source: cq.gov.cn

In 1997, the central government established Chongqing as China's fourth provincial-level municipality (along with Beijing, Tianjin and Shanghai). A river port at a major confluence of the Yangtze River, Chongqing is the trans-shipment hub between the upper reaches of the Yangtze in western China and the Lower Yangtze Valley in the east. In 2010, the central government named it one of five 'national central cities' responsible for coordinating the Great Western Development plan aimed at extending the benefits of the economic boom inland, as well as managing the water reservoir behind the Three Gorges Dam.

In central China, summer continental air masses make Chongqing one of China's 'furnaces' or 'oven cities' and great banyans (*Ficus lacor*) have for years been the city's most common shade tree. In 1986, the banyan was named the official tree of the city. The official website of Chongqing features a page devoted to the City Flower and the City Tree. The official flower, the camellia (*Camilla sinensis*), known to gardeners worldwide, is indigenous to western China. The website cites the fifth-century text *Commentary on the Classics of the Waterways* which mentions the banyan tree. Following the decision in Beijing to establish Chongqing as a new city-region in 1997, swathes of urban buildings were demolished and the historic banyan fell victim to a spate of road widening. The web page featuring the banyan as the City Tree, however, was not updated after 2007. That was the year that the Communist Party Central Organisation Committee named Bo Xilai, former Mayor of Dalian city, governor of Liaoning province, and Minister of Commerce, the incoming Party Secretary of Chongqing. With Bo's arrival in Chongqing the banyan fell into abeyance and was replaced by a new arboreal favourite: the gingko.

Household Registration
(*hukou* 户口 or *huji* 户籍)

The *hukou* is a residency permit or household registration. A form of family registration was used in pre-modern times, and the *hukou* system, which is a modernized and socialist reformulation of the practice, is still in use in the People's Republic today. A person's *hukou* is usually registered soon after birth, based on the mother's residential status. A *hukou* is necessary to receive social benefits, and for the individual to apply for documents such as ID cards and passports. Before the 1980s, the *hukou* system restricted people's ability to move to another city, get married, change jobs or even get housing. Although this is no longer the case, migrants who want to live away from the place of their *hukou* still face extreme difficulties getting their children into school and obtaining medical care and other social benefits. Critics argue that the *hukou* system is both unfair and unsuited to an economy that is powered by migrant workers and graduates who move away from home to start their careers.

In 2003, Sun Zhigang, a young migrant graphic designer, was beaten to death in a Guangzhou police-operated repatriation station, an office empowered to send migrants without proper documentation back to the area of residence specified on their *hukou* documents. The incident, reported by the influential *Southern Weekly* newspaper, led to a vigorous debate about whether China should abandon the *hukou* system entirely. There has since been some loosening of controls, but with 'stability maintenance' being a top priority of the government in recent times (see Chapter 3), it is unlikely that the *hukou* will be abolished in the near future.

3月 2 日

今日主城 48 版

重慶晚報

“白求恩精神示范医院”“雷锋式班集体”“雷锋式学生”

市委市政府昨召开命名表彰大会

薄熙来讲话 黄奇帆等出席

卫生部撤销面粉增白剂

哪些地方可植树？主城18植树点公布

这位女交巡警

武功了得

一招撂翻抢匪

市政府领导分工调整

新上任的副市长吴刚分管教育科技卫生等方面工作

On 2 March 2012, *The Chongqing Evening News* published a front-page story about a speech Bo Xilai gave to a group of doctors on the 'spirit of communism'. Bo reportedly spoke about the PLA martyr Lei Feng, and also reeled off by heart passages from 'In Memory of Norman Bethune', a famous essay by Mao Zedong.
Source: *Chongqing Evening News*

During his previous tenure as Mayor of the northeastern city of Dalian, Bo Xilai remodeled the city's landscape in a process that included an ambitious greening program of the business district. As a result, the environment of the city garnered international attention for its improvement. For the Communist Party the modern appearance of Chinese cities is an indicator of successful urban management, and Bo's high marks for the transformation of Dalian prompted his appointment as Party Secretary of Chongqing, the new city of west China, to which he took his strategy of creating an urban landscape aimed to impress – 'investors look at a city and judge it by how it looks', he declared. He undertook an aggressive re-landscaping of China's most famous 'hill city'. Today, Chongqing's motorways are lined with gingko trees, now described as a 'unique characteristic' of the local environment. Such audacious urban afforestation came at a price: in 2010 alone ten billion *yuan* (US$1.5 billion) was spent on the city's new trees. By contrast, that year the budget for renovating rural schools in the greater Chongqing area – a priority after the 2008 Wenchuan earthquake, was a mere 150 million *yuan*.

Bo's rhetoric bore the hallmarks of a Maoist-era political campaign or voluntarist movement: Chongqing should plant 'ten years' worth of trees in one year, 100 years' worth of trees in ten years.' Other similarities included an emphasis on the participation of large numbers of people and policies

City Branding and City Slogans

The Chinese language readily allows for verbal and written contractions and lends itself to the formulation of pithy slogans. Communist Party propaganda has featured slogans and shorthand expressions since being founded in Shanghai in the early 1920s. In recent decades, companies have used contraction-style slogans for advertising (the Beijing-based Snow-bright Glasses company, *Xueliang yanjing* 雪亮眼镜, for example, took its name from a famous Mao slogan: 'The eyes of the masses are as bright as snow' *qunzhongde yanjing shi xueliangde* 群众的眼睛是雪亮的), while many cities and local governments have adopted slogans for ideological purposes and as tag lines to encourage everything from tourism to general urban development and 'civilized' lifestyles.

In 2010, *Oriental Outlook* magazine (*Dongfang Liaowang Zhoukan* 瞭望东方周刊) observed facetiously that dozens of Chinese cities were branding themselves the 'Oriental Geneva' (*Dongfang Rineiwa* 东方日内瓦), among them Shijiazhuang, Qinhuangdao, Zhaoqing, Kunming, Dali, Chaohu and Wuxi.

The same article noted that in March 2010, Yichun, in Jiangxi province 江西宜春, adopted the slogan 'A City Called Spring' (*Yizuo jiao chunde chengshi* 一座叫春的城市), referring to the character 'chun' 春 in the city name, which means 'spring'. The creators of this clever slogan were seemingly oblivious to the fact that 'to call spring' (*jiao chun* 叫春) is a colloquial expression for the sounds women make during sex. This effectively rendered their slogan as meaning, 'City of Amorous Groans'.

In the last months of 2011, Beijing introduced its own city slogan, one that was more in keeping with the sober tone of traditional Party propaganda. According to official reports, 2.9 million Beijingers voted on a range of appropriate and uplifting words, leading to the choice of four words to epitomize the 'Beijing Spirit' (*Beijing jingshen* 北京精神): Patriotism, Innovation, Inclusiveness and Virtue (*aiguo, chuangxin, baorong, houde* 爱国、创新、包容、厚德).

As of early 2012, Beijing Spirit messages were ubiquitous in the capital: in subway stations, roadside billboards and posters hung up by neighbourhood committees.

Other city slogans that have been used in China in the last few years include:

Shanghai: Wonderful everyday (*Jingcai meiyitian* 精彩每一天)

Chongqing: Although Chongqing was branded 'Red City' (*Hongse zhi du* 红色之都) that was never officially used by the Chongqing government, which promoted the slogans: If you've never been to Chongqing, you don't know China (*Mei daoguo Chongqing, bu liaojie Zhongguo* 没到过重庆，不了解中国) World's Chongqing, Everlasting Three Gorges (*Shijiede Chongqing, yongyuande Sanxia* 世界的重庆 永远的三峡)

Other city slogans include:

Rizhao, Shandong: Blue skies, Emerald seas, Golden beaches (*Lantian bihai jinshatan* 蓝天碧海金沙滩)

Kunming, Yunnan: Every day is Spring (*Kunming tiantian shi chuntian* 昆明天天是春天)

Guangzhou, Guangdong: In one day you understand two thousand years (*Yiri dudong liangqian nian* 一日读懂两千年)

Chengdu, Sichuan: Capital of success, Capital of colour, Capital of cuisine (*Chenggong zhi du, Duocai zhi du, Meishi zhi du* 成功之都、多彩之都、美食之都)

Dongguan, Guangdong: Let fresh splendour blossom every day! (*Meitian zhanfang xin jingcai!* 每天绽放新精彩!)

Ningbo, Zhejiang: Honest, Pragmatic, Open-minded, Innovative (*Chengxin, shiwu, kaifang, chuangxin* 诚信、务实、开放、创新)

Hangzhou, Zhejiang: Exquisite and harmonious, magnanimous and open-minded (*Jingzhi hexie, daqi kaifang* 精致谐、大气开放)

of uniform implementation. The sheer number of trees required led to a feverish nationwide buy-up of gingkos. The sudden appearance of mature trees with forty-fifty centimetre trunks on major thoroughfares of the city indicated that 50-100 years old trees were being traded, reportedly at the cost of some 300,000 *yuan* each (one-hundred times the monthly income of a taxi driver). The mass planting of gingkos was a sign that Bo Xilai and the city had entered an age of conspicuous urban consumption.

Gingko saplings ready for transplanting.
Source: Website of 'Chongqing Professionals Cooperative with Day of Ginkgo', a company that provides trees and landscaping services

The maidenhair-fern-shaped leaves of this delicate-looking tree turn an imperial yellow in autumn. Its ancestry is unassailable. The subtle symbolism was not lost on the Chinese: Bo Xilai was widely known as a 'princeling', a descendant of one of the founders of the People's Republic. In terms of ecosystem planning the gingko was a showy but questionable choice. Gingkos are highly tolerant of sulphur dioxide and resistant to insects. However, they are deciduous and their canopy is relatively small; they provide fewer places for birds to nest and offer less shade during the punishing heat of Chongqing's summer compared to the historic banyans.

Empowered to develop the city in the national interest, Bo Xilai promoted highly visible urban policies such as the mass planting of gingkos, an apt symbol for what in this volume we call 'red rising'. His unprecedented flair for using the media to boost Chongqing and his agenda led to regular coverage about his leadership in the national and international press and helped fuel the idea of a 'Chongqing Model' that was unique to the city and with relevance for the rest of the country. Other campaigns drew on the 'red practices' of the Maoist era, including the 'Sing Red' campaign of staging mass songfests in work places and public parks. The highly publicised crackdown on corruption and organised crime during 2009-2010, the so-called 'Strike Black' campaign, meanwhile resulted in the restructuring of police

Concrete spikes installed underneath freeway bridges in the city of Guangzhou, apparently intended to deter homeless people from taking up residence.
Source: QQ.com/*Southern Metropolis Daily*

services. Police and traffic control platforms were put up all over the city and thousands of extra police officers were deployed on the streets. Local citizens praised the moves for increasing their sense of safety, while the crackdown on organised crime led to over 3,000 arrests and convictions of high-ranking officials.

The Chongqing Model also emphasised the restructuring of state-owned enterprises (SOEs) with the aim of making them more competitive and profitable. After 1949, Chongqing was one of several places in the central and western regions of the country to which crucial industrial and military infrastructure was relocated as part of a national defensive strategy, what was called China's 'Third Front' (the other fronts being coastal and in the north). Rather than dismantling and privatizing state companies, common elsewhere during the country's economic reforms in the 1980s and early 1990s, Chongqing redeveloped state-owned military enterprises as a base for contemporary manufacturing. The leading state-owned enterprise in Chongqing is Chang'an Auto, the Chinese partner of the US Ford Motor Company. It is the third largest manufacturer of automobiles in China and is globally distinctive for locating industrial design, parts manufacture and auto assembly all in one place.

Chongqing has also coordinated investment from international manufacturing firms in a designated technology district, the Liangjiang New Zone. Chongqing Mayor Huang Qifan had previously been the director of Shanghai's Economic Committee (1995-2001) and an economic architect of industrial planning in that city's famous Pudong New Zone. Huang became Vice-mayor of Chongqing in 2001 and Deputy Party Secretary in 2009, then Mayor of the city in 2010. During 2009-2010, the US electronics and computing firm

Hewlett-Packard, the Taiwanese semi-conductor manufacturer Foxconn, and the German chemical producer BASF all set up operations in Chongqing's Liangjiang New Zone. In these ways, like Shanghai's Pudong, the city's economy grew to encompass a range of state-owned and multinational manufacturing concerns. In June 2011, Henry Kissinger visited Chongqing and met with executives from leading firms among a reported 500 US companies operating there (Kissinger also took part in one of Bo Xilai's mass 'Sing Red' choral events and praised the city's achievements). Chongqing's largest heavy industry SOE is the Chongqing Iron and Steel Group. Established in 1890 as the Hanyang Iron Plant in Wuhan, the major city on the central plain of the Yangtze River, it was relocated to Chongqing in the 1930s. In 2010, this state-run corporation established the Chonggang Minerals Development Investment Ltd, a joint venture with the Chongqing Foreign Trade and Economic Cooperation Group. It secured supplies of iron ore by purchasing a majority interest in SINOM Ltd, a Hong Kong-listed company which through its subsidiary Asia Steel Holdings owns a sixty percent stake in the Extension Hill Magnetite Project in Western Australia. Such complex corporate structures were supported by China's emerging financial services industries. They illustrate how Chinese companies have retooled historic industries using state and semi-private capital to take advantage of global production chains.

Major new investment and the relocation of production capacities in central China may appear counterintuitive: China's export industries have flourished largely in the country's coastal areas, in particular the Pearl River Delta and Shanghai. However, new rail capacity has overcome the 'tyranny of distance'. In July 2011, a Eurasian rail service opened with a line linking Chongqing to Duisburg, Germany. The first freight train carrying laptops and LCD screens from Chongqing to Duisburg traveled 11,179 kilometres in just thirteen days, cutting by more than half the average container shipping time between China and Europe and giving Chongqing a competitive advantage over the coastal hubs. As Henry Kissinger learned during his tour, one out of three laptops being manufactured in the world is now assembled in Chongqing.

Red Roofing in Guangzhou

In the summer of 2010, the Guangzhou municipal government augmented the flat roofs of old apartment buildings with PVC boards so that passers-by would be given the illusion that they were sloped, red-tiled roofs.
Source: Singsupplies.com

In the summer of 2010, the Guangzhou city government suddenly informed residents in several areas of the city that the roofs of their apartment buildings had to be renovated. Flat roofs would be augmented with PVC boards so that passers-by would be given the illusion that they were sloped, red-tiled roofs. Part of an unprecedented beautification project, they were designed to impress the hundreds of thousands of international visitors expected to flock into the city for the Asian Games later that year. The move reminded flabbergasted residents, who in some cases protested by occupying their rooftops (although to no avail), that neither middle-class status nor the city's image as open and urbane had diminished the capacity of the government to intervene in their lives, as it had in the Mao era.

Like Chongqing, the Pearl River Delta, funnelling through the heart of Guangdong province, and its provincial capital, Guangzhou, has been at the centre of debates surrounding Chinese urbanization and nation building. As the first region to open to the outside world, the delta has also been a testing ground for new political and economic models. The region is also notorious for showcasing the darker side of the economic boom: sprawling urbanisation, a highly mobile migrant population, labour conflicts, conflicts over land use and development, and woeful air and water quality.

Today, the Pearl River Delta contains nine major cities, all of which have little in common with the riverine rural society of the past. The cities of Guangzhou and Shenzhen are among the wealthiest in the country and nearby Dongguan and Foshan are rapidly becoming key provincial manufacturing centres. To urban planners the integration of these cities seems

Guangzhou's new central business district.
Source: flickr/Arkiben

like an ideal way to increase efficiencies and boost the regional economy. Since the 1980s, economic growth has relied on rapid urbanization; both local and national planners envisage the whole area becoming one vast conurbation: a mega-city of forty-plus million people. There have been modest attempts to integrate service networks in healthcare, transportation and communication across the disparate metropolitan areas; for the most part they remain concentrated in the cities. Large areas of the region remain at least administratively rural.

Cities of national significance like Guangzhou lobby to be included in rankings and lists compiled by the central government to acknowledge their relative standing in the national urban modernization project. Guangzhou was named a 'National Central City' in 2010 and a 'National Civilized City' in 2011. Such labels have limited practical significance. But they reveal the expectation of the central government that urban areas and local administrations will guide and direct modern city life in the name of 'civilization' (*wenming* 文明), a concept with a complex history in East Asia.

As in Chongqing, 'image engineering' is taken very seriously by the government of Guangzhou. In 2010, Guangzhou issued a 'thirty-two word slogan' to encapsulate the 'special characteristics' of the 'Guangzhou way'. The Guangzhou advertising-cum-propaganda push conceptualized the region's particular culture and traditions in terms of 'Lingnan culture', a metonym for the lands south of the Lingnan mountain range, the traditional geographical divide of north and

Constructing Civilization
(*wenming jianshe* 文明建设)

Introduced into the Chinese language from Japan following the Meiji restoration in the nineteenth century, the word 'civilization' (*wenming* or *bunmei* in Japanese) has a range of meanings in China, from civilized to civilization, as well as compliant and restrained; it is sometimes used merely to mean 'polite'.

Ye Jianying (d. 1986), former Vice-president of the People's Republic and Chairman of the Standing Committee of the National People's Congress, first used the expression 'Building Socialist Spiritual Civilization' (*shehuizhuyi jingshen wenming jianshe* 社会主义精神文明建设 – often shortened to *wenming jianshe* 文明建设) in a speech at an official gathering commemorating the thirtieth anniversary of the founding of the People's Republic in 1979.

The speech was highly significant. Delivered when the country was still struggling to recover from the devastations of the Cultural Revolution, the speech, approved by other senior leaders including Deng Xiaoping, noted the importance of economic goals, but it stressed the need to foster a 'socialist spiritual civilization' to match China's material achievements. Party ideologists called the concept a significant development of orthodox Marxism-Leninism and Mao Zedong Thought. In 1986, the government formally launched a program to 'build spiritual civilization', the core elements of which included patriotism, socialist moral codes (fealty to the Party, its goals and rules and regulations) and basic civility. In the 1930s, the then-ruling Nationalist Party had pursued a similar campaign under the rubric of the 'New Life Movement'.

Since the 1980s, Chinese officialdom has used the word 'civilization'/*wenming* in a variety of political contexts, ranging from rhetorical statements about Marxism to campaigns to create 'civilized cities' (*wenming chengshi* 文明城市) in which everything from littering and spitting in public to all forms of anti-social behavior are policed and outlawed. In 2006, China's Internet regulatory authorities ordered websites to censor objectionable content and 'build websites in a civilized way' (*wenming ban wang* 文明办网).

south. The list of special characteristics notes that Guangzhou was China's first international port; it even boasts a mosque dating from the seventh century, and merchants have used the place as a base for trade throughout Asia. The list also refers to more contemporary ambitions to improve the city's ecology and environment. To achieve these 'civilising goals', but more importantly to accommodate increased residential density and reduce its environmental footprint, the city was to be re-oriented along two new axes that cut against the original layout of Guangzhou. The plans support high-rise buildings; predictably, Guangzhou is planning a series of buildings aimed at being among China's tallest. Among them is the Canton Tower designed by the Dutch architects Mark Hemel and Barbara Kuit of Information Based Architecture together with Arup. Its observation deck, spectral night lighting, and curvilinear design have turned what is little more than a giant TV antenna into a local and, it is hoped, international icon.

In contrast to Chongqing, the greening of Guangzhou has adopted a somewhat more democratic edge. Local authorities invited residents to help select plants from a list of one hundred specimens to be used for urban landscaping. In 2010, the city spent nearly 160 million *yuan* on potted plants and flowers for the decoration of roads and highways. The pots were interspersed with kapok trees (*Ceiba pentandra*), the striking orange-red blooms of which are the official city flower – despite not being native to China. The kapok tree, named after its fibrous seedpods, arrived in the era of the early trans-Pacific trade generated by the colonisation of South America. It eventually became the local 'hero tree' for its red color, the symbol of revolutionary Guangzhou in the 1920s when the Communists and the Nationalists constituted a united front against local warlords. In 2011, Guangzhou announced a plan to plant 1,400 kapok trees at key points around the city.

Behind all of these grand, cosmetic gestures, the 'civilising' of the Pearl River Delta has also relied on massive land grabs, forced dispossessions and the demolition of large tracts of old housing stock. For years the

Hong Kong Dogs (*Xianggang gou* 香港狗)
versus Mainland Locusts (*Dalu huangchong* 大陆蝗虫)

On 15 January 2012, a young Mandarin-speaking girl dropped some snack noodles on the floor of a carriage in a Hong Kong mass-transport subway train. In poor Mandarin, a local Cantonese speaker protested about the mess to the girl's family, who argued back, drawing more passengers to join in. In the middle of the quarrel, a Hong Kong woman shouted: 'No use trying to reason with mainlanders, they are always like that.'

The incident, recorded on a mobile phone and uploaded online, generated heated discussion among mainland Chinese and Hong Kong people alike. Are mainlanders all uncouth slobs? Why are Hong Kong people so snobbish? Commenting on an Internet video program, Kong Qingdong, a professor of Chinese at Peking University, said that some people in the former British colony were nothing but 'dogs' with the mindset of a colonised people.

Contributing to the mutual antagonism is what some Hong Kong people perceive as being the abuse by mainlanders of the former British colony's relatively plentiful resources and well-managed amenities. Every year, tens of thousands of pregnant women cross the border from the mainland to give birth in Hong Kong's hospitals in order to take advantage of its superior and publicly-funded health care and to give their children permanent residency in Hong Kong. Mainlanders also go to Hong Kong to shop for luxury and common goods alike, attracted by both the guarantee of quality and lower prices. Some Hong Kong shops have offered mainlanders special treatment: in January 2012, about a thousand Hong Kong residents protested in front of a Dolce & Gabbana store, accusing the owners of discriminating against locals by banning them from taking photos in front of the store while allowing heavy-spending mainlanders free rein with their cameras. A 2008 powdered milk scandal in the mainland that caused infant sickness and some deaths, continues to fuel powdered milk buy-ups by mainlanders in Hong Kong, resulting in shortages. The visible presence of such 'bulk buyers' on the MTR trains, returning to the mainland, contributes to tensions. On 1 February 2012, some Hong Kong citizens paid for a full-page advertisement in a local newspaper complaining about 'locusts', a derogatory reference to the Hong Kong-visiting mainland mothers.

Guangzhou government has been at odds with rural landowners whose farms have been surrounded and forcibly absorbed into the expanded cities. Dozens of 'villages in the city' (*chengzhong cun* 城中村) dot the map. These 'villages' are enclaves of rural land that the villagers sometimes still own collectively. They consist for the most part of substandard apartment buildings that provide cheap rental housing to migrant workers. With narrow alleys and poor sanitation, they appear as holdouts against the modern city. Evictions by developers are not always successful and well-organized opposition from the original inhabitants has meant that large payouts have been made to some villagers, including cash and flats or houses in the new developments. In Guangzhou alone, fifty-two out of 138 urban villages are scheduled for 'redevelopment' during 2011-2015.

A major challenge to plans for the integration of the Pearl River Delta remains the physical fragmentation of the region. Different from London or Tokyo and more like Los Angeles, the delta is an urban area with multiple centres, where localities compete as much as they collaborate, and where many of the metropolitan areas are themselves geographically fragmented. The creation of a mega-city is not merely a matter of reshaping roofs or lining trees with potted plants. Travelling around the region it is easy to appreciate that anything more than the rationalisation of local services can only be achieved through provincial-level government action.

South China's growing mega-city welds the core areas of the Pearl River Delta discussed above with the Hong Kong and Macao Special Administrative regions. The proposed integration of the former British and Portuguese colonies into mainland China's communications and transport networks are particularly controversial in Hong Kong. Local activists and others are wary of seeing Hong Kong incorporated into a vast national project. Shortly after moving from his earlier administrative position in Chongqing, the present Guangdong provincial Party Secretary, Wang Yang, suggested that Guangdong should become China's 'shop' while the hinterland could be the country's 'factory'; Guangdong would to all intents and purposes usurp the role of Hong Kong. Transportation is the key

東莞時報

2012.06.21

汪洋充分肯定
东莞"三打两建"

人社部：现行退休年龄不会立刻调整

穆巴拉克
生命垂危

大巴坠山谷
17人遇难

还剩4天

Front page of *The Dongguan Times* featuring Guangdong Provincial Party Secretary Wang Yang.
Source: *Dongguan Times*, 21 June 2012

Little Yueyue 小悦悦

In October 2011, three-year-old Wang Yue, nicknamed Yueyue, wandered out of her house in Foshan, Guangdong province. She walked into the street next to a neighbouring market and was run over by a van. A few minutes later she was run over again by another vehicle. By the time a woman stopped to help the girl, eighteen other passers-by had ignored the critically injured toddler. Once in hospital Yueyue was put on life support but died soon after.

Footage from a surveillance camera that caught the whole incident was uploaded to the Internet, causing nationwide outrage, and soul searching: How could eighteen people ignore an injured child? A heated debate broke out in the media and online about why people in China avoid doing good deeds. Fear of being a good Samaritan in China is rampant as there have been many reported cases of victims extorting money from those who have helped them or accusing them of causing the accident.

to these integrative moves. As Jeremy Goldkorn notes in Chapter 7 of this book, the national railway project was set back by the Wenzhou rail disaster in mid 2011. After the head of China's railways was sacked for corruption in 2011, the Hong Kong government continued to guarantee high-speed rail services across the delta by funding the most expensive railway in the world, a tunnel line that will, when it opens in 2015, cover the twenty-six kilometres between Hong Kong and Shenzhen at the border with China in twelve minutes.

With large areas of land still controlled by local governments and village collectives, large-scale planning entails complex negotiations. The municipal government is often able to carry out its plans only at a very high cost, or after reaching compromizes with and effectively strengthening local power-holding elites. Local party cadres often debate about whether integration is really possible. For instance, an expensive cross-township bike rental system was scrapped because the two cities could not come to an agreement on the kind of locks that were to be used to safeguard the bikes. Some locals insist that integration will only be a reality when a unified mobile telephone network replaces the numerous local networks that frustrate easy telecommunication.

In late 2011, local disputes over land seizures in the delta made international headlines when the villagers of Wukan protested against local Party developers who had been involved in the illegal sale of collective land without recompense. The villagers forced the provincial authorities to launch an inquiry and promise to return some of the appropriated land. The conflict also culminated in the election of the protest leader as the new village head. This episode, one of many such conflicts around the country that otherwise seldom reach the headlines, was hailed by international and domestic media as a sign that Guangdong was adopting a more liberal attitude towards the protection of the rights of its farmers. Like the concerns in Wukan, most conflicts over rural 'land grabs' are about illegal dispossession and unjust compensation.

As in dynastic times, provincial and regional military leaders are rotated between posts in order to reduce their ability to build up local power bases. The system also guarantees that leaders have experiences running different parts of the country before being promoted to national positions. For an ambitious party leader, a successful stint running the delta can be a stepping-stone to a national political role. Wang Yang is regarded as being aligned with the faction around Party General Secretary Hu Jintao. Wang Yang, like Bo Xilai, was able to use his city as a kind of urban spectacle by which he promoted his ideas (and by association himself) on the national arena.

The 'Cake Debate'

Chongqing and Guangzhou have loomed large in the national debate about the future of China. At stake in the contest between Chongqing and Guangdong were strategies for urban development as well as approaches to ruling the country as a whole. In 2011, the symbolic politics of the two places inspired what was dubbed the 'cake debate'. It was the first time Communist Party leaders used the media to air contesting visions of regional development. In Chongqing, Bo Xilai advocated a more equitable distribution of the wealth generated by the county's economic boom – 'dividing the cake' among the deserving and needy, whereas Wang Yang, the Party Secretary of Guangdong province, promoted continued economic growth in the Pearl River Delta region – 'making an even bigger

The 'Cake Debate' (*dangao lun* 蛋糕论)

The 'cake debate' was one public aspect of the competition between the Chongqing and Guangdong models that played out in the Chinese and international media. Where Guangdong Party leader Wang Yang would uphold the liberal aspects of Deng Xiaoping's reform strategy, making the economic cake as big as possible, the Chongqing Model focused on how to divide the cake (allocate the profits of rapid growth more equitably). The contrasting views reflect a central dilemma of China's economy: is it more important to distribute wealth or to grow the economy at any cost?

cake'. Bo's formulation drew on historic socialist ideals and the way they intersect with contemporary concerns about increasing income inequality, a problem that had become so serious that the government stopped publicizing statistics about the distribution of wealth. Bo proposed the redistribution of wealth through government funding of programs for the public good including the provision of low-cost housing for migrant workers. Referring to Deng Xiaoping's pragmatic acknowledgement that in a market economy some people will become rich first, in July 2011 Bo said: 'some people in China have indeed become rich first, so we must seek the realisation of common prosperity.' A week later Wang Yang responded that: 'division of the cake is not a priority right now. The priority is to make the cake bigger.' This in essence was the 'cake debate'.

The clash of models and the 'cake debate' saw an unprecedented media-fueled conjuncture of national politics, urban planning and contending regional visions in the lead up to the 2012-2013 power transition. While Wang Yang in Guangdong called for continued growth while warning about the limits of self-promotion, Bo Xilai spotlighted the extremes of inequality in Chongqing and the need for greater social equity. In July 2011, the Party Committee of Chongqing adopted a resolution to reduce inequality as measured by the Gini coefficient from 0.45 to 0.35 and highlighted the serious 0.65 figure in Guangdong. Bo also invited members of the Politburo Standing Committee which rules China to Chongqing to witness his achievements.

The 'cake debate' that featured Bo as a champion of egalitarianism and Wang as the paladin of liberalisation camouflaged the important contribution that national-level city planners and thinkers have made to China's overall economic and social innovation. The clash of visions and regional plans show how regional Party leaders project their power through real and symbolic projects. Yet whether in Chongqing or Guangdong, part of what makes a fascinating challenge to our understanding of China is the economic processes unfolding in the country's new cities. By contrast to the economic path followed by advanced industrial economies in which agriculture gave way to manufacturing followed by services industries, the speed of development in China has meant that agriculture, mining, manufacturing and services industries often develop simultaneously and intertwine in ways that have significant implications for social change.

The 'cake debate' was also significant because it unfolded far beyond the traditional halls of power in Beijing, and it was widely discussed in the media. Many observers in China and overseas praised the openness of this 'city competition' in which two governing styles and economic alternatives have been allowed to present such different models for development. Wang became the spokesman for what was loosely termed a 'liberal camp' and Bo the champion of a form of re-jigged socialism. Yet even as the debate suggested possible future directions for other regions and even the country as a whole, it failed to identify clearly political and economic challenges or proffer effective solutions. Nor did it invite different, dissenting or even more nuanced views. Ultimately, the debate gave the 'Chongqing Model' an edge since it appeared to trump the Pearl River Delta with its uneven development and increasing income inequality. It was also effectively a critique of Wang Yang, since Wang was Bo Xilai's predecessor in Chongqing.

In February 2012, the Chongqing chief of public security Wang Lijun, who had previously led the 'Strike Black' anti-crime campaign, turned up at the US Consulate in Chengdu for a highly unusual visit. Wang ultimately left the consulate 'on his own volition'. He was ushered off to the capital to undergo what the official media initially described as 'vacation-style therapy' on grounds that he had suffered some kind of nervous collapse brought on by overwork. The spectacle of the

Guangzhou city centre as viewed from Hua'nan bridge.
Source: flickr/Sam Gao

event – dozens of Chinese security vehicles had surrounded the US Consulate – spread rapidly on the Internet and via mobile phone microblogs and SMS messaging. Reports on both sides of the Pacific suggested that Wang had considered seeking asylum. Some reports claimed that he deposited incriminating documents with US consular staff. As a result Wang Lijun emerged as a pivotal figure in the unfolding drama of the 2012–2013 Dragon Year of political transition. Shortly before his visit to the US Consulate Wang had been dramatically removed from his post as public security chief and reassigned, allegedly as the result of having confronted Bo Xilai with evidence that Bo's wife, Gu Kailai, was involved in the death of the British businessman Neil Heywood. Wang had previously come under official investigation for corruption in an earlier position in a different city. While Wang disappeared into Party-imposed 'therapy', the media revealed Bo Xilai vacationing in a different way, in Kunming, Yunnan province – the base of the Yunnan military region established during the Sino-Japanese War by Bo Yibo, his exalted father, on whom his legacy has depended. In such incidents the historic landscape comes to life and underscores how cities transmit significant, complex symbolic meanings in China's critically decisive national debates.

Soon a terse official statement announced that Bo himself had been relieved of his duties and put under investigation. Government-organized mass singing events were cancelled and whatever had been 'red' in Chongqing began to fade. In 2011, Chongqing Satellite TV had been taken over by the local government, turned into a public interest channel and been forced to drop commercial advertising. In the wake of Bo Xilai's fall, the station quietly returned to its former advertising-supported format. In the following weeks, international media followed up the multiple strands of the mysterious, lurid story involving Bo, Gu, Wang, Heywood and, tangentially, Bo and Gu's 'playboy' son, Harvard University student Bo Guagua. Journalists traced leads between China, the UK and the US in pursuit of the truth behind this deadly Chinese Communist soap opera.

Meanwhile, domestic reports on Chongqing's massive security apparatus hinted at allegations that officials had wiretapped the phones of members of China's national leadership while they were in the city, including President Hu Jintao. Reports of deep fault-lines in 'red Chongqing' began to emerge, including accounts that lower level officials had disagreed vehemently with Bo's policies and shocking allegations of abuses of authoritarian power by Bo and his followers.

The central government appointed as Bo's interim successor Zhang Dejiang, a Vice-premier and Politburo member who had preceded Wang Yang as Party Secretary in Guangdong. On 16 March, the Chongqing People's Congress approved an additional thirty billion *yuan* investment for the city's automobile industry in a signal of confident support for the economy-as-usual. By May, the Chongqing government began to erase all evidence of Bo-era slogans and campaigns, and the Chongqing Urban Planning Exhibition Hall, the largest in the country, closed an entire floor showcasing the 'Chongqing Model'.

CROSS-STRAITS RELATIONS

In January 2011, the wealthy mainland Chinese businessman Chen Guangbiao announced his intention to visit Taiwan before the Chinese New Year with NTD500m (US$16.5m) in donations for low-income Taiwanese families. Purportedly inspired by Bill Gates's 'Giving Pledge', the money was to be handed out in hongbao 紅包*, or red envelopes in the traditional Chinese practice, with the inscription: 'The day is cold, the ground freezing, but the people's hearts are warm. The Chinese nation is one family and a fire in the winter'* (天寒地凍人心暖、中華民族一家親，冬天裡的一把火).

The visit, which occurred towards the end of President Ma Ying-jeou's first term, created a media storm in Taiwan. In a telephone survey by the newspaper *Apple Daily*, which is always ready to stoke controversy, 36.16 percent of respondents agreed with the statement: 'If he has money to bring, it is a good thing and he should be thanked.' But 39.8 percent agreed with the question-response: 'Who does he think he is? Bringing money humiliates the Taiwanese people!'

Cross-straits relations (*liang'an guanxi* 兩岸關係) have evolved in complex ways since the 'hot stage' of the

Chinese Civil War officially wound down some thirty years ago (when the two sides agreed to cease their desultory, ritualistic, every-other-day shelling of islands and coastline).

The term 'cross-straits relations' refers to the intersecting political, military, economic, cultural and social relationships between Taiwan and mainland China. They have an institutional basis in governmental organisations, such as the Mainland Affairs Council (*Dalu weiyuanhui* 大陸委員會) in Taiwan, and the Taiwan Affairs Office (*Guowuyuan Taiwan shiwu bangongshi* 国务院台湾事务办公室) in the People's Republic of China. Because neither state recognizes the other, relations are also institutionalized at the 'private' level through the Straits Exchange Foundation (SEF, or *Haixia jiaoliu jijinhui* 海峡交流基金會) and the Association for Relations Across the Taiwan Straits (ARATS, *Haixia liang'an guanxi xiehui* 海峡两岸关系协会). Since the mid-2000s, there have also been meetings at the highest level between the Chinese Communist Party (CCP) and the current ruling party of Taiwan, the Chinese Nationalist Party (KMT).

Cross-straits relations are also an economic relationship, as Taiwan's economy integrates with that of the mainland through two-way trade, investment and tourism. Taiwanese people have been able to travel to the mainland since the early 1990s for tourism and business and from 2008, Taiwan has allowed mainland tourists, first in groups and then as individuals. From less than 100,000 in 2008, the number rose to over two million mainland visitors in 2011.

Despite the economic links, military tensions remain palpable across the straits, with the deployment by the mainland of an increasingly formidable array of weapons aimed at Taiwan. 'Cross-straits relations' can in this context stand as a shorthand for a complex mix of regional military tension, US-China relations, Chinese expansionism, US regional hegemony, and Taiwanese nationalism. Indeed, the term, whether in English or Chinese, is commonly employed in centres of power such as Washington, Brussels, Tokyo or Canberra to avoid naming either side and so reproducing a discourse of Taiwan as either differentiated from or as a part of China. 'Cross-straits relations' as a phrase acknowledges only the most irrefutable, empirical facts of geography and the presence of a stretch of ocean between two coasts.

Overlapping and interposing histories ensure, of course, that cross-straits relations are much more than the multidimensional interface of capital, people and military hardware that provides the facts by which we can measure them.

The People's Republic of China, founded in 1949 and led by the Chinese Communist Party, claims Taiwan as part of the territory of China. It refers to it as 'Taiwan province'. Its decision-makers and spokesmen have expressed that claim in different ways over many decades in rhetoric that has reflected mainland politics and an evolving understanding of Taiwan's socio-political development. These range from emotional appeals to 'Taiwan compatriots' (*Taiwan tongbao* 台湾同胞) to belligerent threats and displays of military power.

As for the island of Taiwan, the state is officially known as the Republic of China. The Republic was founded on the mainland in 1912, at the end of the Qing dynasty. At the time the island of Taiwan was a colony of Japan, ceded in perpetuity by the Qing in 1895. Following the Japanese surrender in World War II in 1945, the Republic of China, led by the KMT under Chiang Kai-shek, took control of the island. In 1947, after eighteen months of disastrous and corrupt governance by the KMT administration, the native population of Taiwanese, that is, those with generational ties to the island, and who refer to themselves as 'natives' (*bensheng ren* 本省人), rebelled. The bitter legacy of the brutal suppression of the 'February Twenty-eighth Uprising' led to the emergence of the modern Taiwanese independence movement. In 1949, the

Nationalists lost the Civil War to the Communists and relocated the national government of the Republic of China to Taipei. A million or more Nationalist refugees and demobbed soldiers arrived to live among a hostile population of nearly five million Taiwanese.

Despite complicating factors like the intermarriage of Taiwanese and mainlanders (called *waisheng ren* 外省人), resulting in a new generation with mixed heritage, this history continues to play out in Taiwan's divisive and often rancorous democratic politics. National identity is the subject of a vigorous and self-aware debate in Taiwan. In the rhetoric of this debate, Taiwan is divided between the 'greens' and the 'blues' – those who support self-determination for the Taiwanese and Taiwanese cultural nationalism, and those who support close relations with mainland China and a broader, Chinese cultural identity. (Green symbolizes the island's natural beauty for Taiwanese nationalists; blue is the representative colour of the KMT). The blues claim the ability to manage cross-straits relations in the interests of Taiwan, while the greens accuse the blues of selling out the island to the People's Republic.

On Taiwan, in areas like trade and politics, cross-straits relations are characterized by ambiguous boundaries between the official and unofficial, the public and the secret. Within the Taiwanese electorate there is no consensus, as a result, about the state of cross-straits relations at any one time. Hundreds of thousand of Taiwanese live and work on mainland China. But there is no reliable, publicly available information on their precise number and political affiliation. Relations (or non-relations) between the People's Republic and Republic of China are intersected by those of the Communist and Nationalist parties; the 'truth' about the relationship between China and Taiwan is contested and politicized.

In the late 1980s, the KMT let go of its claim to be the legitimate government of all of China. (The Communist Party still loudly trumpets itself as the legitimate government of all China, including Taiwan.) In a democratic Taiwan, this accords with electoral sentiment: surveys reveal that the vast majority of Taiwanese reject the idea of unification with the People's Republic, preferring, at the very least, to maintain the status quo of the island's de facto sovereignty.

From 2000 to 2008, for the first time since the KMT assumed control of the island in 1945, a party other than the KMT governed the Republic of China, when President Chen Shui-bian of the Democratic Progressive Party (DPP) won the presidential election in 2000. The DPP is the party of Taiwanese nationalist politics, established by an older generation of Taiwanese who were educated under the Japanese as well as a younger generation of anti-KMT and pro-democracy activists and Taiwanese nationalists who grew up under KMT authoritarianism. In his first term, Chen moderated the rhetoric of Taiwanese nationalism, taking significant steps to reach out in a conciliatory manner to mainland China. However, understanding that the DPP's ultimate goal was an independent Taiwan, Beijing's policy towards Taiwan in Chen's first term was to use every opportunity to accuse it of 'provocation' in its pursuit of Taiwanese self-determination. Beijing also exploited the mishandling of Taiwan's relations with the US by the DPP government. The Chen government misread the shift in US policy after 11 September 2001 and pursued referenda legislation to enable plebiscites (for example, on a formal declaration of independence) at the same time as failing to secure arms procurement bills through the legislature, stretching the status quo of cross-straits relations while assuming ever greater reliance on US military protection.

Chen was re-elected to a second term in 2004, signalling Taiwan moving further away from unification with mainland China. For the People's Republic, this was considered a failure of its Taiwan policy. Cross-strait relations entered a downward spiral. Playing off the domestic politics of division, the Chen government's rhetoric and policy positions became increasingly shrill and explicitly anti-China.

Beijing was thus much relieved by the return of the KMT to power with the election of Ma Ying-jeou in 2008, and with his re-election in 2012. Ma came to office with the stated aim of improving relations with the mainland. He would do this in a distinctive way, with cross-straits policies that deliberately operated at the level of the tacit or the unspoken.

In an attempt to improve relations with mainland China, Ma announced a policy called the 'Three Nos': 'no unification, no independence and no use of force'. It builds on the so-called '1992 Consensus', the outcome of talks between the SEF and ARATS in Singapore in 1992 in which both sides agreed that there is one China but each side interprets what that means and leave that interpretation unspoken in any negotiations. 'Mutual non-recognition of sovereignty' (*hu bu chengren zhuquan* 互不承認主權) and 'mutual non-denial of jurisdiction' (*hu bu fouren zhiquan* 互不否認治權) allows each side to agree that they do not recognize the other, to agree to disagree as it were.

Ma Ying-jeou's goal was to 'engage in negotiations on issues of more pragmatic concerns while shelving our political disagreements'. The centrepiece of his first term was the Economic Cooperation Framework Agreement (ECFA) or, in Chinese, *Haixia liang'an jingji hezuo jiagou xieyi* 海峽兩岸經濟合作架構協議. ECFA is a preferential trade agreement that eliminates tariffs on 539 goods from Taiwan to China and 267 goods in the other direction. ECFA is notable for being especially generous in its terms towards Taiwan.

In keeping with the policy approach of the Ma administration, the agreement itself was not signed by either of the governments of the People's Republic or the Republic of China, but by the representatives of ARATS and the SEF. It is an agreement between states that accepts that neither side recognizes the other. The document uses language such as 'both sides' (*shuangfang* 雙方), or the 'Taiwan side' (*Taiwan fangmian* 台灣方面) and the 'mainland side' (*dalu fangmian* 大陸方面). There is no talk of either 'province' or 'nation' in regards to Taiwan.

Ma Ying-jeou won a strong victory in the presidential election in January 2012, yet opinion polling shows him to be a notably unpopular president. His approval rating dropped below twenty-five percent shortly before the inauguration for his second term in May 2012. The gap between what is said and what is left unsaid by the Taiwan government about relations with China has created a well of unease and uncertainty among the Taiwanese electorate in which neither the Taiwanese nationalism of the DPP nor the rosy rhetoric of the KMT with its language of 'win-wins' (*shuangying* 雙贏) expresses the reality of how the people of Taiwan experience cross-straits relations.

It was against this background that Chen Guangbiao arrived on the island with his *hongbao*, bringing on a 'water-cooler moment' (*remen huati* 熱門話題) in Taiwan's national conversation with which its political rhetoric is unequipped to come to terms. In a Chinese cultural context the *hongbao* is a gift that expresses reciprocal social relations of dependency. It passes from parent to child, from boss to worker. Chen Guangbiao's visit spoke of a social understanding of Taiwan's relations with China in which the people of Taiwan recognize at a symbolical level that a rising China is more and more able to dictate the terms of cross-straits relations – Chen Guangbiao positioned himself as the patriarch or boss over Taiwan in the symbolic language of red envelopes. It is a far cry from the threats, shrill nationalism and military intimidation of the 1990s and 2000s; but for many, the metaphorical significance of the envelopes is just as controversial.

—*Mark Harrison*

3

THE IDEOLOGY OF LAW AND ORDER

Susan Trevaskes

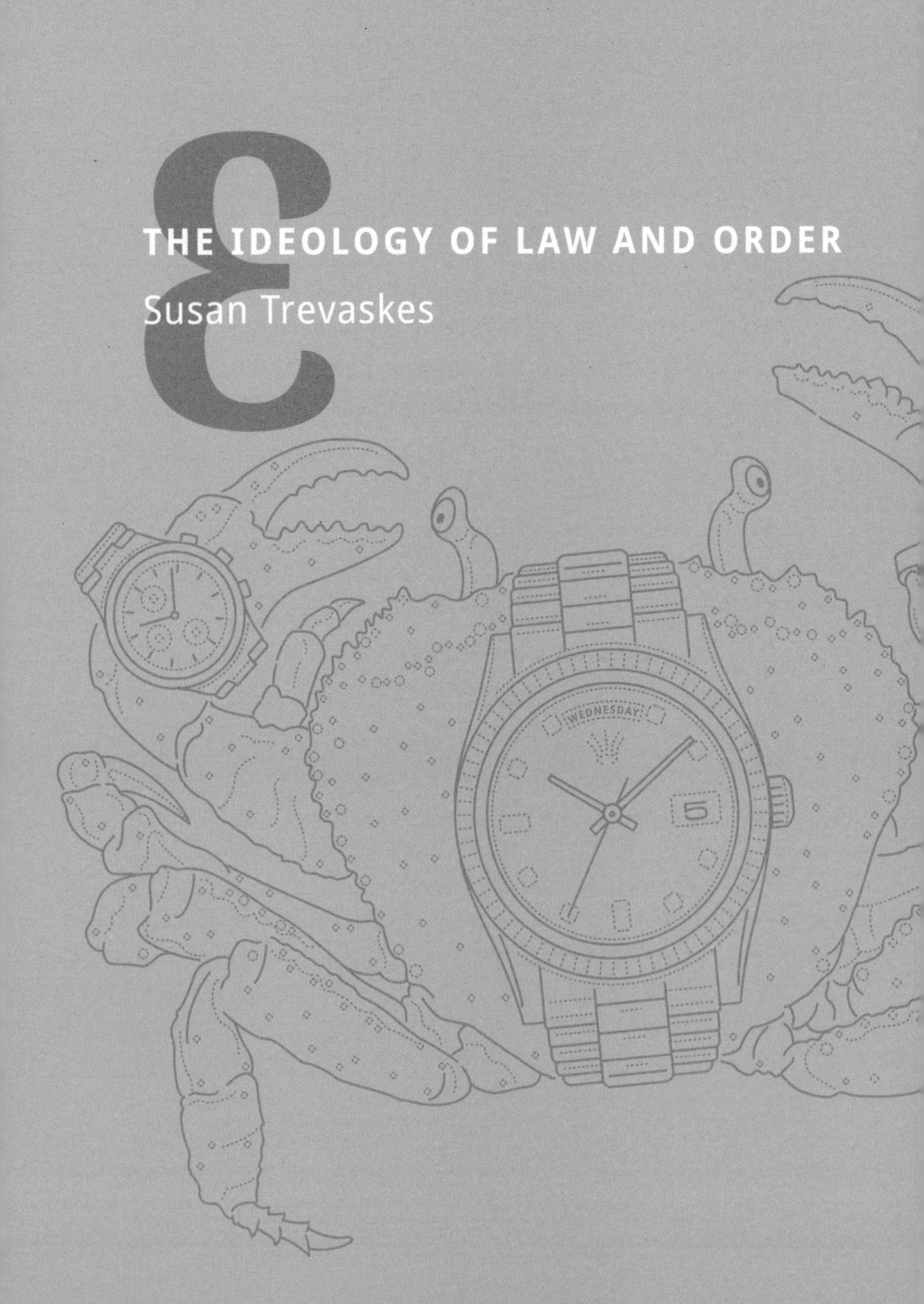

JUSTICE STANDS at the intersection between state and society in all of its dimensions. It is the expression of relations between the vast majority of China's people and the relatively small coterie who govern them – the Chinese Communist Party. As more people resist the interference of power-holders in all aspects of their lives as well as the abuse of their social and economic rights, the Party has come to regard such behaviour as arising threat, an alternative source of legitimate power and justice. The collective, if often inchoate, power of the average citizens and the importance they have come to place on justice today pose direct challenges to China's 'red rising' – that is the increasingly assertive party-state and its goal of 'maintaining stability'.

During the years 2010-2012, China was riven by social tensions. Dysfunction in local political structures over many years fuelled a thirst for justice. While the country's rapid rural and urban development (discussed in the previous chapter) have benefitted the national and indeed the international economies, land seizures by unscrupulous developers with the help of corrupt party-state officials have sparked public outrage, and protest. In these boom years individuals and various groups in China have increasingly resorted to collective and individual resistance – protests and other forms of overt dissent including strikes, demonstrations and riots in an effort to secure social and economic rights. Increasingly, people are expressing their anger not just about inequalities of wealth and opportunity but also inequalities that limit access to the legal system and impartial justice.

Ideology has been central to the philosophy and practice of justice throughout the history of the People's Republic. Political rhetoric is often used to rationalize measures of social control, such as policing operations and regulations designed to modulate and manipulate social conduct. Ever since the founding of the People's Republic, the Party has determined the state's responses to crime and unrest – including the nature of judicial decision-making in criminal trials. As social disturbances and legal contestation have come into sharper focus in recent years a version of former Party Chairman Mao Zedong's all-encompassing approach to social control has competed at the local level with the 'harmonious society' model promoted nationally since 2005.

In the lead up to the transition year of Chinese party-state power of 2012-2013, law and order became a critical arena in which both the outgoing leadership as well as the incoming contenders for ultimate power attempted to accrue political capital. In the first half of the 2000s, reformers within China's legal system had begun to make significant headway in their efforts to create a corps of professional judges and institute a less draconian regime of punishment for criminals. Although these reforms remained largely in place in 2012, they co-existed with the increasingly egregious actions of both civil and armed police in the suppression of rising dissent. The future of the legal reforms will depend on the outcome of the leadership transition itself.

Propaganda poster: 'Everybody participate; collectively build an harmonious community.'
Source: Baidu Baike

Two contrasting approaches shaped the legal landscape during the post-Beijing Olympic years, 2008-2012. The first was the 'Chongqing initiative' or model that pursued a two-pronged policy summed up in the slogan 'Sing Red, Strike Black'. The charismatic and mass mobilization 'red campaigns' of Chongqing are discussed in the preceding chapter. The 'black' refers to Chinese mafia-style syndicates and other criminal activity. Like many rapidly developing areas in China in which local power and economic opportunity were relatively unrestrained by suitable checks and balances, Chongqing was rife with corruption and organized crime when Bo Xilai became the municipality's Party chief. In 2009, Bo and his security forces launched the 'strike black' anti-crime campaigns. Thousands were rounded up and tried for crimes including accepting bribes, other forms of economic crime, assault and murder.

While all this was happening in the south-west, Party General Secretary Hu Jintao and Premier Wen Jiabao were determining national 'social stability' policy settings. These policies aimed to enforce social stability at all costs; the goal was defined as consolidation of an 'harmonious society'. In contrast to Bo Xilai's approach, this agenda favoured what were called 'stability maintenance operations' – a strong police presence at rallies, protest meetings and in dealing with individual cases of disruption (real or imagined) – rather than a Mao-style mass campaign approach such as championed by Bo Xilai. Competing political camps infused political ideologies of control into justice and security agendas on both national and local levels. They did so to align themselves and their approaches with the quest for national stability/unity – for the sake of their own political advancement. This contest over the styles of control and the kinds of justice they deliver is of crucial importance to the Party: it is at the core of it credibility as the sole source of state power and authority.

Zhou Yongkang, often referred to in the international media as China's 'top cop'. As the ninth member of the Standing Committee of the Communist Party's Politburo, Zhou has overseen security forces and law enforcement agencies in recent years.
Source: Baidu Baike

One of the egregious failures of the Hu-Wen era (2003-2012) was that the Beijing-based Party elite did not successfully build into local government operations a substantive form of oversight or moderation that could effectively – and not merely rhetorically – curb corruption and abuses of power. Over the first three decades of the post-Mao era Open Door and Reform policies initiated in 1978, apart from critical periods of popular protest such as the mass nationwide uprising of 1989, people had generally been willing to forfeit political engagement in exchange for assured social and economic rights. But the local configuration of power in villages, townships and cities across the nation is such that over recent years many millions have become increasingly aggrieved as they have seen even these rights eroded. Local power-holders sanction rapid economic development that tolerates, if not encourages, the seizure of agricultural land and allows unregulated factory production that often has serious environmental consequences. When people felt that they had exhausted all avenues of redress for the plunder of their economic and social rights mass protests have erupted.

The 'Mass Line' and 'Harmonious Society'

In China the practice of and debates around law and order have been shaped by the Maoist concept of 'social contradictions', that is social or political activities that cause discord, crime or dissent within the ranks of 'the people' (that is the majority of citizens), or between the people and their enemies. Today 'enemies' are defined as individuals or groups suspected of destabilizing society, threatening the territorial integrity of the nation or questioning the ultimate authority of the Communist Party. These days, 'social contradictions' is a term often used euphemistically to describe social conflicts between the disaffected masses and the objects of their disaffection: local government officials, developers and, in some cases, company bosses.

In the period 2010-2011, approximately 100,000 mass protests occurred as a result of local injustices and abuses of power. The gathering momentum of online expressions of dissatisfaction (a topic discussed also in chapters 5 and 7 in this volume) helped fuel unrest in the streets.

The nationwide social anomie was in part exacerbated by the political transition that was slowly unfolding in the lead up to the 2012-2013 renewal of Party and state leaders in Beijing. Without an open political process, a free media, or regular channels for political contestation in which differing socio-political agendas could be aired, some of the aspirants for the top jobs in China sought to bolster their political capital by demonstrating their ability to maintain 'stability and unity'. This made the landscape of law and justice in China, hitherto dominated by a single, dominant Party ideology, contested territory.

A propaganda poster from the Chaoyang District Government, Beijing: 'If you, me and him are civilized, all families will live in harmony.'
Photo: Geremie R. Barmé

In the Mao era (1949-78) justice in the People's Republic was underpinned by a policy of class struggle and the use of mass trials. These events were staged not only to impose the 'proletarian dictatorship' but also to educate (and caution) the population at large. The mass line was essentially a means used to mobilize popular participation in national economic and revolutionary goals. For its part, 'mass-line justice' sought to transform the 'diffuse and unsystematic' ideas of the masses and meld them in 'a concentrated and systematic way' so as to resolve social frictions between and within classes.

In twenty-first century marketized China, such concepts of social (and overt) class contradictions belong to a different era. Today, the authorities still speak of pursuing the 'mass line', but this is little more than a rhetorical device, stripped of significant content or meaning. Generally, the state now asserts itself not through mass mobilizations but in the overt application of state power via vast police actions, sometimes in the form of anti-crime campaigns intended to punish 'enemies of the masses', that is corrupt officials and organised crime.

'Insist on leadership by the Party, develop democracy to the fullest, do everything according to the law. Diligently carry out elections for representatives at district, county, village and town levels.'
Photo: Geremie R. Barmé

A more voluntarist aspect of the old mass line reappeared, however, in recent years in the form of the 'Sing Red' campaign men-

Harmonious Society (*hexie shehui* 和谐社会)

The concept of the 'harmonious society' was originally introduced at the National People's Congress in 2005 and is associated with Hu Jintao. It was developed into a fully blown Party resolution in 2006 that included a blueprint for social and political governance; its proclaimed goals included producing more equitable economic and social outcomes by reducing the egregious disparities in income and living conditions between China's haves and have-nots. The mantra-like formula 'harmonious society' is repeated *ad nauseam* by officials and in the official media, but in popular usage it has acquired a negative connotation. It is often used as a satirical euphemism for the government's efforts at maintaining stability, including censorship and the suppression of dissidents.

Chinese Internet users, who are inclined to mock all political slogans, created a slang pun on 'harmony': river crab (河蟹, pronounced *héxiè*, homophonous with 'harmony' or *héxié*). To be censored is sometimes referred to as 'being harmonized' or 'being river-crabbed', and 'river crab' sometimes indicates censorship.

'Sing Red, Strike Black' (*changhong dahei* 唱红打黑)

In 2009, the Chongqing Party Secretary Bo Xilai announced a campaign to revive China's red, or revolutionary-era culture and to rein in criminal activity. This campaign went under the rubric of 'Sing Red, Strike Black'. 'Sing Red' signified the need to 'sing red [or pro-Party and patriotic] songs, read red classics [the works of Mao and other leaders], recount red stories [of the revolution and patriotic valour] and pass on [to the next generation] red maxims'. 'Strike Black' was short for 'strike down social darkness and eliminate evil', which refers to organized criminals.

As police cracked down on organized crime, restrictions were placed on TV and radio stations: reducing entertainment programs and advertising in favour of 'red' revolutionary programming. Mass events were organized at which tens of thousands of participants sang Mao-era songs.

The 'strike black' element of the campaign ensnared prominent business people, government officials and even the city's former police chief, who was convicted and executed. While the campaign drew criticism from some liberal intellectuals and people who were persecuted during the Cultural Revolution, leftists who idealized Mao's rule (or at least aspects of it) praised it wholeheartedly.

The movement halted abruptly following Bo Xilai's dismissal in March 2012.

tioned earlier that aimed, through the collective experience of revolutionary and patriotic culture, to evoke and reaffirm mass unity. Bo Xilai, the Party Secretary of Chongqing who features throughout this volume, introduced and actively propagated this approach with the advice of his think tank supporters to create what has been dubbed the 'Chongqing Model' (for more on this see Chapter 2).

The expression 'harmonious society', meanwhile, has been the dominant form of official rhetoric used by the Beijing authorities to bind fractured social relations in the decade from 2002 to 2012. 'Harmonious society' was formulated to deal head-on with the dramatic rise in the social tensions triggered by China's unprecedented and uneven economic development. Up until about 2007, the year prior to the Beijing Olympics, the 'harmonious society' strategy generally favoured a kid-glove approach to social issues, aiming to ensure greater social stability and public harmony and to present a more humane and welcoming face to the outside world.

Both the 'red politics' of the Chongqing Model and the 'harmonious society' strategy of Beijing shared a common presumption: that the interests of 'the masses' are at one with those of Party elites. In reality, over recent years the chasm between the masses and the country's social-political elites, never inconsiderable, has only widened.

An undertaking to narrow the gap between incomes and social opportunities was written into a state plan to support the construction of the 'harmonious society' in the mid-2000s. But such promises were at best vague and unrealizable. After 2007, the rhetoric changed. Instead of addressing the problems and injustices, the Party leadership turned its focus on the protests and petitions these sparked among the restive masses themselves. It declared that people and groups who created social unrest, that is those who were protesting in increasing numbers against abuses of power and the disparities in wealth, should be dealt with through so-called 'stability maintenance' operations.

'Stability maintenance' (*wei wen* 维稳, an abbreviation of *weihu shehui wending* 维护社会稳定) is a catch-all term covering a range of policing methods from the crackdown on open dissent widely reported in the international media to anti-crime campaigns. Thus, after 2007, the 'harmonious society' was less about 'building' a certain kind of society and more about 'protecting' the status quo against those who dared to dissent through 'stability maintenance'.

The face-off between powerful elites and aggrieved non-elites has led to a twofold crisis of confidence. On the one hand, the people have lost faith in the party-state's ability to address issues of the abuse of power. On the other, the officials have lost confidence in the ability of political

Stability and Unity (*anding tuanjie* 安定团结)

By 1974, as a result of nearly a decade of extreme revolutionary politics, China remained politically torn and volatile. Although he had been the ultimate progenitor of years of chaos, Mao increasingly saw the need to restore order. That year he called on Party leaders to pursue a policy of 'stability and unity'.

Deng Xiaoping initially contested this directive on ideological grounds, but Mao overruled him by stating: 'Stability and unity does not mean giving up class struggle'. In 1977, after Mao's death, Deng was reinstated and became the de facto leader of the Party. 'Stability and unity' remained the premise for the Party's work; Deng even stated: 'Stability crushes everything else' (*wending yadao yiqie* 稳定压倒一切). The phrase 'stability and unity' came to be associated with Deng, despite its early use in a campaign against him.

'Stability crushes everything else' was eventually replaced by the Jiang Zemin-era 'culture of harmony' (*hehe wenhua* 和合文化) and then by Hu Jintao's 'harmonious society'. All have aimed to preserve the hard-won social stability and political unity that dates from the start of the Reform era in late 1978.

Mass Line (*qunzhong luxian* 群众路线)

The 'mass line' was a method of leadership designed by Mao Zedong that sought to 'learn from the masses' in general, and the peasantry in particular, by gathering their ideas and systematizing them as a basis for social and political action.

The mass line, first articulated by Mao in 1927, was an attempt to adapt Marxist-Leninist doctrine to China's particular socio-political conditions. The mass line was supposed to ensure that the Chinese Communist Party would run a government by the people and for the people. Mao later criticized the Soviet leader Joseph Stalin for being out of touch with the masses.

As Mao himself said:

> To link oneself with the masses, one must act in accordance with the needs and wishes of the masses. All work done for the masses must start from their needs and not from the desire of any individual, however well-intentioned. It often happens that objectively the masses need a certain change, but subjectively they are not yet conscious of the need, not yet willing or determined to make the change. In such cases, we should wait patiently. We should not make the change until, through our work, most of the masses have become conscious of the need and are willing and determined to carry it out. Otherwise we shall isolate ourselves from the masses.
>
> —*'The United Front in Cultural Work'* (30 October 1944)
>
> The people, and the people alone, are the motive force in the making of world history.
>
> —*'On Coalition Government'* (24 April 1945)

and legal institutions to ensure social stability by solving social problems through the legitimate exercise of the law. It is as if, in recent years, the party-state has lost faith in its own promise to provide institutional autonomy and the rule of law.

Mass-Line Justice: the Bo Xilai Formula

By 2010, Bo Xilai's 'Chongqing Model' was for driving the conversation on issues of justice and policing, on the Internet, in communities and in the capital Beijing itself. He boldly coloured his socio-economic and justice policies red, justifying his approach as being one that 'puts the people first' (an update of the old Maoist slogan about 'serving the people'). He also claimed that it a 'necessary corrective' to the political and economic approach laid down by Deng Xiaoping during his 1992 Tour of the South that 'development is an inescapable necessity' (*fazhan shi ying daoli* 发展是硬道理). In its place, Bo attempted to situate 'the people' at the centre of socio-economic policy and he proposed to do so by improving the living and working conditions of Chongqing's millions of peasant migrant workers (*nongmingong* 农民工), for example providing cheap rental housing for Chongqing's large, and economically vitally important, population of peasant migrant workers.

重慶商報

文强伏法

一段黑恶江湖的终结：文强昨上午被执行死刑

一场大快人心的胜利：市民拉横幅放鞭炮庆祝

江北再造六个"北城天街" 奢侈品购物馆9月开业

百余富豪今聚重庆

我市高考录取明天开始
有疑问请打这四部电话

9日-10日18:30至23:00
南滨路部分路段管制

想当相扑运动员
170公斤胖娃还要增肥

加拿大房产全球巡展

8 July 2010: the execution is announced of Wen Qiang, former head of the Municipal Judicial Bureau of Chongqing, for a number of crimes ranging from protecting organized crime and accepting bribes to rape. His conviction came as a result of the 'Strike Black' campaign.
Source: *Chongqing Economic Times*

The other side of Bo Xilai's policy, 'Strike Black', was to achieve a more 'equitable' distribution of justice. It was in the name of the masses that Bo pursued a much-celebrated 2009 campaign to rid Chongqing of organized criminals and their 'protective umbrellas' in government. He revived Mao-era tactics such as exhorting the masses to report and denounce suspected criminals. It was such strategies and the language in which they were framed that gave Bo's anti-crime campaign the political cachet it required to distinguish his approach from that of his rivals. Although his campaign to 'Sing Red, Strike Black' was restricted to Chongqing, the effects were felt nationwide.

Three corruption-related cases in Chongqing dominated national media reports on crime control in 2010 and 2011. The head of the municipal Bureau of Justice and former Deputy Police Chief, Wen Qiang, was convicted of having taken bribes in excess of 100 million *yuan* and was executed in 2010. The 'Chinese mafia' crime boss Gong Gangmo was gaoled for life for a spate of violent and economic crimes. His lawyer, Li Zhuang, became a household name when he was charged, tried and gaoled for allegedly helping his client falsify evidence. The case against Li was widely regarded by China's legal world as a travesty of justice and a frame-up. In an open letter to his colleagues in Chongqing one of China's most famous legal scholars, He Weifang, went so far as to say that the actions taken by Bo Xilai and the Chongqing police force against Li had set the course of the rule of law in China back thirty years.

Yao Jiaxin 药家鑫

In October 2010, a twenty-one year-old junior at the Xi'an Conservatory of Music by the name of Yao Jiaxin accidentally hit Zhang Miao, a twenty-six-year-old woman, with his car. Fearful that she would report his licence plate number and demand compensation, Yao stabbed the young woman to death. In the weeks that followed, Yao's extraordinary cold-bloodedness raised the profile of the case, and rumours circulated on the Internet that he had a powerful family that would help him escape punishment. These rumours later turned out to be false. Following his arrest, Yao admitted that the reason he killed Zhang was that he assumed from her peasant-like features that she might try to take advantage of the situation and extort money from him.

For a time, Yao's trial and appeal were one of the most talked-about issues in the Chinese media. Online opinion was overwhelmingly in favor of a death sentence. Yao was executed in June 2011.

Li Zhuang 李庄

Li Zhuang was, until recently, a Beijing-based lawyer. He became embroiled in the politics of Bo Xilai's 'Sing Red, Strike Black' campaign in late 2009 when he was seen to have provided too rigorous a defence for the Chongqing crime boss Gong Gangmo. Gong claimed that he had been tortured by police, but when he recanted, police authorities accused Li Zhuang of 'inciting a client to give false testimony.'

As a result, in January 2010, Li was himself arraigned in court and sentenced to thirty months in gaol. Immediately after the sentence was read in court, Li openly accused prosecutors of breaking a plea deal. The sentence was reduced to eighteen months on appeal. Months prior to his release in April 2011, prosecutors brought further charges that were later dropped due to a lack of evidence. Li's case is seen as being significant as it sent a clear message to lawyers to keep their defence work in line with the political interests of Party authorities.

Li Zhuang, now free, is a frequent commentator on social affairs on his *Sina Weibo* microblog.

These Chongqing dramas were hardly the only instances of badly behaved privileged urbanites that made justice news over this period. But they certainly did further erode the credibility of and community confidence in the prospects of decent governance and justice. The public also expressed outrage over the handling of less high-profile criminal cases than those involving Chongqing's crime lords and their political cronies. Two examples outside Chongqing are the case of Yao Jiaxin and the 'My Father is Li Gang' incident (outlined in Chapter 5). Both involved relatively well-off young men who, having each accidentally run over and killed people, attempted to escape justice. Both cases gained instant national notoriety and demonstrate how quickly public anger can turn against individuals perceived as having used their power or status to gain unlawful or unfair political, economic or social advantage – or to escape legal sanction. These were not members of the party-state bureaucracy, or nomenclatura, but individuals of only relatively modest social status who nevertheless had taken advantage of their personal networks to evade responsibility for their actions.

Hu Jintao and Wen Jiabao Maintain Stability

In March 2011, it was announced that China's annual budget for 'stability maintenance' was over 650 billion *yuan*, a sum in excess of official figures for national defence. The news raised eyebrows both in China and abroad, even though such an escalation of police budgets and powers had been evident before the August-September 2008 Beijing Olympics. As early as 2007 the Party had begun to act against individuals who generated 'disharmony' by participating in or fomenting 'mass incidents'.

The international media tends to focus on individual cases of repression of defence lawyers, grassroots human rights activists, dissident intellectuals like the 2010 Nobel Peace Prize Laureate Liu Xiaobo, net activists and troublemaking artists like Ai Weiwei. The Chinese authorities' attention, by contrast, is really concentrated on 'mass incidents' (*qunti*

Peasant Workers (*nongmingong* 农民工, often shortened to *mingong* 民工)

A *mingong* or peasant worker is a person whose *hukou* (household registration, see Chapter 2) identifies him or her as a farmer but who has migrated, usually to a city, in search of work. *A Survey of China's Peasant Workers* (*Zhongguo mingong diaocha* 中国民工调查), a book published in 2005, claimed that there were more than 300 million *mingong* in China, including the children of *mingong* growing up in cities but still tied to their home village by their household registration.

Mingong are typically people with relatively little education who work on construction sites and in factories. In cities like Beijing and Shanghai, many university graduates from rural areas who have failed to obtain an urban *hukou* are also officially registered as *mingong*.

A less politically correct alternative to *mingong* is the term *mangliu* 盲流, literally 'blind floaters', one which suggests the unchecked flow of rural poor into the cities. The pejorative use of *mingong* by urbanites has given the term a derogatory meaning, and a number of alternatives have emerged, including 'new city resident' (*xinshimin* 新市民) and 'new contract worker' (*xinxing hetong gongren* 新型合同工人).

shijian 群体事件). A 'mass incident' could be anything from a sit-in, march, rally or strike to a full-blown street demonstration organised to protest against injustices or abuses of power. Such protests might involve ten people or more than 1,000 and, in some cases, over 10,000. According to Chinese reports, there has been an average of over 100,000 mass incidents annually. Many protesters are poor and vulnerable individuals. Threats to their already limited social and economic access to resources (a home or a low-paying job) can easily spark an emotional confrontation with the responsible authorities. Relatively benign incidents, easily resolved but allowed to fester by local authorities, frequently escalate from 'small disturbances' (*xiao nao* 小闹) to become 'major disturbances' (*da nao* 大闹). Such disturbances – protests – are almost invariably directed against government officials, local developers or businesses. The situation, paradoxically, benefits the central authorities. The strategy of 'localising grievances while insulating the Centre' successfully encourages a perception that the central government is sympathetic in principle to the aggrieved, poor and vulnerable people involved in such protests.

Around sixty-five percent of China's mass incidents relate to the misappropriation of agricultural land. The Chinese Academy of Social Sciences estimates that fifty million farmers had their land seized in 2010, with that figure increasing annually at a rate of three million. Increasingly, people are also protesting en masse in response to environmental threats to their health, livelihood and homes by polluting industries and government actions. A typical example is the October 2010 Wenchang Incident in Hainan province. Thousands of people protested against the failure of local government officials to notify them before releasing the waters of a local reservoir inundating hundreds of properties. In one of the largest protests of 2011, tens of thousands of residents in the northern city of Dalian forced the authorities to close a paraxylene chemical plant. A storm had damaged the dyke around the plant, sparking fears that paraxylene made at the plant could spill into the water system and inflict enormous damage. Mass protests like these occur because people do not have effective, conventional dispute-resolution mechanisms at their disposal. As the commentator Tang Hao put it: 'When local governments use unconventional methods to build polluting projects, the public is forced to resort to unconventional means to protect their interests.'

Other incidents can be sparked by a single individual taking action against a perceived injustice, such as in the case of the October 2010 tax riot in Huzhou city in Zheijiang province on China's south-east coast. An argument between a local tax col-

Main entrance of the Supreme People's Court, Beijing, which is located in the former Foreign Legation Quarter.
Source: Wikimedia Commons

Stone lions, which traditionally stood in front of imperial government buildings adorn the entrance to the Supreme People's Court, Beijing.
Source: Anthony Ellwood-Russell

A courtroom, Supreme People's Court, Beijing. The court boasts 340 judges.
Source: flickr/Seth Nelson

Stability Maintenance (*wei wen* 维稳)

Since 2005, the Chinese government has allocated vast amounts of money and resources to quash organized resistance to its authority. Revolutions overseas, the growing use of mobile communications and digital networking, as well as labour conflicts and ethnic unrest have all had an impact on China's stability maintenance campaign. Added to this is an awareness that local corruption and malfeasance by party-state officials have generated resentment and protest, that there are limited avenues for complaint or redress and that rapid economic development has generated serious social inequalities.

The overall strategy of using police force to maintain social stability and to enforce the official version of social harmony is a campaign known by the expression *'wei wen'*, a shorthand for *weihu shehui wending* 维护社会稳定, or 'maintain social stability'. Charged with 'maintaining stability' are local police in public security bureaus across the nation and parapolice belonging to the military's expanding contingent of People's Armed Police (PAP). Stability maintenance incorporates 'preventative' activities such as building extensive CCTV surveillance networks in major cities such as Chongqing, as well as maintaining a strong police, military police and private security presence at protests and rallies. Stability maintenance also involves Internet censorship, paid informants, security contractors, the harassment of activists, and neighborhood watch-dog groups.

'Wei wen' was a much-used term in March 2011, following online calls for a 'Jasmine Revolution' in China. The term and the execution of related policies are associated closely with Zhou Yongkang, a key member of the Party's leading Politburo and head of China's security services slated for retirement in late 2012.

Rights Protection (*wei quan* 维权)

Wei quan is a shortening of the expression *weihu hefa quanyi* 维护合法权益, 'protect legal rights'. It is a term that came into use in the early 2000s to refer to a grassroots network of activists and lawyers who have tried to defend the rights of Chinese citizens. Despite harsh restrictions and persecution by the government, some lawyers and intellectuals persisted in organizing demonstrations, writing letters of appeal, pushing reform through petitions and the media, and defending victims. They are known as *wei quan* or rights activists.

Government reactions to these grassroots activities have at times been extremely harsh, with reported instances of detainment and torture. Use of the Internet, including blocked websites like Twitter, by activists has unnerved the government, and it is not unusual for prominent rights activists to be 'invited to drink tea' (*qing hecha* 请喝茶), that is, to attend a compulsory meeting with security officers to explain postings on Twitter or other activities over a seemingly innocent cup of tea.

lector and a textile business owner quickly escalated into a protest involving hundreds of people enraged at local tax hikes.

Accidents or violence in which ordinary people were victims and local officials then perpetrators led to particularly explosive incidents. The Kunming riot of March 2010 was sparked when urban management officers

Demonstrations in Weng'an, Guizhou province, after allegations of a cover-up connected with a girl's rape and murder turned violent.
Source: Myspace.cn, Zonaeuropa.com

(*chengshi guanli xingzheng zhifa renyuan* 城市管理行政执法人员, *chengguan* for short; a particularly unpopular form of roadside bureaucrat) tipped over a tricycle cart being ridden by a sixty-year-old female peddler, resulting in her death. Hundreds of witnesses to the accident surrounded the government vehicle and beat up the officers.

The most dramatic and influential mass incident in recent years occurred in Wukan township in Guangdong province, previously mentioned in Chapter 2. Starting out as a protest against official land grabs and the illegal sale of agricultural land to developers, a demonstration in late 2011 quickly morphed into China's largest local uprising in recent memory. The vast majority of the town's residents crowded into the streets and pitted themselves against local Party and policing authorities. After years of economic deprivation at the hands of illegal land dealers who were in business with local Party chiefs, residents rose up, took

Inner Mongolia Riots, May 2011

One of the most noteworthy mass demonstrations in 2011 occurred in Inner Mongolia, a Chinese territory bordering Mongolia. The situation was sparked by the death of an ethnic Mongolian herder named Merger who, on 10 May, tried to stop a convoy of coal trucks that had been damaging grazing pastures and harming goats by driving through the grasslands. Witnesses said that a driver deliberately ran over the herder. The incident spurred over a thousand demonstrators, including some students, to take to the streets in Xilinhot in the biggest show of people power in Inner Mongolia in over twenty years.

In a situation with some parallels in Xinjiang and Tibet, many ethnic Mongolians blame Han-owned companies operating mines in Inner Mongolia for not sharing their wealth with the indigenous population. The riots were quelled only when paramilitary police came out in force against the protesters. The driver of the truck was tried for homicide, sentenced to death and executed. The provincial government also announced new rules concerning grassland protection.

to the streets and stormed government offices in their thousands. When one of the protest leaders who had been taken into custody by police died, the incident escalated further. The township was placed under siege and food and fuel supplies were cut off by local and provincial public security and military police.

Throughout December 2011, the plight of Wukan attracted national attention. Sensing an opportunity to present an alternative to both Bo Xilai's red campaigns and the Hu-Wen leadership's bully-boy crackdown style, the Guangdong provincial Party leader and nemesis of Bo Xilai, Wang Yang, turned events to his own political advantage. He sent in his deputy to negotiate with the protesters. When, at the end of the month, Wang promised that the local officials would be brought to justice and fresh (and free) local elections would be held both police and protesters backed down. Wang Yang declared a victory and claimed that this was a new model – the 'Wukan approach' – to resolving social disputes.

This mix of politicking, mass incidents and stability maintenance activities in the post-Olympic years was made more volatile by a series of 'disappearances' of civil rights lawyers, men and women known as advocates of 'rights defence', or *wei quan* in Chinese. The lawyers Teng Biao, Jiang Tianyong and Tang Jitian, who met to talk about the case of blind civil rights activist Chen Guangcheng, then under house arrest, were inexplicably 'disappeared' by police. They eventually reappeared and were subsequently all placed under strict surveillance and then house arrest. These arrests and disappearances coincided with Chinese protests inspired by the 2010-2011 Middle East and North Africa protests (discussed in Chapter 5).

Police detained the Beijing civil rights lawyer Ni Yulan, a woman with a long history of conflict with the security forces, for various lengths of time during 2010-2011 for her protests and defence work on behalf of people who had been forcibly evicted from their homes to make way for demolitions. In 2009, she was under detention for nine months and denied contact with her family. In April 2011, police took Ni and her husband into custody again for 'creating a social disturbance'. Later in July that year, she was additionally charged with fraud for allegedly claiming that she was a lawyer so as to win sympathy for her case and for financial gain. On 10 April 2012, Ni was convicted on both charges and sentenced to two years and eight months imprisonment. Her husband, Gong Jiqin, was also convicted of 'creating a social disturbance' and sentenced to two years in prison. Others, such as the rights lawyer, Jiang Tianyong, who disappeared for two months from February 2011, later spoke to the press about having been tortured while in custody. The veteran activist Zhu Yufu, detained in March 2011, was arrested again the following month on charges of inciting the subversion of state power. Some were so intimidated by the authorities that they declined to comment publicly on their disappearance and periods of detention. The list of lawyers disappeared and detained in recent years also includes Tang Jitian and Liu Shihui, both of whom were whisked away by security personnel. Tang Jitian remained under house arrest until the end of 2011. He was reportedly sent back to his hometown in the north-eastern province of Jilin seriously ill, having contracted tuberculosis while in detention. Police took away the intellectual dissident Xu Zhiyong in May, while Gao Zhisheng, one of China's most famous rights lawyers who had, among other things, also defended Falong Gong adherents was still missing at the end of the year.

Chen Guangcheng 陈光诚

Chen Guangcheng is China's most recognized legal activist, sometimes referred to as a 'barefoot lawyer' after the 'barefoot doctors' of the Cultural Revolution era who served people outside formal state structures. The self-taught blind lawyer's fame dates from the mid-2000s when he mounted legal challenges against local authorities in Linyi, Shandong province, who forced late-term abortions and sterilizations on local women in order to comply with national one-child policy quotas. Chen was gaoled for four years and three months on charges of 'damaging property and organising a mob to disturb traffic'. After his release in September 2010, he and his family were immediately placed under house arrest.

In February 2011, after a home video illustrating the harsh conditions of Chen and his family's confinement was released on the Internet, his wife reported that their house was invaded by over seventy public security personnel and that they were badly beaten. Thirty-odd supporters attempted to draw attention to their plight by visiting their village in late 2011, but dozens of security personnel set upon them and beat them as well. Other would-be visitors include journalists, European diplomats, lawyers, intellectuals and the Hollywood actor Christian Bale. None managed to evade local toughs to see Chen.

Chen's predicament attracted widespread support from bloggers in China and human rights organizations in the West. Yet, as leading legal scholar Jerome Cohen asserts: 'Chen Guangcheng never saw himself as a "troublemaker" bent on damaging social stability and harmony. Indeed, he wanted to improve stability and harmony by using legal institutions to process social grievances in an orderly way as prescribed by law. His only mistake was to accept the law as it was written, as a true believer in the power and promise of China's legal reforms.'

In late April 2012, Chen dramatically escaped from his hometown of Linyi and travelled to Beijing where, with the help of supporters, he found temporary refuge in the American Embassy. After some days he was transferred to a local hospital where he was treated for injuries sustained during his flight. In May, Chen was allowed to travel overseas with his immediate family to pursue his legal studies in New York.

The blind lawyer Chen Guangcheng, now the country's most prominent rights activist, ran afoul of local police when he helped people protesting against forced late abortions. His disappearance became a *cause célèbre* among rights-conscious citizens and a focus of international attention on China's human rights record. In May 2012, he dramatically escaped house arrest in rural Shandong province, travelled to Beijing and eventually was allowed to leave China with his immediate family to pursue legal studies in New York.

Conclusion

Wei wen (stability maintenance) and *wei quan* (rights protection) are concepts that are now at the forefront of China's 'law and order' agenda. Law is the subject of widespread and intense contention in China today. Events of recent years suggest that the 'everything else' in Deng Xiaoping's 1980s' maxim 'Stability crushes everything else' (*wending yadao yiqie* 稳定压倒一切) includes the law as well. Overall, the authorities favour striking down with brute police force any social activity that is deemed to threaten stability. The definition of what exactly constitutes 'stability-threatening' activities has expanded with the intensification of political infighting within the upper echelons of the Party and state mechanisms. The crackdown on threats to 'stability' appears to serve both as a prerequisite for a Harmonious China and a means of shoring up the very future of the Party's hold on national power.

Stability and unity have long been core political concerns in China from the Maoist era 'stability and unity' through to the present. Confronted by increased public dissent, stability and unity have once more become the dual principles supporting the Party-dominated legal system and dominating its approach to governing a nation that is experiencing exacerbated conflict between various elites and average citizens. The 'social contradictions' (to use the Maoist vocabulary), that the authorities still favour, at the heart of China's justice landscape, show that the main tension in the country is not between the authorities and a few rogue dissidents, but between China's ultimate interest group – the Party – and a building source of opposition: the people themselves.

4

4

UNCERTAIN NUMBERS, UNCERTAIN OUTCOMES

Jane Golley

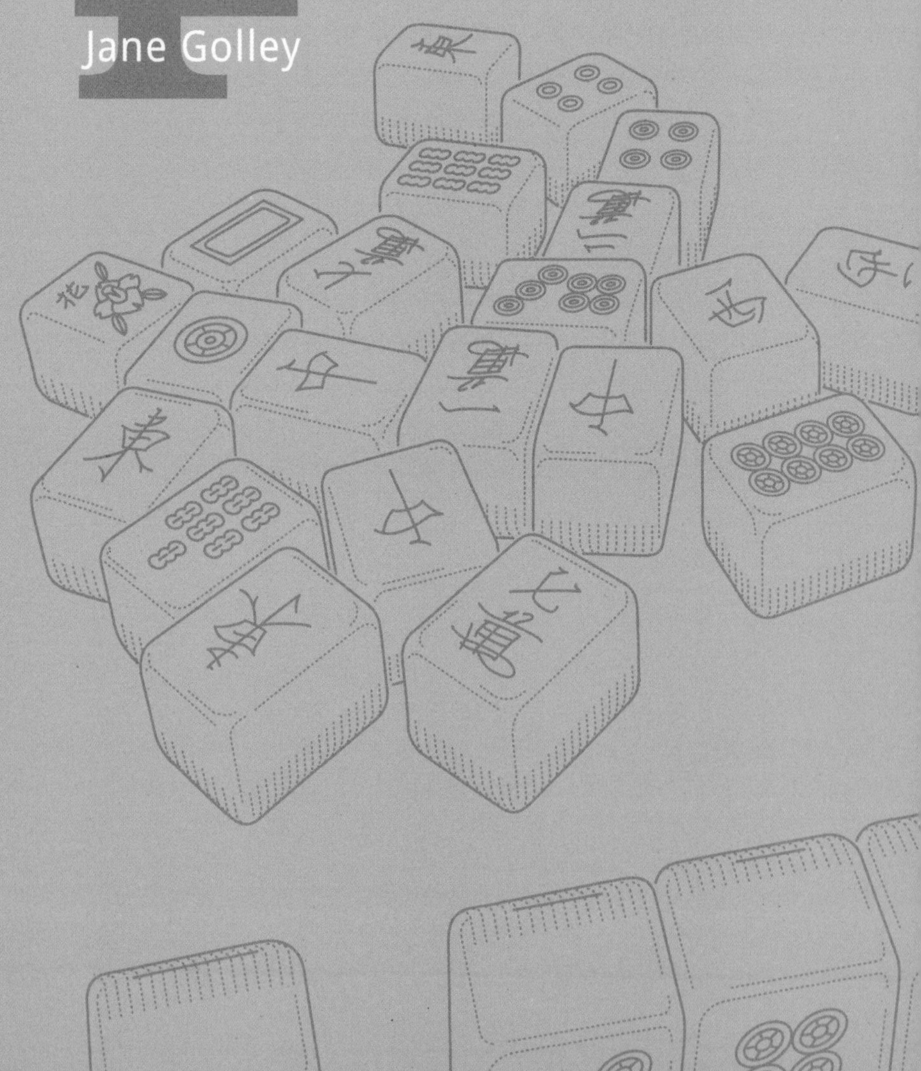

SOME OF the numbers that have been collected, concocted, analysed and debated in recent years illustrate the potentially serious nature of China's economic, social and political challenges. Ongoing debates regarding fertility rates, the pending exhaustion of rural surplus labour, the end of the demographic dividend, gender imbalances, income inequality and government debt make it virtually impossible for anyone to predict particular outcomes with precision. Accurate assessments of China's socio-economic outlook require more accurate collection and reporting of numbers. Meanwhile, great care must be taken in interpreting those that are available.

In April 2011, the International Monetary Fund hit the headlines in China and abroad with the announcement that China's Gross Domestic Product (GDP), in purchasing power parity (PPP), would surpass America's in 2016, making it the largest economy in the world. Already the world's second largest economy, with an official rate of GDP growth returning to over ten percent in 2010 after only a slight slump in 2009, and with official estimates of foreign exchange reserves at over US$3 trillion in 2011, it seemed reasonable when Premier Wen Jiabao offered to help debt-ridden Europe at the World Economic Forum's annual meeting in Dalian, China in September 2011. He said:

A propaganda poster (now known as a 'public service announcement') exhorts citizens to treat male and female children equally. Despite such campaigns, China has a sex ratio of 108 males to 100 females (UN World Population Prospects 2010).
Source: Imagine China

> We have been concerned about the difficulties faced by the European economy for a long time, and we have repeated our willingness to extend a helping hand and increase our investment [there].

Yet the European Union's per capita GDP in 2010 of US$32,537 was more than seven times that of China's of US$4,382, with Europe's (and the world's) richest economy, Luxembourg, being fifty-five times richer in terms of GDP than China's poorest province, Guizhou. China's leaders already face growing international pressure to reform their exchange rate regime, capital markets, financial and banking sectors, and even their style of government. They also must deal with a daunting list of internal development and reform issues relating to the ageing of the population, income inequality, health care and social security, rebalancing the economy, environmental deterioration and poverty. It is clear that China's leaders have their hands full with internal and external challenges alike.

The Sixth National Census

The results from the Chinese government's Sixth National Census in 2010 were released in April 2011, followed by a surge of media commentary and academic analysis. The demographers Zhongwei Zhao and Wei Chen noted that the 2010 Census recorded a number very close to that revealed by annual population survey data for 2009, which they take as an indication that the census data is in fact quite accurate. They also note that the United Nation's population projections for China for 0-14 year olds in 2010 were thirty-eight million higher than the census results, projections that were based on total fertility rates (TFR) of 1.8, 1.7 and 1.64 children per woman for the periods 1995-2000, 2000-2005 and 2005-2010 respectively. These two pieces of information, alongside a few others, enabled them to calculate the fertility rates that would have resulted in the true Census population results for 2010, which they put at 1.6, 1.45 and 1.45 for the same three periods above. This leads them to conclude that China's fertility rate is considerably lower than the officially reported level, and has been since the mid-1990s.

One cannot help but wonder why the National Population and Family Planning Commission (NPFPC) would consistently report a TFR that hovered so closely to 1.8. Indeed, the official TFR was a flat 1.8 from 1999 to 2005, and it was within two hundredths of 1.8 since 1994 (fluctating between 1.82 and 1.78). Given the vast number of factors that determine fertility rates – including the level and pace of economic development, urbanisation, female education, increases in labour force participation rates, improved life-expectancy of new-born children, costs of a competitive education system, and family planning policies and their efficacy – it seems improbable that China's TFR would have maintained such stability over such a dynamic time period. Zhao and Chen suggest that the 'selection' of this number 'seems not to be an arbitrary or anecdotal action', but a matter of convenience. For example, being just under the replacement level (of 2.1, the fertility rate required to maintain a constant population), it can create the illusion of having achieved the desired objective of slow and steady population reduction without greatly affecting the overall age structure of the society. Moreover, it indicates that family planning policies have succeeded in bringing fertility rates down, and therefore deserve further funding and support.

While this provides some logic for the actions of officials within the NPFPC, it does not justify their being allowed to get away with this misreporting over such a long time period. Figure 1 illustrates the projected populations based on official data (OD), data collected by the United Nations (UN) and Zhao and Chen's (ZC) revised population figures. The differences between the most credible estimates (ZC) and the least believable (OD) of China's total population reach 112 million for 2030 and 180 million by 2050. Zhongwei Zhao rightly concludes that: 'Differences of nearly 20 percent in estimated fertility levels and of [over] 100 million people in projected population size are by no means negligible.'

Accurate population and fertility data are crucial for understanding the economic implications of demographic change in China, as elsewhere. Has China's demographic dividend already ended or does it have decades to play out? Just how rapidly is the population ageing? Is China really running out of 'surplus labour'? And what should be done in response? Without accurate data, it is very difficult to say. Below I consider some of the economic implications of getting the population numbers wrong.

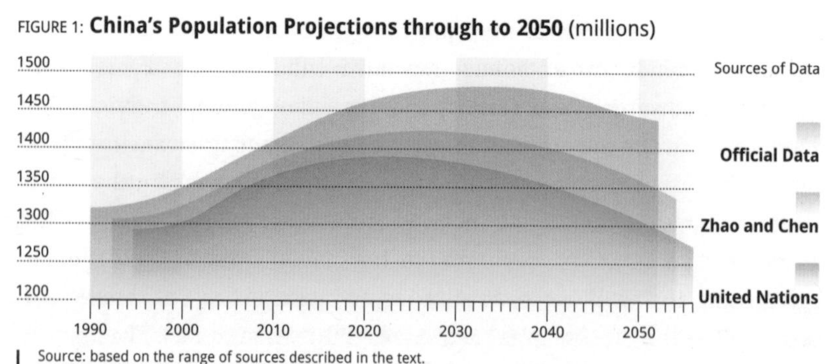

FIGURE 1: **China's Population Projections through to 2050** (millions)

Source: based on the range of sources described in the text.
For more information, see the Online Notes to this volume at: www.TheChinaStory.org

The Demographic Dividend

Will grandpa eat the demographic dividend?
Economists worry that China will 'get old before it gets rich'.
Source: Imagine China

There is a growing body of evidence to suggest that the potential demographic 'dividend', 'gift' or 'bonus' associated with a country's demographic transition towards slower fertility and population growth, and therefore a growing share of the population engaged in – rather than depending on – the workforce, can be quite substantial. This issue was the focal point of the Asian Development Bank's Asian Economic Outlook for 2011. Perhaps no country has benefited more from such a transition than China. According to some estimates, the change in the age structure of China's population over the last two decades could explain fifteen to twenty-five percent of its record-breaking stretch of high economic growth.

Cai Fang, a member of the National People's Congress Standing Committee and Director of the Institute of Population Studies at the Chinese Academy of Social Sciences, has written a string of papers on this topic, including a recent one entitled 'The Coming Demographic Impact on China's Growth: the age factor in the middle-income trap'. Cai emphasises that the economic benefits of China's expanding workforce are rapidly coming to an end. This will reduce the advantages China enjoys in labour-intensive industries at a time when the workforce is ill-equipped to compete with developed economies in technology- and capital-intensive industries. As a result, China could fall into a 'middle-income trap', that is, failing to make the transition to high-income status. Finding ways out of this trap will be necessary to prevent China from 'getting old before getting rich', a situation in which it would face the challenges of an ageing society without the necessary reources.

Rod Tyers and I have studied the impact of demographic change on China's economic performance using a global economic model that incorporates the age and gender structure of sixteen geographic regions, of which China is one. In projecting through to 2030, this kind of modelling work necessarily involves assumptions about how various demographic parameters will change over time – including birth rates, sex ratios at birth, age-gender specific death, immigration and emigration rates, life expectancies, and labour force participation rates. While agreeing with Cai Fang that most of China's demographic dividend lies in the past, our work shows that, under alternative assumptions about fertility rates, it is not necessarily over. With the right policy decisions, it could plausibly last for at least another decade. An obvious criticism of our work would be that it relies on the United Nations Population Projections for China's population data including on fertility rates, which, as shown above, may well be overstated.

The End of Surplus Labour?

A typical factory with a business based on cheap labour.
Source: Imagine China

A related debate, in which population figures matter, centres on China's rural labour force and the extent to which it is 'surplus' to rural development, and hence available at low wages to fuel urban industrial development, particularly in the labour-intensive factories in south-east China, and in Guangdong. Following media reports of labour shortages in Guangdong from 2004, a number of academic studies have claimed that China is either close to, or has already reached, a turning point in economic development in which the supply of rural surplus labour has been exhausted, resulting in labour shortages and rising wages in the urban sector. A special issue of the *China Economic Journal* in 2010, published by the China Center for Economic Research at Peking University, was dedicated to this topic. It is also something that featured regularly in articles published in *Caijing* magazine and Chinese newspapers in 2011.

Yet there is also considerable empirical data showing that, despite some evidence of rising wages in urban areas, there is little to suggest that a labour supply shortage is the cause. Instead, because of policies that still hinder many rural workers from migrating to cities, Chinese industries may be denied access to millions of under-employed low-income rural labourers. This, combined with evidence of low migration rates and a high degree of 'churning' – migrants over their early twenties who return to their villages – immediately raises the question of why more rural workers are not migrating to urban areas. A thoughtful policy response would be to reduce the institutional barriers to cross-regional migration. Population projections through to 2020 based on the hypothesis that all barriers to migration were eliminated suggest that the number of migrants could more than double, from the current estimate of 150 million to around 300 million.

How do the results of the 2010 Population Census then feed into this debate? The 2010 Census reported that China had 940 million people between the ages of fifteen to fifty-nine (a group often referred to as the 'working age population'). This is fairly close to the UN 2010 estimates of 915 million (a difference of about twenty-four million or three percent). However, the gap between these sources is much larger for children aged 0-14 – that is, China's future workforce. The 2010 census reports this number as being 222 million compared with the UN's 261 million, a gap of over thirty-eight million or fifteen percent.

At face value, it may be tempting to conclude that, as the Chinese population is lower than hitherto thought, the end of the country's labour surplus must be nigh. But it is not that simple: we need to know how this reduction is distributed among various population groups. For example, if the thirty-eight million 'missing children' are all rural residents, then the labour surplus would come to an end more rapidly. However, if they are all urban, this will not necessarily be the case. The point is that accurate measures of the population, and its distribution across age and space, are crucially important for understanding China's growth and future economic potential.

Sex Matters

Another important question is whether these 'missing millions' are male or female? According to the United Nation's *World Population Prospects* (the 2010 Revision), China has a sex ratio of 108 males to 100 females, the highest gender imbalance of any country in the world.

An imbalanced sex ratio is a common demographic feature in many countries, especially in East, South and Southeast Asia, where a combination of cultural preferences for sons, the desire to reduce the size of families, and the introduction of Ultrasound B technology that can detect gender have resulted in a rise in sex-selective abortions in recent decades. With China's one-child policy added to the mix, the results have been dramatic. According to one recent estimate, China's sex ratio at birth was just 1.07 in 1980, only just above the natural rate of 1.06, rising to 1.12 in 1990, 1.18 in 2000 and reaching 1.22 in 2007. Assuming that the survey methods used in the cited studies are reliable, China currently has somewhere between thirty and forty million 'missing women' or 'excess men'.

According to Columbia University's Shang-jin Wei and his co-authors, Qingyuan Du and Xiaobo Zhang, this has resulted in 'male excess savings'. According to this theory, in a population with a rising ratio of

Urban and Rural Populations and Incomes

Data from China's National Bureau of Statistics (NBS) released in January 2012 showed that there were more people living in cities than in the countryside for the first time in China's history. Other statistics from 2011 released by NBS include:

- the number of urban dwellers increased by twenty-one million to hit 690.79 million at the end of 2011, accounting for 51.27 percent of the country's total population. The rural population fell by 14.56 million to 656.56 million;
- China's total population increased by 6.44 million during 2011 to 1.34 billion;
- the income gap between urban and rural residents narrowed. Urbanites' average income was 3.13 times of that of rural people, down from 3.23 in 2010 and 3.33 in 2009. Rural residents' per capita income rose 17.9 percent year-on-year in 2011 to 6,977 *yuan*. Per capita disposable income of urbanites was 21,810 *yuan*, up 14.1 percent from one year earlier; and,
- the survey results showed that the per capita wage income of rural residents rose 21.9 percent to 2,963 *yuan* in 2011, with wages accounting for 42.5 percent of rural residents' incomes. Media reports attribute the increase in rural residents' wages to rising incomes of migrant workers. This is a change from the trend noted by the NBS in early 2010, described by *China Daily* in an article titled: 'Urban-rural Income Gap Widest Since Reform'.

men to women, men try to out-save each other in order to be competitive in the marriage market. Wei and Zhang demonstrate that per this 'competitive saving motive', the rise in China's sex ratio can explain half of the increase in Chinese household savings as a share of disposable income (from sixteen percent in 1990 to thirty percent in 2007).

Wei and Zhang take this idea further in their exploration of the sexual foundations of economic growth. They find support for the hypothesis that China's sex ratio imbalance may stimulate economic growth through entrepreneurial activity and hard work – not because males are inherently more entrepreneurial, but because when the sex ratio is high they are more driven to increase wealth in order to be competitive in the marriage market. Their claim is supported by empirical evidence that men in regions with relatively high gender imbalances are more willing to accept dangerous and unpleasant jobs and work longer hours.

And it doesn't stop there. Du and Wei show how China's rising gender imbalance accounts for more than one half of the current account imbalance between China and the United States. They conclude that although China's 'sex ratio imbalance is not the sole reason for global imbalances, it could be one of the significant, and yet thus far unrecognised, factors.' The high rate of savings helps to generate the vast pool of foreign exchange reserves that the People's Bank of China invests overseas, primarily in the US, giving China global economic and political heft. According to William Overholt of Harvard University:

> The recycling of China's huge foreign exchange reserves was far from the only source of the tsunami of liquidity, but it was one of the largest. Chinese leaders have angrily denied that Chinese funds and inexpensive exports played this role, but ultimately it is a simple fact. Conversely, Western politicians have been far too quick to blame Chinese currency policies when the actual problem stemmed from the U.S. bubble demand, combined with high Chinese savings rates...

In combination, if one were to credit both the findings of Wei and his colleagues and Overholt's analysis, an argument could be made that China's rising sex imbalance was largely responsible for the global financial crisis!

Of course, such a conclusion relies on a range of some questionable numbers. The accuracy of the fertility rates quoted by Wei and Du are perhaps the least problematic. In their model of marriage and savings, both sexes maximise utility, something that is jointly determined by wealth and love. To set up the 'love parameter' for their calibrations, Wei and Du value a lasting marriage at US$100,000 per year (on top of one's own income), which is about two times the average income per worker during the period 1972-1998. On this basis they set the mean of 'love' = 2! To attribute the global financial crisis to China's gender imbalance on the basis of these assumptions would be going too far.

Economic models such as these earn economists a bad name. Yet as long as you don't take the numerical results to be accurate forecasts (which they are not intended to be), such models provide a crucially important means for understanding dynamic and complex processes. China did not cause the global financial crisis. But there is some evidence to suggest that China's rising gender imbalance helps explain that country's high savings rates, from which global macroeconomic consequences follow. A deeper understanding of the impact of gender imbalances on the economy would require accurate measures of all sorts of things, including 'valuations' of love, and sex ratios at birth. While we cannot expect the Chinese (or any other) government to devote resources to measuring and reporting on the former, we can and should expect them to accurately measure and report the latter.

An Harmonious Society?

A homeless man with Ronald McDonald.
Source: Flickr.com/denisvlr

The misreporting of population and fertility data is not an imminent threat to China's economic stability. However, in recent years there has been growing concern that the misreporting and/or poor measurement of its economic data might be.

The economist Nouriel Roubini became famous for having predicted a 'catastrophic' global financial meltdown that central bankers would be unable to prevent in July 2006. In 2011, he and Dani Rodrik were two of the more pessimistic commentators on the Chinese economy. Writing in The *Financial Times* on 23 August 2011, Dani Rodrik pointed out that other predictions for the Chinese economy are 'largely extrapolations from the recent past and they overlook serious structural constraints', most critical of which is to reorient the economy 'away from export-oriented manufac-

Top Ten Problems of Public Concern

In December 2011, the Chinese Academy of Social Sciences (CASS) published a list of the top ten problems of concern to citizens in China. It was based on a survey of 6,468 people over the age of eighteen, drawn from five major cities, one hundred counties and 480 villages across the country. Respondents were given a list of problems and asked which ones worried them. The percentage of respondents who expressed concern about each item is as below:

1. Soaring commodity prices: 59.5 percent
2. Health care availability and cost: 42.9 percent
3. Income and wealth gap: 31.6 percent
4. Governmental corruption: 29.3 percent
5. Unemployment: 24.2 percent
6. Housing prices: 24 percent
7. Retirement pension for the elderly: 16.6 percent
8. Food safety: 15.9 percent
9. Education costs: 10.9 percent
10. Environmental pollution: 10.3 percent

The Gini Coefficient and Bo Xilai

In January 2012, *Caixin* magazine reported:

> For the eleventh year in a row, Chinese officials say they cannot publish the nation's Gini coefficient – a common measure of income inequality used worldwide.
>
> ...The Gini coefficient, which measures income distribution on a scale of zero to one, indicates a relatively reasonable income gap if the number is between 0.3 and 0.4. A Gini index between 0.4 and 0.5, however, signals a large income gap.
>
> The main reason [for not publishing China's Gini coefficient], the National Bureau of Statistics (NBS) Director Ma Jiantang said on 17 January 2012 is that data on high-income groups is incomplete. Some experts criticized the announcement, saying the government is looking for reasons to de-emphasize China's significant wealth gap...
>
> ...The last time Chinese officials published a Gini coefficient was in 2000, when they announced that China's 2000 figure was 0.412. A 2011 NBS report said that the 2011 'Gini coefficient is a little bit higher than that in 2010', but did not elucidate either year's figures...

Other media reports noted that the week before Bo Xilai was ousted as Chongqing Party Secretary, he told reporters that China's Gini coefficient had exceeded 0.46.

The *Caixin* report also highlighted the following:

- in its Twelfth Five-year Plan for 2011 to 2015, published before the fall of Bo Xilai, the Chongqing Municipal government committed to bringing down its Gini ratio from 0.42 to 0.35. This was the first time a local government had included Gini coefficient goals into its Five-year Plan.
- according to a 2007 China Reform Foundation report, 4.4 trillion *yuan* in 'grey income', or undeclared income, of urban residents had not been accounted for in official statistics, amounting to twenty-four percent of China's total GDP.

turing and towards domestic sources of demand, while managing the job losses and social unrest this restructuring is likely to generate.'

In 2011, Roubini discussed the possibility of a 'perfect storm' that could again threaten the global economy, with China's role in this storm related to its overreliance on exports and fixed investment: 'Down the line [in China], you are going to have two problems: a massive non-performing loan problem in the banking system and a massive amount of overcapacity [that] is going to lead to a hard landing.'

For China's sake, and that of the rest of the world, it would be nice if Roubini turned out to be wrong this time around. Unfortunately, it doesn't really make sense to look to China's official statistics to convince oneself that he will be, as the Chinese leadership itself seems willing to admit. In early 2011, Derek Scissors, an economist at the Heritage Foundation in the United States, concluded that it was not credible that the Chinese economy was growing at an annual ten percent, as it was officially claimed. Scissors starts with the admission in late 2010 by Li Keqiang (set to become China's premier in 2012) that China's official GDP figures were 'for reference only'. Li was also quoted as saying that bank lending, rail cargo and electricity consumption were the best indicators of 'the true health of the Chinese economy'. Scissors uses this 'Li Keqiang theory' to argue that China's actual economic performance was stronger than officially reported in 2010 and weaker in 2008-2009. Differing from the common view that Chinese economic data is universally over-reported, Scissors suggests that a more 'nuanced view is that the Party is obsessed with stability, and this obsession leaks into data reporting such that the highs and lows of China's economic performance are both dampened.'

Of the indicators mentioned by Li Keqiang, bank lending is the most complex. Commercial bank lending accelerates with economic growth, while policy-driven bank lending is used counter-cyclically to bolster activity during a slow down. Although the amount of commercial bank lending is on the rise in China, most lending is still policy-driven, and it is a major instrument for stimulating economic growth. Scissors examines the official figures for growth rates of GDP and loans in China over the past decade and argues that the lending required to achieve below-average GDP growth in 2010 was worryingly high. He acknowledges that aggressive lending might have been appropriate for the weakening economy in 2008-2009. But he contends that in 2010 this was a major policy mistake, with the 'forced policy lending' undoing a decade of banking sector reforms. With myriad worrying figures including official estimates of hidden local government debt at RMB10 trillion (US$1.5 trillion) and rising, and with Li Keqiang himself saying that bank lending is a key indicator of China's economic health, Scissors's analysis provides little room for optimism.

Nor does Carl Walter and Fraser Howie's 2011 book titled *Red Capitalism: The Fragile Financial Foundations of China's Extraordinary Rise*, which provides a detailed account of the complex maze that consti-

Rich and Poor

In 2008, the World Bank reported that 29.8 percent of China's population was living on less than US$2 per day. According to a report released by the National Bureau of Statistics (NBS) in January 2012, the average annual income of China's rural residents in 2011 was 6,977 *yuan* (about US$ 1,100, or about US$3 per day). Estimates of the annual incomes of China's very poorest are much lower: in remote parts of the country as low as 1,500 *yuan* (about US$240, or about US$ .66 per day).

At the other end of the scale, the Hurun Rich List, an annual compilation of information about China's richest people, said that in 2011, the average net worth of China's 1,000 wealthiest people was around five billion *yuan* (US$924 million).

Bo Xilai's son Bo Guagua's tuition fees at Harvard were reported to be US$90,000 for his two-year program, while in 2009, the media reported the troubles of a man from Hubei province was having paying the tuition fees for his son at a local primary school after they were raised from 200 to 325 *yuan*. Though China has officially abolished tuition fees for students during the nine-year compulsory education period, schools still manage to find ways to collect money. The 325 *yuan* covered books, insurance and milk.

The minimum wage in Shanghai:
1,280 *yuan* per month.
The minimum wage in Shenzhen:
1,500 *yuan* per month.
The average monthly earnings in 2008 of Fu Yucheng, president of CNOOC (one of China's large state-owned oil companies):
1.004 million *yuan*.

The most expensive houses in China, according to media reports cost eighty to ninety million *yuan*. In December 2010, a CCTV news report showed President Hu Jintao visiting subsidized housing in Beijing whose residents said they were paying seventy-seven *yuan* a month. The number became a meme on the Internet to mock CCTV's propagandistic report: most urbanites, especially in large cities like Beijing, did not appear to know anyone with access to such cheap housing.

tutes China's state-owned banking and financial system. They extend the definition of 'public debt' to include not only the debt obligations of the central government and the Ministry of Finance (combined they are about twenty percent of GDP), but also of the four 'policy banks' and the Ministry of Railways, plus local government debt and even non-performing loans in state asset management companies, based on the argument that the central government would not allow any of these bodies to fail. This results in an estimate of 'true public debt' to GDP at 77.3 percent for 2011, well above the 'red line' international standard of sixty percent, and massively higher than twenty percent, the commonly reported figure that suggests that government finances are in good order. These findings are echoed in the IMF's recent warning to China of the possible perils ahead in the country's heavily state-controlled banking and financial system. Their report argues that 'state controls over the economy were partly to blame for soaring property prices, excessive bank lending and mounting local government debt, and that these were among the growing risks that threatened to undermine the country's economic boom.'

During recent years then it is little surprise that analysts in China have alleged that 'the state advanced while the people are in retreat' – that is, the state's domination of the economy mitigates against further economic opening and reform. Whether or not this is as problematic as Walter and Howie and the IMF suggest depends very much on whether the numbers they have used in their analyses – most of which were drawn from official sources – are accurate or not. What exactly Li Keqiang meant by 'for reference only' is not clear – and it's certainly not encouraging.

On top of banking and financial sector reforms, China faces an urgent need for reforms in public finance and government administration, according to Christine Wong, who reviewed China's public investment infrastructure for the World Bank in 2011. Wong describes the proliferation of off-budget local investment corporations (LICs). Under the stimulus program of 2008-2010, these grew in number to more than 10,000 nationwide, with a total debt rising to RMB10 trillion by the end of 2010.

China's Top Ten Richest

The *Hurun Rich List*, an annual compilation of information about China's richest people, noted that in 2011 there were 271 US$ billionaires in China. It was called a 'record year for China's rich'.

The *Rich List* also notes that thirty percent of China's top fifty richest people are delegates to the National Party Council or the Chinese People's Political Consultative Conference. The top ten people (all men) on the 2011 list were:

1. Liang Wen'gen 梁稳根
Wealth: US$11 billion
Age: 55
Company: Sany
Industry: Heavy machinery

2. Zong Qinghou 宗庆后 & family
Wealth: US$10.7 billion
Age: 66
Company: Wahaha
Industry: Soft drinks

3. Li Yanhong 李彦宏 (or Robin Li)
Wealth: US$8.8 billion
Age: 43
Company: Baidu
Industry: Internet

4. Yan Bin 严彬
Wealth: US$7.8 billion
Age: 57
Company: Ruoy Chai
Industry: Red Bull drinks, property, investments

5. Xu Jiayin 许家印
Wealth: US$7.2 billion
Age: 53
Company: Evergrande Property
Industry: Property

6. Wang Jianlin 王健林
Wealth: US$7.1 billion
Age: 57
Company: Wanda
Industry: Property

7. Wu Yajun 吴亚军 & family
Wealth: US$6.6 billion
Age: 47
Company: Longfor Properties
Industry: Property

8. Liu Yongxing 刘永行 & family
Wealth: US$6.4 billion
Age: 63
Company: East Hope
Industry: Aluminum, agricultural feed

9. He Xiangjian 何享健 & family
Wealth: US$6.3 billion
Age: 69
Company: Midea Group
Industry: Home appliances

10. Yang Huiyan 杨惠妍 & family
Wealth: US$5.6 billion
Age: 30
Company: Country Garden
Industry: Property

With the banking sector's limited capacity to appraise the credit-worthiness of LICs and even of local governments, whose finances are complex and non-transparent and for which little public information is available, Wong concludes that bailouts will be required for local governments and the Ministry of Railways. Such bailouts will divert resources away from the 'harmonious society' policies discussed in Chapter 3 of the present volume.

This sentiment is also reflected in the 2011 work of Xiaolu Wang and Wing Thye Woo. They have written on China's 'grey income': not the income of an ageing population, but about the mis-reported household income particularly among the richest and most well-connected households. Their evidence shows that inequality in China is widening, despite the Communist Party's recognition that social stability requires not just continuing high rates of economic growth but also the diffusion of the benefits of growth across society. In fact, they claim that the income of the wealthiest ten percent of Chinese households is not twenty–three times that of the poorest ten percent, as reported in the official data, but sixty-five times. Based on these findings, they conclude that:

The skyscrapers and elevated ring roads that Beijing city planners dub the 'Central Business District' (CBD).
Source: Flickr/Trey Ratcliff

> Unless the government could stay largely uninfluenced by the rent-seeking lobbying of capital owners and other special interest groups, the free competition of the market economy would inevitably be replaced by the monopolistic practices of crony capitalism. Such a development would accentuate income inequality, economic inefficiency, and social conflict. To avoid these serious threats to economic development and social harmony, institutional reforms are essential, especially in the public finance system and government administrative system.

While the numbers behind this conclusion do not threaten imminent collapse, they are worth noting.

In the 2012-2013 transition period, a weakened European economy will substantially reduce the demand for Chinese goods in its largest export market. It is unclear just how much worse the global economic climate could become, or what China can do to prevent another crisis, if anything. They will have their hands full with domestic issues (as noted elsewhere in this volume). These range from the potential for social unrest as the gap between the haves and have-nots continues to widen, to dealing with ageing before affluence and the (possibly) fragile state of the country's public banking and financial systems. The accurate reporting of the numbers that shape expert opinion and public perception both inside and outside China would help China considerably in facing this wide range of internal and external challenges.

CHINA'S TOP TEN

HUDONG ENCYCLOPAEDIA'S TOP TEN WORDS OF 2011

Below is a selection of top ten lists and annual reviews of 2011 published by various organizations including the official Xinhua News Agency, commercial Internet companies and the neo-Maoist website Utopia.

Hudong Encyclopaedia *(*Hudong baike 互动百科*) is a Wikipedia-style crowd-sourced online encyclopedia run by a Beijing Internet company. In January 2012, Hudong Encyclopaedia released a list of the top ten words and phrases of 2011, chosen by their editors. The list was published in affiliation with the* People's Daily *Public Opinion Survey Office.*

Limit, Restriction (*xian* 限)
The word of the year was 'limit' or 'restrict'. In 2011, foreign countries had to restrict government spending and limit greenhouse gas emissions, while in China there were limits placed on

apartment purchasing and car use, and restrictions on broadcast of entertainment shows on TV. The organizers also said that 'resources are always limited… Humanity must come to a new understanding of "limits"; this is the only way to ensure the harmonious development of nature, the environment and society.'

Holding Up (*hold zhu* hold 住)

The English-Chinese hybrid phrase '*hold zhu*' means something like 'keep it up' or 'keep holding the attention of an audience'. It was first used in a Taiwanese TV talent show in which a deadpan contestant wearing cartoonish makeup demonstrated in front of a live audience how to '*hold zhu*' the stage no matter how embarrassing the situation, for example by putting her bra on top of her head to look like a Qing-dynasty princess. Video clips of the show were uploaded to the Internet, and the phrase became popular among mainland Chinese. In 2011, '*hold zhu*' was frequently used in advertisements, newspaper headlines and Internet postings to mean capturing the attention of a crowd, or to refer to a daring performance of some kind.

Steve Jobs (*Qiaobusi* 乔布斯)

Chinese Apple fans mourned the death of Steve Jobs with as much fervour as their fellows in other countries. In the days following Job's death on 5 October 2011, people organized mourning ceremonies outside Apple stores in Beijing and Shanghai, where they left burning candles, flowers and once-bitten apples. 'Why doesn't China have its own Steve Jobs?' was a question asked by dozens of newspapers and in hundreds of Internet forums. Even the *People's Daily* ran an article praising the genius of Steve Jobs.

High-speed Rail (*gaotie* 高铁)

In late July 2011, two high-speed trains collided, killing forty people and injuring nearly two hundred in Wenzhou, an eastern city near Shanghai. The accident brought the topic of China's high-speed rail program under extreme scrutiny from the media and the public (see Chapter 7 for further details).

Gutter Oil (*digou you* 地沟油)

The widespread use of gutter oil – oil recycled from food waste and sold to restaurants for use in cooking – was one of the food scandals of 2011 that most alarmed the public. The *Chongqing Evening News* estimated that about three million tons of gutter oil is consumed annually in China, but this figure is a guess, because the gutter oil business is illegal and gutter oil vendors do not report their sales figures.

In December 2011, following an exposé published by Xinhua News Agency about the gutter oil industry in Beijing, Tianjin and Hebei, the Ministry of Public Security launched a blitz against the trade in gutter oil. Police arrested more than 700 people and seized 60,000 tons of gutter oil. However the fear of gutter oil remains a widespread reason that some people avoid eating out.

School Bus (*xiaoche* 校车)

On 16 November 2011, a school bus operated by a kindergarten collided head-on with a coal truck in Qingyang, Gansu province. Nineteen children and two adults were killed in the accident. The bus, a nine-seat van modified to carry more passengers, had sixty-two children on board at the time of the crash, along with the two adults. News of the crash caused outrage on the Internet, especially because the week after the Gansu crash reports appeared in the press about the government's donation of twenty-three new school buses to Macedonia. Internet users contrasted the government's largesse to foreigners with its miserliness towards its own people. Pictures showing American school buses that survived collisions with other vehicles unscathed led to a popular belief that the US government built school buses according to military standards. Media pundits and microblog users called for more to be done to protect the safety of Chinese school children.

Guo Meimei (*Guo Meimei* 郭美美)

Guo Meimei was a young woman who uploaded pictures to her Sina Weibo microblog of herself with a white Maserati car, and of a closetful of Hermès handbags. She also claimed to be a manager of the China Red Cross: the combination of showing off her wealth (called *xuanfu* 炫富 on the Internet) and her association with a charitable organization that had previously come under scrutiny for corruption caused public outrage. Guo turned out not to have an official position at the Red Cross, but the negative publicity severely damaged the organization's reputation and greatly reduced donations from the public.

Hurt No More (*shangbuqi* 伤不起)

Originating in an Internet posting about how difficult it is to study a foreign language, the expression '*shangbuqi*' is used to mean that someone has been so hurt by their experiences that they simply cannot be hurt any further.

PM2.5

PM2.5 refers to air pollution particles smaller than 2.5 micrometres in diameter that may pose a more serious health risk than larger particles. This measurement has been used by the US Embassy's air quality monitor and Twitter feed for several years, but PM2.5 numbers were not previously reported by China's air quality monitoring stations, which only noted the numbers for larger pollutants. (For more on PM2.5, see Chapter 7.)

Salt Rumours (*yaoyan* 谣盐)

This is a pun/homonym referring to the word for 'rumour', which is also pronounced *yaoyan*, although written as 谣言. The phrase refers to widespread rumours that radiation from the Japanese nuclear disaster that followed the 2011 earthquake and tsunami would result in people even in China suffering from a lack of iodine. This led to a run on salt in China; worried citizens stockpiled vast quantities of iodized salt, which they thought could combat radioactive contamination of food and water.

Occupy Wall Street
(*zhanling Hua'erjie* 占领华尔街)
Despite some censorship of the debate surrounding the protests in the US and elsewhere, news of the Occupy Wall Street demonstrations was widespread in the Chinese media and on the Internet. In October 2011, a small crowd of leftists activists in Zhengzhou, Henan province, organized a demonstration in support of the US protesters.

Sina Weibo *is the most popular of the Twitter-like microblog services in China. In December 2011, Sina published their list of the top news stories of the year. They did not disclose the methodology behind the compilation of the list, but the top item about the Wenzhou high-speed rail accident on 23 July certainly trended strongly. As noted in Chapter 7 of this book, that train accident was the major news story of 2011, one in which Weibo played an important role.*

Train Accident
(*dongche shigu* 动车事故)
The accident at Wenzhou left over forty dead and resulted in a month of questioning of what some bloggers called China's 'blood-stained GDP' model and corruption and other problems at the Ministry of Railways (see Chapter 7 for details).

Microblogs and the Anti-Child-trafficking Campaign
(*weibo daguai* 微博打拐)
Rural development scholar Yu Jian-

rong launched a campaign on Sina Weibo to reunite kidnapped children with their families. Yu encouraged Internet users to upload photos of child beggars to Weibo, as many of them are assumed to have been kidnapped and forced by gangs into professional begging. Some critics complained that the campaign infringed on the beggars' right to privacy.

Li Na Wins the French Open

(*Li Na Fawang duoguan* 李娜法网夺冠)
The female tennis player Li Na won the French Open in June 2011, the first Chinese player to win a Grad Slam singles title.

The Japan Earthquake

(*Riben dizhen* 日本地震)
The earthquake and tsunami that hit Japan in March 2011 was closely watched on the Chinese Internet. Some commentators admired the orderly way that Japanese citizens dealt with the natural disaster. There was also widespread *Schadenfreude*, with some Internet users recalling China's past sufferings at the hands of their eastern neighbour and saying that the Japanese deserved what they got.

Guo Meimei Incident

(*Guo Meimei shijian* 郭美美事件)
This relates to the scandal surrounding Guo Meimei, a young woman who uploaded pictures of her expensive handbags and luxury cars to Weibo and boasted about a position with the Chinese Red Cross that it turned out she didn't actually hold (see 'Hudong Encyclopaedia's Top Ten Words of 2011' above, and Chapter 8 for further details).

Steve Jobs Passes Away

(*Qiaobusi qushi* 乔布斯去世)
Chinese Apple fans mourned with as much emotion as their fellows in other countries (see 'Hudong Encyclopaedia's Top Ten Words of 2011' above for more information).

Xie Na and Zhang Jie's Grand Nuptuals

(*Xie Na Zhang Jie dahun* 谢娜张杰大婚)

Celebrity gossip: the TV personality Xie Na married the singer Zhang Jie.

Soul Searching and Little Yueyue

(*Xiao Yueue yinfa fansi jujue lengmo* 小悦悦引发反思拒绝冷漠)

A toddler in Foshan was the victim of a hit and run accident and then ignored by passers-by. Video footage captured by a surveillance camera was widely circulated on the Internet, causing a soul-searching discussion online and in the media about contemporary morality (see Chapter 2 for further details).

The Death of Osama Bin Laden

(*Ladeng zhi si* 拉登之死)

Osama Bin Laden's death at the hands of US special forces troops was big news in China, as everywhere else. Reactions ranged from criticisms of American hypocrisy over legality and human rights, and admiration of Bin Laden for standing up to the US, to delight that a terrorist had met his just deserts.

TV Sensation: *A Surprise at Every Turn*

(*chuanyueju 'Bubu jing xin' rebo* 穿越剧《步步惊心》热播)

A Surprise at Every Turn was a popular TV show about a woman who time travels from contemporary China back to the eighteenth century. In recent years, the concept of time travel became so popular in books, TV and film that, in early 2011, Chinese TV regulators introduced restrictions on similar works that encouraged audiences to speculate about the past, or indeed the future (one in which, presumably, China would no longer be a one-party state).

XINHUA'S 2011 TOP TEN NEWS STORIES

***Xinhua News Agency** published a list of the top news stories of 2011 in English and Chinese. Xinhua's original English-language descriptions of each item are given below.*

Measures to Cool off the Property Market

China launched a series of tough government measures to cool off the property market, including higher mortgage rates, a ban on third-home mortgage loans and purchase restrictions. The State Council, or China's Cabinet, introduced a policy package urging enhanced efforts to ensure the healthy development of the property sector and to promote the construction of affordable housing units for low-income families.

Food Safety Scandals

Food safety scandals erupted in great number in 2011. Authorities busted farmers for adding clenbuterol, a known carcinogen, to pig feed in order to grow leaner pigs.

Government Spending Restrictions

More than ninety central government departments publicized their 2010 and 2011 spending on government-funded overseas travel, receptions and official cars upon an order issued after an executive meeting of the State Council in May.

Further Criminalization of Drunk Driving Offenses

China's amended Criminal Law criminalized all drunk driving incidents starting 1 May. The previous law imposed criminal penalties on drunk drivers only when they caused serious traffic accidents.

Wenzhou High-speed Train Crash

On 23 July, a high-speed train rammed into a stalled train near the city of Wenzhou in the eastern province of Zhejiang, leaving forty dead and over 190 injured.

Ninetieth Anniversary of the Communist Party

In a speech delivered on 1 July at a ceremony marking the ninetieth founding anniversary of the Chinese Communist Party (CCP), Hu Jintao, General Secretary of the CCP Central Committee, hailed the Party's achievements and stressed efforts for the future development of the country and the Party.

Shenzhou-8 Docks with Tiangong Space Lab Module

The launch and safe return of the Shenzhou-8 unmanned spacecraft marked the successful completion of China's first space docking mission, with the spacecraft docking with the Tiangong-1 space lab module.

CCP Central Committee Plenary Session Focuses on Culture

The Seventeenth Central Committee of the Communist Party concluded its Sixth Plenary Session in October, adopting a landmark guideline for improving the nation's cultural soft power and promoting Chinese culture. The Central Committee also pledged enhanced efforts to promote the healthy and positive development of Internet culture.

Centenary of the 1911 Xinhai Revolution

A gathering was held on 9 October to commemorate the one hundredth anniversary of China's 1911 Revolution, which ended 2,000 years of imperial rule in the country by toppling the Qing dynasty.

Ethics and Morality Debates

Ethics and morality were heavily discussed in the public sphere, with two incidents stoking debate. In July, a woman in east China's city of Hangzhou caught a two-year-old girl who plunged from the window of a tenth floor apartment, winning praise from people across the country. However, in late August, a bus driver in East China's Jiangsu province stopped to save an old woman who was hit by a three-wheeled vehicle, only to find himself held accountable for the accident.

UTOPIA'S LIST OF TRAITORS

***In December 2011**, the Maoist website Utopia published a poll inviting readers to rank China's Top Ten Traitors, that is men and women deemed to have sold out China to foreign interests, or whose ideas and activities were seen as compromising national integrity. The site was shut down in early April 2012 in the aftermath of the fall of Bo Xilai, one of Utopia's heroes. The final selection of China's Top Ten Traitors was not announced.*

The Top Ten Traitors were to be chosen from a shortlist of eighteen, listed below with the likely reason for their inclusion:

1. Economist **Mao Yushi** 茅于轼 for liberal economic ideas, especially privatisation and his criticism of Mao Zedong.

2. History teacher **Yuan Tengfei** 袁腾飞 for his middle-school history lessons critical of Mao.

3. 'Science cop' **Fang Zhouzi** 方舟子 for his anti-Chinese medicine activism and support for genetically modified crops.

4. Wu Jinglian 吴敬琏 for liberal economics.

5. Diplomat **Wu Jianmin** 吴建民 for his calls for 'rational patriotism' rather than boycotts after an incident in 2010 over the disputed Diaoyu (or Senkaku) Islands.

6. CCTV host **Bai Yansong** 白岩松 for his promotion of 'universal values' and opposition to a boycott of French supermarket Carrefour after the Olympic Torch Relay fiasco in Paris.

7. Military scholar, biographer of Mao Zedong and Lin Biao, **Xin Ziling** 辛子陵 for his 2010 open letter calling for an end to media censorship.

8. Retired government official **Li Rui** 李锐 for his writings promoting political reform and his revisionist views of Mao.

9. Legal scholar/law professor **He Weifang** 贺卫方 for his liberal ideas and criticism of government policy.

10. Stephen N.S. Cheung 张五常 for his liberal economic ideas.

11. Zhang Weiying 张维迎 for his liberal ideas and promotion of the further transformation of the Chinese economy.

12. Economist **Li Yining** 厉以宁 for his liberal economic ideas.

13. *Southern Weekly* Deputy General Editor **Xiang Xi** 向熹 for his newspaper's liberal tendencies.

14. Former *People's Daily* Deputy Editor-in-Chief **Huangfu Ping** 皇甫平 for publishing articles supporting reforms and criticism of Mao's legacy.

15. Writer, incarcerated Nobel Prize winning dissident **Liu Xiaobo** 刘晓波 for his critical writings, support of 'universal values' and activism.

16. Former doctor of Mao Zedong, Mao biographer **Li Zhisui** 李志绥 (deceased) for his book *The Private Life of Chairman Mao*.

17. Peking University journalism professor **Jiao Guobiao** 焦国标 for his 2004 essay 'Denouncing the Central Propaganda Department'.

18. Former *People's Daily* Editor-in-Chief/publisher **Hu Jiwei** 胡绩伟 for his support for press freedom and his petition for the repeal of the declaration of martial law during the 1989 Tiananmen crisis.

5

5

DISCONTENT IN DIGITAL CHINA

Gloria Davies

THE DIGITAL age has brought new complexity and new conundrums to China's one-party rule. While dissidents continue to be summarily arrested and charged with serious crimes, official rhetoric and *vox populi* now jostle for attention on the Internet.

The McDonald's store on Wangfujing, Beijing, where online postings called for 'Jasmine Movement' protesters to meet on 20 February 2011. Most of the people who gathered on that day were foreign journalists, police officers and shoppers curious as to why there were so many police and cameras at a fastfood outlet.
Source: Wikimedia Commons

In China, 2011 turned out to be the year that people were simply not allowed to 'say it with flowers' – at least not jasmine flowers as the government, panicked over the potential ripple effects of Tunisia's 'Jasmine Revolution', placed a nationwide ban on the much-loved jasmine. As popular revolt spread across the Middle East during what became known as the 'Arab Spring', Chinese rights activists saw an opportunity to initiate their very own 'Jasmine Movement'.

In February 2011, a loose worldwide coalition of anonymous Chinese netizens posted notices on Twitter and Chinese-language websites hosted outside China urging people to assemble at select venues in thirteen Chinese cities at 2:00pm on 20 February. This was to be the first of a series of weekly rallies protesting against the state and Party's abuse of power. They weren't called rallies but 'collective strolls' (*jiti sanbu* 集体散步). The notices circulated briefly on QQ and other mainland-based microblog services before they were censored by the Internet police.

On the day of 'Jasmine protest', the anonymous organizers of the movement posted an open letter on the Internet. Addressed to China's National People's Congress the letter demanded government accountability and concerted action against corruption and misrule. The letter-writers insisted that the planned rallies were a demonstration of public concern, not an overt threat to the existing political system. The organizers claimed:

> We don't care if China implements a one-party system, a two-party system, or even a three-party system, but we are resolute in our request that the government and its officials accept oversight by ordinary Chinese people. Furthermore, we call for an independent judiciary. This is our fundamental demand.

Not surprisingly, the letter was immediately suppressed.

Police, meanwhile, were turning out in force at the chosen protest venues. In Beijing, a modest crowd of around a hundred people gathered outside the McDonalds in Wangfujing, the premier shopping mall in China's capital. The police dispersed the crowd before a single slogan was ut-

Collective Strolls (*jiti sanbu* 集体散步)

Though public protest is largely banned in China, over the last few years a milder form of demonstration has developed. 'Collective strolls' allow citizens to express dissatisfaction in a non-explicit yet overt fashion. Participants in such strolls do not hold up banners or chant slogans. The apolitical and leisurely connotations of the word 'stroll' (*sanbu*) help soften the confrontational aspect of protests. It also makes it easier to avoid Internet censorship of keywords like 'demonstration' so that participants can organize online.

Group walks have usually been launched in wealthy coastal cities in reaction to concerns about the environmental impact of infrastructure or industrial projects. Such protests are rarely in response to issues of fundamental governance, human rights or the legitimacy of the rule of the Party. They tend to be, to use an American expression NIMBY – Not In My Backyard – protests. In early 2011, there were calls for Chinese citizens to organize a 'Jasmine Revolution' in China. Some included the suggestion that protests take the form of collective strolls.

The expression 'collective stroll' first appeared online in June 2007, when people in the city of Xiamen, Fujian province, took to the streets to protest against a paraxylene (PX) factory that was under construction and that they feared would pollute their neighborhood. In January 2008, homeowners in Shanghai who disagreed with land acquisitions for the building of an extension of the city's famous Maglev high-speed train put on another collective stroll. In August 2011, residents of the city of Dalian organized a collective stroll in protest over another PX factory that, according to media reports, drew over 12,000 people.

All of the above-mentioned protests were successful in their aims. Construction on the PX factories in Xiamen and Dalian was halted. There has been no follow-up in the media about new plans for these factories; they will presumably be built in places where people are poorer and less networked and easily prevented by local toughs from collective strolling.

tered. In the weeks that followed, an increased police presence in Beijing and other cities ensured that the movement would not gain any visibility, let alone traction. China's 'Jasmine Movement' was over before it began. Nonetheless, this brazen if toothless attempt to hold the party-state to account caused acute anxiety among the Party's leaders. They swiftly moved to place a blanket ban on the word 'jasmine' (*molihua* 茉莉花) on the Chinese net. One casualty of the censorship was a video featuring Hu Jintao, the Party General Secretary and President of the People's Republic, singing the well-known Chinese folk song 'Lovely Jasmine Flower' (*Hao yi duo molihua* 好一朵茉莉花). It was something that beleaguered Chinese netizen activists widely gloated over.

Official panic mounted as the scent of jasmine spread through the Middle East. Guangxi province in south-west China cancelled its annual International Jasmine Festival in Heng county. Heng county boasts of China's largest jasmine plantation; it is locally known as 'the hometown of jasmine'. Regardless of the economic impact on growers, sales of the flower and the plant were also halted. Meanwhile, local police in Beijing called in flower vendors to force them to sign pledges not to stock jasmine. One jasmine grower was described 'glancing forlornly at a mound of unsold bushes whose blossoms were beginning to fade' as he observed that the plant had plunged to a third of its previous market value.

The logo of the Jasmine Cultural Festival in Hengxian, Guangxi province, cancelled in 2011 due to official sensitivities surrounding the word 'jasmine'.
Source: Molihuajie.com

The mainstream media in China was characteristically silent about the ban on jasmine. Three months passed before the authorities felt sufficiently confident to allow Guangxi to hold its jasmine festival after all; only in August did Heng county finally become a hive of jasmine-related activity once more. The belated festivities included a gala concert featuring well-known celebrities like the Taiwan Mando-pop groups Shin and F.I.R., the Taiwanese singer-producer Jonathan Lee (Li Zongsheng) and

Jasmine Revolution

(*molihua geming* 茉莉花革命)

Inspired by the Jasmine Revolution in Tunisia and the Arab Spring in February and March 2011, anonymous Internet users urged their fellow citizens to have their own 'Jasmine Movement', and protest for democracy. The messages circulating online called for weekly rallies, sometimes using the term 'strolls'. The first rally on 20 February 2011 attracted a handful of curious observers and a few people who appeared ready to protest. These were outnumbered by scores of foreign journalists and hundreds of uniformed and plain-clothes police.

The online calls led to a massive deployment of security forces nationwide, at least thirty-five arrests and the harassment of the foreign media. The harsh especially harsh treatment in 2011 dealt to activists, lawyers, and civil-society advocates like the artist Ai Weiwei seemed to stem from the government's fear that a Jasmine Revolution really might materialize.

China's own pop stars such as Allen Su (Su Xing), winner of Hunan Satellite TV's 2007 Superboy contest – a highly popular national talent show based on the 'Idol' format.

Over the years, after an initial hostility to pop music in the early 1980s, the Chinese government has come to support and encourage this type of entertainment. It generates revenue while conveniently projecting an image of cultural 'openness', both locally and internationally. In 2011, such gala concerts and shows had the effect of distracting public attention away from the most egregious suppression of dissent and protest in recent years. Singers crooned and dancers pranced while hundreds of activists and social critics were called in for questioning and threatened into silence, many detained, some indefinitely, for an alleged connection with the 'jasmine' threat. The more risible aspects of the crackdown, so poignantly illustrated in the misfortunes of the lowly jasmine, its cultivators and vendors, contributed to the tabloid view of an 'unfree' China posing a threat to the 'free' world.

Yet by simply equating China with autocratic rule, the notion of 'the China threat' reduces the complex realities of life and society in the world's most populous nation to a black-and-white image of an oppressor state bearing down on its abject people. Such cartoons loom large each time there is a political crackdown in China. But as Peter Ford noted in *The Christian Monitor* in late 2011, most informed observers of China agree that: 'What China wants is pretty straightforward and unexceptionable: to be prosperous, secure, and respected.'

The party-state's draconian (and frequently counter-productive) actions exact a heavy toll on the country's rights movement and activists. At the same time, relations between the state and society are in a dramatic state of flux. Despite the best efforts of the authorities to control the flow of information in and out of the country, international and local events now have a direct, immediate impact on public opinion in the People's Republic. The Internet has to an extent turned the once formidable force of state censorship into a blunt tool of limited use, one that is far from uniformly successful in deterring the public airing of complaints and grievances. In the digital age, the state must brace itself for myriad, unpredictable public responses every time it exercises coercive power.

Voices in Contention

For most of the twentieth century and since, mainland China has known only one-party rule. It began in 1928 with the Nationalist or Kuomintang government under Chiang Kai-shek, the enemy-predecessor of the Chinese Communist Party which, following a vicious civil war and defeat in 1949, removed the Republic of China to Taiwan. One-party rule in China has generally resorted to a set of national values and beliefs – an ideology – to foster unity and kept them alive in society at large. Formal education, propaganda campaigns and other forms of instruction in the workplace and local community inducted young people into this set of values and beliefs.

The economic reforms that the Chinese Communist Party under Deng Xiaoping introduced from late 1978 required a more flexible approach to the life – and the mental world – of China. By combining elements of Party ideology with the notion of economic liberalization the theoreticians came up with the slogan: 'socialism with Chinese characteristics'. Unlike the first fifty years of one-party rule between 1928 and 1978 (first under Chiang Kai-shek then, after 1949, under Mao Zedong), post-Maoist China has seen

The Top Ten Celebrities of 2011

1. Andy Lau (Liu Dehua 刘德华) – popular Hong Kong singer, producer and philanthropist.

2. Jay Chou (Zhou Jielun 周杰伦) – Taiwan-born pop star who debuted as a Hollywood actor in *The Green Hornet* (2011).

3. Faye Wong (Wang Fei 王菲) – Beijing-born and Hong Kong-based pop star.

4. Jackie Chan (Cheng Long 成龙) – Hong Kong actor, director, kungfu star and eternal celebrity.

5. Yao Ming 姚明 – superstar basketball player for the Houston Rockets who retired in 2011 due to injury.

6. Donnie Yen (Zhen Zidan 甄子丹) – Hong Kong's most popular action star; played Guan Gong, the God of War, in the Chinese blockbuster *The Last Bladesman* (2011).

7. Zhang Ziyi 章子怡 – an actress once described by *Time* magazine as 'China's gift to Hollywood', best known outside China as the star of *Crouching Tiger, Hidden Dragon* and *Memoirs of a Geisha*.

8. Jet Li (Li Lianjie 李连杰) – martial arts actor, film producer and international star who has appeared in over forty films.

9. Fan Bingbing 范冰冰 – popular actress sometimes called 'China's Monica Belluci'.

10. Zhao Benshan 赵本山 – China's most successful comic performer; has a wise-guy persona.

a more fluid use of ideology, combining Party propaganda with marketability.

The 2011 crackdown shows how the Party now defends its authority. While suppressing information in China about the detention of well-known rights activists like Ai Weiwei, Chen Yunfei, Jiang Tianyong, Ran Yunfei, Tang Jitian and Teng Biao, some of whom have been mentioned in Chapter 3, the state-run media trumpeted the government's achievements in economic and social reforms. In an editorial titled 'China is Not the Middle East', the official Communist Party mouthpiece, *People's Daily*, reminded its readers of the government's ceaseless toil on the nation's behalf. Published on 3 March 2011 in Chinese and English, the editorial was clearly intended both for a local and an international readership.

It described the situation in China as one which: 'the Chinese can fully participate in and discuss affairs of state, under the existing legal system and democratic system.' It warned that those who 'incite unrest' posed a threat to the orderly and timely achievement of social and political reforms and that 'street corner politics' only hindered and exacerbated existing inequalities. The article lists some of the government's achievements, such as the expansion of the tertiary educational sector and the enrolment of one in four Chinese between eighteen and twenty-two in col-

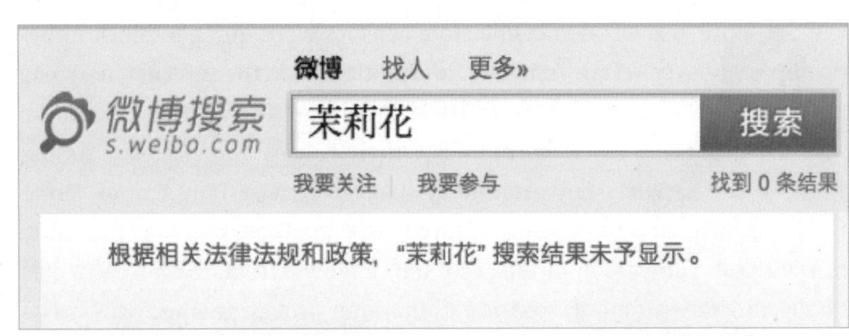

A screenshot of the message that Sina Weibo has shown users searching for jasmine flowers 茉莉花 from March 2011: 'According to relevant regulations and policies, results for a search for "jasmine flowers" cannot be displayed.'
Source: Sina Weibo

lege education. No mention was made of the major cases of corruption and fraud that have bedevilled the haste of China's own 'education revolution', or the protests they've engendered. Instead, it presented one-party rule as a form of conscientious and caring governance: 'Chinese leaders have always accorded with the public will', the writers declared. 'They pursue developmental and reform strategies to solve the problems that have emerged in the process of development and reform.' This tautology, which is typical of China's official voice, reflects a lack of vision beyond immediate short-term goals and offers its lame conclusion that: 'China is not the Middle East'. It's a negative comparison that, without irony, casts China as a lesser evil: a more benign autocracy, not like those others being overthrown by their angry and fed-up citizenry.

The authorities invoked 'social justice' as a guiding principle throughout the 2000s even as popular anger mounted due to government inaction on social injustices such as corruption, threats to public health and safety and rising living costs. They typically blamed misinformation, rumours and Western media reports for the undermining of public confidence in the party-state. Official unease only increased as it became evident how easy it was for people to bypass official controls to organise mass rallies and protests via social media.

An Internet-user cartoon mocking 'Green Dam' (*Lüba* 绿坝) censorship software introduced in 2009 which was intended to protect China's youth from pornography and harmful political ideas.
Source: Danwei Media

While state censors were quick to block undesirable information from the Internet, netizens were just as fast in getting around the blocks to publicize their causes and protests. As the prominent blogger-activist Ran Yunfei wrote on 19 March 2010 in a post that was promptly censored but widely circulated on websites outside China, one proven method was a Hydra-headed assault: large numbers of Internet users, each registering multiple microblogs to publicize a given piece of blocked information, which could easily be assembled like a jigsaw.

In response the authorities have invested untold (and unreported) sums in improving what it calls the Golden Shield Project, the official name of what is colloquially known as China's 'Great Firewall'. Still, net users are becoming more adept at what they call 'climbing over the wall' so as to gain access to information posted on the Internet outside China. Jonathon Keats, a columnist for the US-based *Wired* magazine, wrote about the highly permeable nature of the Great Firewall: 'it resembles less a fortress than a speed bump.' Its real effect is predominantly psychological insofar as it deters the many who are either indifferent to censorship or too lazy to circumvent the system.

As Chapter 7 goes into in more detail, as people learn how to scale the Great Firewall, the state censors develop newer and more sophisticated ways to stymie them. Within China, the lack of transparency in which the state operates and the severity of punishments meted out by the legal system ensure that most website owners err on the side of caution in filtering information on their own initiative. This lack of transparency is also reflected in wildly varying estimates of China's Internet police force. In September 2002, the BBC made an educated guess that there were already 30,000 'net cops'. The mainland media offers far more modest figures; He

Guangping, the head of the Public Security Bureau of Guangdong, a province with a population of over one hundred million, stated in January 2011 that the province employed fewer than 1,000 Internet police officers.

Coupled with the Internet police is an army of commentators (of equally unknown number) hired to post online comments in support of the official position on any given issue, or to provide disinformation. In mid 2008, the *Far Eastern Economic Review* estimated the number of commentators at around 280,000. In late February 2011, coinciding with the government crackdown on activists and social critics mentioned above, people who were able to access Twitter in China noticed a flurry of pro-government posts. The contents ranged from attacks on China's 'Jasmine Movement' for being treasonous, through to the condemnation of the US as seeking to destroy China, its rival, by promoting democracy. Added to this was a torrent of abuse and profanities launched against the protesters. It was reported that several of the microbloggers even adopted the names of Chinese activists and dissidents. These Internet dissemblers are derided as the 'Fifty-cent Gang', an epithet based on a widely held belief that they are paid fifty Chinese cents per comment or post.

In 2010-2011, online sales of stuffed toys that looked like alpacas spiked. This was because the animal was associated with the anti-establishment Chinese Internet slang term 'Grass Mud Horse' (*caonima* 草泥马), which had first appeared in early 2009 (see the Chronology for details).
Source: Danwei Media

Government officials have at other times been keen to make a show of magnanimity in response to criticisms of the party-state's propaganda drive and the Fifty-cent Gang. This is part of a relatively new official rhetorical strategy aimed at presenting one-party rule in a benign light. In an age of instant messaging in which things quickly go viral, the Chinese party-state is straining to pre-empt and placate public anger. So it neither defends nor confirms their existence, letting them cop flak for unpopular policies and displaying a tolerant face while continuing its knee-jerk suppression of dissent in real life.

Fifty-cent Gang (*wumao dang* 五毛党)
Fifty-cent Gang refers to Internet commentators hired by the Chinese authorities to post comments favourable to party-state policies in an attempt to shape and sway public opinion for fifty Chinese cents or *wumao* a pop. The term is also used in a derogatory sense to refer to anyone who speaks out in support of the Chinese government, its policies and the Communist Party (the assumption being that you'd have to be paid to do so).

An incident that occurred at People's University in Beijing on 22 April 2010 illustrates how keen officialdom was to win the people's trust. Wu Hao, a leading propaganda official from Yunnan province and a popular media figure, was giving a speech about the new era of transparency in official communications. Just before Wu ascended the podium, a young man approached and showered him with fifty-cent bills. The man later identified himself as Wang Zhongxia, a graduate of the university. When subsequently interviewed about the incident, Wu said: 'the protest of a Chinese netizen was perfectly normal' and that, as a government official, he even found the experience instructive. He kept one of the fifty-cent bills as a memento, claiming that it would spur him on to serve the people better. Wu contended that his calm response to a calculated insult was evidence that China had become 'a more and more open society and nation'. He added a caveat: 'we must not allow such actions to become a regular occurrence as it is not what the masses need.'

Other Party members who yearn for the ideological certainties of the Maoist era believe this sort of thing shows that the Communist Party lacks a clear sense of direction, principle and backbone. Discontent with the Party's retreat from core socialist-communist values has long been part of public discourse. With the further acceleration of state-led market expansion throughout the 1990s, there was plenty of social commentary about the large numbers of people who were using Party membership to advance their careers and make money. As the commentators included disgruntled Party elders and revolutionary veterans who served under Mao, the ruling leadership allowed some latitude for this type of criticism, curtailing it only when it started to attract wider attention.

In February 2011, as Geremie Barmé notes in the concluding chapter to this volume, a group calling itself the Children of Yan'an Fellowship mounted an articulate challenge from the left. With the sense of entitlement and self-worth befitting the progeny of Mao-era party leaders, the group's members produced a document – 'Our Suggestions for the Eighteenth Party Congress' (the one scheduled for late 2012; see Chapter 10). They published this advice on their website and encouraged substantive political reform through a return to core Maoist values. The appearance of this document roughly coincided with the open letter issued by the organizers of China's 'Jasmine Movement'. Both documents invoked the idea of egalitarian justice. But whereas the 'Jasmine Movement' did so in the context of the rights of citizens and the need for an independent judiciary, the Red revivalists focused on ideological retro-rejuvenation and an affirmation of party-state rule.

In the 1950s, 'red' symbolized class struggle, the guiding logic of Party rule under Mao. A leading slogan of the day spoke of the need for the country to be led by people who were 'red and expert'. Expertise (technical, scientific, educational) had to be matched by a zeal for fighting bourgeois thinking and capitalism. It was neither class struggle nor the end of capitalism that excited China's twenty-first century 'reds'. They were also beneficiaries of China's capitalist transformation. Some of their number, such as Bo Xilai, the erstwhile flamboyant Party Secretary of Chongqing discussed in several places in this book, visibly enjoyed the limelight, which may well have also contributed to the downfall of both him and his lawyer-businesswoman wife, Gu Kailai, in 2012. It was obvious they were not poor. (The net worth of individuals belonging to China's political elite remains unknown but is a favourite topic of speculation on the Internet.) We need to keep this complicated ideological (and rhetorical) landscape in mind as we consider an event that kept China's one-party system under critical scrutiny in the global media between 2010 and 2011.

Google and Dissent

When Google shut down their mainland-based search engine, some Internet users laid flowers at the Google offices in Beijing as a sign of mourning.
Source: Flickr.com/JoshChin

The event was Google's statement of 12 January 2010 that the company was contemplating the closure of its China operations. Google announced that it would no longer censor search results on its mainland-based portal Google.cn (established in January 2006 and subject to the same restrictions as other mainland-based portals). Users would instead be re-directed to its unrestricted Hong Kong-based portal. The company also identified a barrage of cyber-attacks originating in China on Google's infrastructure and services, noting in particular the hacking of gmail accounts held by mainland- and overseas-based rights activists and advocates. Although no mention was made of the criticism Google.cn had attracted previously for complying with China's censorship system, the statement sought to assure

Google users that a 'new approach' was underway, one that was: 'consistent with our commitment not to self-censor and, we believe, with local law [in China].'

The media in China and abroad closely covered the issue. Google's stance led to hostile exchanges between the US and Chinese governments and was the subject of vast amounts of commentary in China and internationally about Internet freedoms and the future of China's media landscape. If critics of Chinese government censorship and rights abuses outside China welcomed Google's statement as a belated affirmation of its ethical motto 'Don't be evil', mainland users of Google.cn mourned the portal's demise.

On 21 January, nine days after Google's announcement, US Secretary of State Hillary Clinton addressed an audience at the Newseum in Washington. Urging 'the Chinese authorities to conduct a thorough review of the cyber intrusions that led Google to make its announcement', Clinton infuriated China's pro-government commentators by likening state censorship to a virtual Berlin Wall. She said that just as that wall eventually fell, 'electronic barriers' would ultimately prove no match for the human need to communicate and to share information. 'Once you're on the Internet,' she said, 'you don't need to be a tycoon or a rock star to have a huge impact on society.'

These remarks by 'Secretary of State Xilali' (as she is known in the Chinese media) deeply offended the Chinese government. An article appeared in the *People's Daily* three days later under the byline Wang Xiaoyang condemning Google for insinuating that the Chinese government was involved in the cyber-attacks. Alluding to Clinton's Newseum address, the article accused 'certain Western politicians for smearing China', alleging that China and Chinese Internet companies were as much victims of hacking as Google. While this clash of official views became a focus of international media coverage outside China, the mainland media were restricted to publicizing the official Chinese position. The Chinese media ran plenty of articles berating Google for making 'false accusations'. One titled 'Google Ought to Examine its Own Actions and Apologize to China!' enjoyed particularly wide circulation on the net. Some websites presented this article as 'expert commentary' because the author, Deng Xinxin, was a professor at the Communication University of China in Beijing. Alternative, independent views more sympathetic to Google's position appeared only to be censored immediately. They did, however, circulate freely outside China.

Hacker (*heike* 黑客)

In March 2009, a Canadian organization with public and private funding called Info War Monitor published a study that revealed the existence of 'Ghost Net', a cyber spying organization apparently based in China that had hacked into hundreds of foreign commercial and government servers. In January 2010, Google famously pulled the servers of its search engine from China, redirecting China-based users to its Hong Kong server. On Google's official blog, the company explained that one reason for this move was that Google and twenty other foreign companies had been the target of hacking attacks originating in China. Security experts and members of the US military establishment have made similar allegations. The Chinese government's routine denials of such allegations have done nothing to reassure potential victims, and the 'cyberthreat' from China remains a favorite topic of hawkish Internet commentators as well as security experts in the United States and elsewhere.

In April 2012, hackers claiming allegiance to the Anonymous group boasted that they had defaced or hacked into hundreds of Chinese government websites, prompting a spate of international media reports. As it turned out, the affected websites all belonged to small, provincial government organizations; no one from Anonymous has yet released any particularly sensitive information from Chinese government servers.

Also, in the days following Google's statement, Chinese Google fans laid tributes of candles, cards, floral bouquets, and other symbolic objects on a slab outside the company's ten-storeyed headquarters at Tsinghua Science Park in Beijing that featured the company logo. Security guards removed these daily offerings. When challenged, one guard replied that without an official permit, floral tributes were illegal. The phrase 'illegal floral tributes' soon went viral on the Internet as a symbolic protest against state censorship. Naturally, the phrase was quickly blacklisted. Flowers did not have much luck on the Chinese Internet in 2010-2011.

In a poll conducted from 13-20 January 2010 by NetEase, the company operating China's highly popular 163.com portal, 77.68 percent of 14,119 respondents wanted Google.cn to stay in China. By April, the furore surrounding Google had died down, though it was briefly revived in June

2010 when the company reported more recent cyber-attacks from China. The *People's Daily* promptly published another op-ed deriding Google for stooping to slander and betraying 'the spirit of the Internet'. In the end, Google did not withdraw from China, despite its declining share of the mainland's Internet traffic market (Baidu being one of its successful competitors) and frequent complaints from Internet users in China about interruptions to Google services. At the time of writing, Google.cn remains in operation but any attempt to access the portal outside China is automatically redirected to Google.com.hk.

Google's fate inspired pensive remarks from the Shanghai-based essayist Han Han, China's leading online literary celebrity and independent commentator (for more on Han, see Chapter 7). Between December 2009 and January 2010, two influential Chinese-language magazines – *Asia Weekly* in Hong Kong and Guangzhou's *Southern Weekly* – named Han Person of the Year. In April 2010, he came second in *Time* magazine's 100 Poll (in which readers cast votes for the world's one hundred most influential persons); he garnered 873,230 votes. (The Iranian opposition politician Mir-Hossein Mousavi was number one with 1,492,879 votes.) By the end of 2009, he was China's most popular blogger, his blog attracting some three hundred million hits. By July 2011, that number exceeded five hundred million.

In March 2010, an interviewer asked Han for his views on Google's imminent departure from China. He replied that any candid response was pointless, as it would be immediately censored (as this remark was). Nonetheless, the transcript of the interview circulated on the Web outside China (after appearing briefly on his blog), and savvy mainland netizens were able to access and read it via proxy servers. Han expressed regret about Google's departure but observed that the company had overestimated the interest of China's netizens in accessing uncensored content. He claimed uncharitably that most mainland Chinese were so preoccupied with making money they didn't care about censorship.

Liu Xiaobo 刘晓波

Liu Xiaobo is a writer who has, since the mid-1980s, been a high-profile figure, first as a literary critic, cultural provocateur and firebrand, then as an activist in the 1989 protest movement. Following his release from prison in 1991, he became an outspoken advocate of political reform and human rights. In 2008, Liu was a key figure in the drafting and propagation of Charter 08, a rambling document calling for democracy and human rights in China and modelled on the Czechoslovak Charter '77. In December that year, Liu was detained for his Charter 08 activism on charges of 'inciting subversion of state power'. On Christmas Day 2009, he was sentenced to eleven years imprisonment and two years deprivation of political rights. Liu was awarded the 2010 Nobel Peace Prize for 'his long and non-violent struggle for fundamental human rights in China'. The Chinese authorities reacted with a frenzy of vitriol and condemnation of the Nobel Prize committee – and even of Norway itself and its government (which plays no role in the selection of Nobel laureates).

Han also remarked that if Baidu (China's largest Web company) were to offer people RMB10 (US$1.57) to install a browser that would not only block Google but impose even greater search restrictions, he was willing to wager that more than half of China's 200 million netizens would gladly accept. Han was wrong on one point, however: he had greatly underestimated the size of the mainland online population. Official figures produced at the time by the state-run China Internet Network Information Center (CNNIC) in its June 2010 survey put China's online community at 420 million. But Han Han's remarks were not surprising: his blog posts often criticized government corruption and public apathy.

When Han accused his fellow-netizens of docile compliance with censorship, he made it clear that he was letting off steam in the hope of encouraging greater awareness in China. In mid-2011, he told Evan Osnos of *The New Yorker* that he opposed 'hastening multiparty elections' as the Party was simply too powerful: 'they are rich and they can bribe people.' Summarizing Han's position, Osnos wrote: 'Outsiders often confuse the demand for openness with the demand for democracy but in domestic Chinese politics the difference is crucial.' Indeed – although Han's blog posts are frequently censored, he has not been harassed or arrested for them.

The limits of political tolerance in China become clear when we compare the government's relatively benign attitude toward Han Han with the harsh treatment meted out to Liu Xiaobo, China's best known dissident and recipient of the 2010 Nobel Peace Prize. Liu was most recently arrested in December 2008, at the end of China's successful if troubled Olympic year, for co-authoring and organizing Charter 08 – a petition that, in essence, demanded an end to one-party rule and an immediate transition to a multi-party democracy. Twelve months later, he was sentenced to eleven years in gaol on the charge of attempting to subvert state power.

China's party-state interpreted the award of the Nobel Peace Prize on 8 October 2010 to Liu Xiaobo as a serious politically motivated affront. Outside the country there was intensive media coverage of the ensuing diplomatic tensions between Norway and China as well as the many international petitions demanding Liu's release from gaol. The Chinese government initially blocked this surge of news but when censorship proved futile, it moved to condemn the Nobel Committee for allegedly perverting the award's aims. The state-controlled media repeatedly and uniformly referred to Liu as a 'criminal'. The Chinese official phrase for staying 'on message' is 'maintaining a unified calibre' (*tongyi koujing* 统一口径). In the case of Liu Xiaobo, this consisted of condemning the Nobel Peace Prize; denigrating and attacking Liu Xiaobo's character; criticizing Liu's Western supporters as being either misinformed, actively anti-China or both; and, publicizing any international support for China's position. As Benjamin Penny notes in the following chapter, there were even attempts in China to organize a 'counter-Nobel Peace Prize' called the 'Confucius Peace Prize' in protest.

To achieve a convergence of opinion, the government powerfully utilized the full array of information technologies not only in print and TV media but across digital media platforms: websites, online forums, blogs and microblogs. But the Chinese public enjoyed access to these same digital technologies. 'Microblog fever' played a critical role in spreading the news of Liu's Nobel award. As traffic soared on the Twitter hash-tag '#Liu Xiaobo', mainland netizens who accessed the service via proxy servers began forwarding the contraband news within China. Because the name 'Liu Xiaobo' was banned on the mainland Internet, coded substitutes soon appeared such as the English-language 'Dawn Wave', a literal translation of 'Xiaobo'. One group of feisty human rights activists in Guizhou – one of China's poorest provinces – called on netizens to flood the Internet with the message: 'Good news! A mainland Chinese has won the Nobel for the first time.' A tit-for-tat ensued with pro-government articles and comments countered by oblique defences of Liu's award.

My Dad is Li Gang!

(*Wo ba shi Li Gang!* 我爸是李刚!)

According to the National Bureau of Statistics, there are 149,594 people in China whose ID documents carry the name Li Gang. On 16 October 2010, the name gained national notoriety when twenty-two-year-old Li Qiming 李启铭, apparently drunk, drove his car onto the campus of University of Hebei in Baoding, knocking down two young women. When campus security guards tried to detain Li Qiming he is said to have shouted: 'Charge me if you dare. My dad is Li Gang!' One of the women, twenty-year-old Chen Xiaofeng, died in hospital. Outraged Chinese Internet users discovered that the Li Gang who was Li Qiming's father was deputy director of a district Public Security Bureau in Baoding.

The outcry on the Internet brought the incident to the attention of the central government. Li Qiming was tried and sentenced to six years in prison.

The Li Gang incident epitomized a ballooning social problem: the misbehaviour, often involving expensive automobiles, of the spoiled children of officials and rich business people, known as *guan erdai* 官二代 and *fu erdai* 富二代 respectively.

Such defiant activity is the product of a society that is being opened up by the easy flow of information across digital platforms. Over coming years, with digital technology becoming more affordable, rural dwellers and the working poor will swell China's online population. Whereas the authorities are still confident they can guide and mould public opinion with regard to international news in which China has a stake, such as Liu's Nobel Prize, they take a far more cautious approach when dealing with local incidents that touch a nerve among Chinese citizens.

In October 2010, Liu's Nobel inflamed mass public sentiment far less than a drunk-driving incident in the city of Baoding in Hebei province, in which a female university student was killed and another injured. Chen Xiaofeng and Zhang Jingjing were roller-skating along a narrow lane on the Hebei University campus when they were hit by a car driven by Li Qiming, the son of the local deputy police chief. In recent years, road casualties caused by China's 'second-generation rich' (*fu erdai* 富二代, the progeny of the wealthy, often with powerful Party connections) have outraged ordinary citizens because of the leniency normally shown to the

An Internet joke that circulated following the 'My Dad is Li Gang!' incident showing a road sign Photoshopped to read: 'Friend: Drive slowly, your dad is not Li Gang!'
Source: Hudong.com

culprits. When campus security guards arrested Li, he shouted: 'Go ahead, charge me if you dare, my dad is Li Gang!' Netizens promptly inundated the Internet with parodies and permutations of 'My dad is Li Gang!' (*Wo ba shi Li Gang!* 我爸是李刚!) lambasting the abuse of power among China's rich. State censors tried to contain the public reaction by blocking reports about the incident but it proved too irresistible, even for CCTV (China Central Television). On 21 October, the national broadcaster aired an interview with a tearful Li Gang, who apologized on his son's behalf. The next day a report featured a weeping and contrite Li Qiming; he was later sentenced to six years in gaol. Before the case was heard in court, Li's father paid 466,000 *yuan* (US$73,750) as compensation to the dead girl's family and 91,000 *yuan* (US$14,400) to the injured girl, with half this sum being payment for her hospital treatment.

In January 2011, when the official Xinhua News Service released its 2010 list of 'Top Ten Buzzwords on the Internet in China', 'My dad is Li Gang' was ranked number four and stood out as the only politically sensitive catchphrase. The fact that it was listed at all indicates something of a new willingness to heed the simmering discontent about the wealth gap.

The inequality now affecting every aspect of Chinese society has lent particularly ambivalent impetus to the revival of 'red culture'. Given rampant official corruption, the Maoist rhetoric of egalitarianism, minus its original anti-capitalist tenor, has popular appeal while justifying the continuation of one-party rule. Egalitarian rhetoric was the staple fare of a much poorer China where political campaigns and ideological witch-hunts co-existed with dreams of national prosperity. Back then the Communist Party enjoyed a monopoly on defining what was 'red'. In the digital present-day, ordinary netizens and the Party elite alike can contend among themselves and with each other over the true value and utility of Maoist ideas and ideals.

In the weeks that followed the removal of Bo Xilai from all of his official positions on 15 March 2012, the Party leadership in Beijing held back from pronouncing on the 'red' campaigns that were Bo's trademark from 2009. Still, on the eve of Bo's dismissal on 14 March 2012, Premier Wen Jiabao, a known opponent of Bo, delivered a widely noted speech (discussed in the introduction to this volume). In it he called for renewed efforts at political reform to safeguard against the recurrence of a 'historical tragedy on the scale of the Cultural Revolution'. Wen's remarks were a barely veiled attack on Bo, whose flaunting of 'redness' tacitly accused his critics of being less than genuine socialists. To forestall speculation about factional strife in the Party's upper echelons, the state's Publicity Department (formerly known as the Central Propaganda Department) soon issued a directive forbidding mainland news outlets from publishing extended commentaries on the Premier's speech.

The Chinese party-state generally prefers to stress its socialist credentials while downplaying its Maoist origins. A highly publicized *People's Daily* editorial of 11 April 2012 urged Chinese citizens to 'maintain a high level of ideological unity' with the Politburo in Beijing and to 'raise high the great banner of socialism with Chinese characteristics'. The editorial was at pains to reassure its readers that 'China is a socialist country ruled by law' in which 'there is no privileged citizen before the law'. Such grandiose if content-free declarations together with zealous state censorship and state-sponsored rumours meant that Chinese Internet coverage of the unfolding drama around Bo, his wife Gu Kailai and their coterie was highly restricted and monitored, not to mention biased against the purged Bo. Yet, the politically engaged were just as determined to publicize their views on this issue as the state censors were to suppress them. And so yet again, irrepressible coded debate continued to thwart any official hope for 'ideological unity'.

6

6

SEARCHING FOR A SAGE TODAY

Benjamin Penny

IN RECENT years, Chinese leaders have acknowledged that the country's famed rapid development has also resulted in increased social inequality, environmental degradation and community unrest. Official attempts to revivify elements of the Maoist heritage that began in Chongqing, the 'red culture' discussed throughout this volume, was one attempt to find a past ideological model to serve present-day society. A sage from a much earlier period, Confucius, has also been promoted by President Hu Jintao as providing values for rebuilding social cohesion while maintaining secular authority. The search for paragons led some also to Laozi, the Taoist philosopher, as well as to one of his latter-day adherents and promoters, the celebrity Taoist priest Li Yi. In the late 2000s, Li Yi's 'temple spa' outside Chongqing became a haven for the nouveau riche, who sought there spiritual balm for the anxieties of modern life – until, that is, Li's spectacular fall from grace in late 2010.

A tourist poses in front of a statue of Confucius that appeared on 11 January 2011 on the eastern flank of Tiananmen Square outside the National Museum of China. It disappeared without explanation on 21 April the same year.
Photo: Danwei Media

On 11 January 2011, a 9.5-metre bronze statue of Confucius appeared outside the entrance to the recently refurbished National Museum of China along the eastern flank of Tiananmen Square in the heart of Beijing. *China Daily* reported that the sculptor, Wu Weishan, 'meant to present Confucius as a peak in the history of Chinese philosophy and culture… When passers-by look at his eyes, they may feel a kind of spiritual communication with the ancient wise man.' One such passer-by was also quoted approvingly: 'Confucian wisdom transcends time and space. In my opinion, Confucianism is at the core of Chinese values. It can still guide us in daily life.' Opinion about the statue was not, however, all positive. The prominent leftist website Mao Flag demanded its removal and in a *People's Daily* online poll taken about a week after its unveiling, some sixty-two percent of the 820,000 respondents expressed opposition to it.

Early on the morning of 21 April, the statue disappeared. The untoward arrival of the Sage, followed by his equally sudden departure, led to fevered speculation on Chinese blogs as well as in the international press about what it all might mean. Did the erection of the statue signal the final and complete rehabilitation of Confucius after the vitriolic attacks on him in earlier decades of the People's Republic? Did its removal indicate a change of mind among the inner circles of the leadership? Could Confu-

The statue of Confucius 'internally exiled' to the courtyard of the National Museum of China.
Photo: Geremie R. Barmé

cius's disappearance even be a response to the negative reaction of ordinary Chinese, as evidenced in the poll results? And perhaps most significantly, was the *volte-face* by the authorities a manifestation of a shift in the power balance between Party factions leading up to the leadership changes in 2012-2013?

Not surprisingly, the opaque nature of Chinese succession politics and the close control that the Communist Party maintains over information fuelled idle speculation. People immediately saw in the fate of the Confucius statue an augury of Party factional politics. Its removal was viewed by some as being one more sign of the then increasing influence of Bo Xilai, the Chongqing Party Committee Secretary and member of the Politburo, famous for his 'Sing Red' campaign and support for the Maoist legacy in general, something discussed in other chapters. Following the 2008 Beijing Olympics ideological differences amongst China's leaders became more evident. But while political reform has been mooted it is unlikely that the Chinese Communist Party could in the future rename itself the Chinese Confucian Party, a suggestion made only half in jest. Equally unlikely, though, is the idea that in the second decade of the twenty-first century the Party could genuinely contemplate a Maoist revival.

Harmonious Confucianism

One thing is certainly clear: Confucianism in a form approved by the Party is alive and well in today's China. It has attained a respectability unimaginable during the country's revolutionary era. In its current anodyne form – far removed from the subtle and rigorous arguments of the Confucian philosophical tradition – China's party-state uses the sage's teachings to help justify repressive actions and policies. Much of the social and political coercion of recent years, topics discussed at length by Susan Trevaskes in Chapter 3, is pursued in the name of creating 'harmony' and an 'harmonious society'. When President Hu Jintao launched the program to build

Confucius (*Kongzi* 孔子)

Many of the most important Chinese political, philosophical and literary figures of the twentieth century regarded Confucianism as the ideological foundation of a repressive and backward society and culture and an autocratic, hierarchical political system. They saw Confucianism as the root cause of China's weakness: it fostered servility in the people, enforced inequality (including gender inequality) in society, was more concerned with the family than the individual, and entrenched rote learning and self-destructive, ritualistic behaviour rather than intellectual inquiry and rational action. The first major wave of anti-Confucianism was in 1919, as part of the progressive May Fourth Movement, which saw Confucianism as inimical to democracy and science. By the Cultural Revolution in the mid 1960s, the Communists further vilified Confucius as the chief representative of ancient China's slave-owning aristocracy, calling him Kong Lao'er – colloquially 'Confucius the prick'. In the early 1970s, the Party leadership linked him with Mao Zedong's then arch-enemy and erstwhile closest comrade-in-arms Lin Biao in the 'Criticize Lin, Criticize Confucius' campaign.

Confucius was born in the state of Lu – roughly equivalent to modern Shandong – in 551 BCE. He died in 479, long before China had been unified by the Qin. Best known as the author of *The Analects* (*Lunyu* 论语), a book of his sayings and recollections compiled after his death by disciples, he worked as a scholar official, first in Lu, then later for the rival states of Wei, Song, Chen and Cai. The legend has it that in each place he expounded his theories of good government and human relations, but remained disappointed that they were never put into practice.

After Confucius's death his disciples, and their disciples, preserved and developed his ideas, forming different schools of interpretation. The Han dynasty (206 BCE-220 CE) adopted 'Confucianism' as its legitimizing ideology. But Confucianism, also known as the 'Teachings of the Scholars' (*Rujia* 儒家), continued to change and adapt itself to differing circumstances in subsequent dynasties. The Confucianism that survived into the nineteenth century was an 'harmonious society' at the February 2005 meeting of China's National People's Congress, he proclaimed that: 'As Confucius said, "Harmony is precious".' This allowed, and indeed helped to generate, a wave of enthusiasm for Confucius.

The statement, 'Harmony is precious' (*he wei gui* 和为贵) comes from the primary Confucian classic, *The Analects*. In that book, however, the line is not attributed to Confucius himself but to his disciple Youzi. It has gained slogan-like currency in contemporary Chinese. But the full sentence in *The Analects* is: 'Harmony is precious *when performing the rites*.'

deeply influenced by a form that had appeared in the Song dynasty (960-1279) and is usually called Neo-Confucianism (credited to Zhu Xi, 1130-1200) and the Ming-dynasty philosopher Wang Yangming (1472-1529).

In the twentieth century Confucianism continued to have its defenders, both in politics and philosophy. A stream of thought called 'New Confucianism' (as opposed to Neo-Confucianism) appeared in the Republican period. Developed outside the People's Republic after 1949, it began to claim adherents in mainland China from the early 1980s. They reasoned that the moral verities of Confucianism could help fill the moral and ideological vacuums left by the collapse of state Maoism and construct a modern state untainted by undesirable Western liberal values. Outside the mainland, one of the main proponents of New Confucianism – which essentially justifies an authoritarian state – was Lee Kwan Yew of Singapore. His push for 'Asian values' during the 1990s exemplified this trend.

Beginning in the mid 1980s, the Communist Party allowed and occasionally encouraged the rehabilitation of Confucianism. Discussions of the relevance of Confucianism to modern problems have saturated academic and public spheres. From early in the new millennium Confucius became the name the Chinese government chose to represent China to the rest of the world, even calling the Chinese cultural and language learning centres being set up across the globe with state funding 'Confucius Institutes'.

On 11 January 2011, a bronze statue of Confucius was erected outside the entrance to the newly renovated National Museum of China on the east side of Tiananmen Square. There was neither official explanation nor any ceremony. The leftist website Mao Flag (maoflag.net) objected, and published an article calling for its removal. Illustrating the article was an image of the statue with the character for 'demolish' (*chai* 拆) photo-shopped over it. On 21 April, the statue disappeared, again without any explanation in the media or from official sources. It reappeared in an internal courtyard of the National Museum.

The 'rites' were the codified rules of behaviour that governed formal rituals, individual decorum as well as that of the family and strict regulations for the conduct of interpersonal relationships. But then perhaps Hu's use of the adage betrayed the real meaning of China's present politics of 'harmony': to make people behave according to a set of norms determined by officialdom and its changing priorities.

The background to Hu's move to proclaim 'harmony' as the primary social good resulted from the realization that the benefits of thirty years of economic growth were distributed unevenly; a small number of people enjoyed extraordinary wealth while the vast majority still struggled. Social services such as medical care have become too expensive for many to afford, the cost of housing has skyrocketed, and the effects of pollution are appalling. Creating an harmonious society was meant to help alleviate these ills. Policies aimed at building a more equitable society encompassed undertakings to improve China's 'democratic legal system', protect human rights, increase employment, narrow the wealth gap, improve public services, promote moral standards, and secure public order as well as protect the environment.

More cynical, and perhaps realistic, observers also see behind these noble sentiments a warning against any attempt to question or undermine the power of the Communist Party. Indeed, the invocation of Confucius and notions long ascribed to Confucian thought such as the importance of maintaining proper social hierarchies, the need for loyalty and respect towards those in superior positions, made Hu's call for 'harmony' seem, for some, like a strident call for the shoring up of authoritarianism. Rulers in China from imperial times have consistently and morbidly feared 'chaos', understood as a collapse of social bonds and relationships, a state of turmoil, of upheaval and overturning, or even a challenge to their own authority.

Along with the Party's use of a repackaged Confucianism to further its current goals, the enthusiastic invocation of the Sage is also part of an effort to forge a new national image, both at home and overseas. If Confucius now represents 'harmony' and 'peace', these noble virtues are emptied of any particular relationship to his actual thought, except in the most diluted form. The Sage himself, meanwhile, has ended up as an amorphous symbol for Chineseness that can be deployed for almost any nationalist purpose. Despite the appearance and the disappearance of the Confucius statue, the ancient Sage as palimpsest is still a potent power in China: his name means everything, even as it means nothing in particular.

Logo for the Confucius Institute, an organization intended to promote the party-state's version of Chinese language and culture.
Source: Confucius Institute website at Chinese.cn

The Sage Put to Use

One of the first instances of Confucius being used as a national brand came with the establishment of Confucius Institutes. This state-funded program is ostensibly the equivalent of Germany's Goethe Institute, France's Alliance Française and Italy's Dante Alighieri Society. Like them, Confucius Institutes are intended to promote internationally the study of the national language and culture. The first Confucius Institute opened in 2004 in Seoul. Now there are some 350 of these institutes in 105 countries, as well as another 500 'Confucius classrooms' in schools. There are nine Confucius Institutes in Australia, located in tertiary education institutions, as is typically the case in most countries, with the number of school-based Confucius classrooms growing. Concerted opposition to the program has, however, limited their growth. Criticisms have focused on the possible threat to academic freedom they represent by being located in universities: topics sensitive to the Chinese government such as Tibet, Taiwan or Falun Gong cannot be discussed in the fearless way we expect to be the norm in academic institutions.

More problematic, Confucius Institutes are perceived as a tool of China's soft power diplomacy. 'Soft power' refers to a state or other international actor attaining their objectives through such means as culture, education or reputation rather than through military or coercive measures. Another less well-aired but equally cogent criticism of the Institutes is that in their language programs, they promote a very particular view of what 'Chinese' is and how it should be written (that is, *Putonghua* 普通话, or 'Standard Chinese', and in simplified characters). This curriculum excludes the very many other forms of Chinese currently spoken in the Sinophone world (Cantonese, Shanghainese, Hokkien, etc.) as well as the traditional writing system, effectively rendering the language learner, in the words of one recent critic, 'semi-literate'. Whatever the underlying politics of the Confucius Institute program, it should be clear that it has very little to do with Confucius himself. Indeed, students trained exclusively in their language programs would be unlikely to be able to read *The Analects*.

A leaflet for the Confucius Peace Prize, first awarded in 2010 as a riposte to the Nobel Peace Prize given to Liu Xiaobo.
Source: Baidu Baike

Confucius Institutes are only one example of the controversial appropriation of the philosopher's name for institutions and events that have, or seek to have, official sanction. Perhaps the most egregious is the 'Confucius Peace Prize', an idea first proposed by one Liu Zhiqin, the chief representative of Zurich Bank in Beijing. Liu suggested the establishment of this prize as a response to the awarding in October 2010 of the Nobel Peace Prize to the dissident writer and thinker Liu Xiaobo. Liu Zhiqin's advocacy of a new, Chinese-sponsored peace prize published in November 2010 began with a strident critique of the Nobel Committee:

> The Nobel Peace Prize Committee won Liu Xiaobo while losing the trust of 1.3 billion Chinese people. They support a criminal while creating 1.3 billion 'dissidents' that are dissatisfied with the Nobel Committee... However, the Chinese people's discontent or questioning will not change the prejudice of the proud and stubborn Noble Prize Committee members... it has become the mind-set of the current Westerners that they will oppose whatever China supports and support whatever China opposes. In order to make them change their mind-set, more appropriate ways need to be adopted...

The first Confucius Peace Prize was awarded in December 2010 to Lien Chan, Chairman Emeritus of the Nationalist Party and former Vice-president of the Republic of China on Taiwan. It was awarded in recognition of his famous 2005 trip to the mainland. Lien's meeting with Hu Jintao on that occasion was the highest-level contact between the Communists and Nationalists since 1945, when Mao Zedong had met Chiang Kai-shek in Chongqing. Lien was chosen by the 'Confucius Peace Prize Committee' (described in the Chinese media as being an NGO) from a shortlist that is said to have included Bill Gates, Nelson Mandela, and the Chinese-government-endorsed Eleventh Panchen Lama. The director of Lien's office commented on the prize: 'We've never heard of such an award and of course Mr Lien has no plans to accept it.' In September 2011, the Chinese Ministry of Culture announced that the prize had been cancelled. This was followed three weeks later by an announcement cancelling an alternative award – the Confucius World Peace Prize – that was to have been run by the China Foundation for the Development of Social Culture, an organization under the Ministry of Culture. Despite this, a second prize *was* awarded in 2011, this time to Vladimir Putin by the China International Peace Research Centre, a new Hong Kong registered organization headed by the poet Qiao Damo, who was a member of the original Confucius Peace Prize committee and who had apparently nominated himself for the 2010 prize. Like Lien Chan before him, Putin failed to appear at the award ceremony in Beijing. His prize was accepted in his stead by two Russian exchange students.

Another recent event in the world of Confucius appropriation, this one with strong government support, was the 2010 film *Confucius* starring the Hong Kong star Chow Yun-fat in the title role. It was supposed to open in 2009 – the sixtieth anniversary of the founding of the People's Republic, and the 2,560th of the birth of Confucius (according to the traditional dating). The première was delayed allegedly because the authorities feared that it would be overshadowed by the much more popular US film *Avatar*. Initially, the idea that Chow Yun-fat, a Hong Kong star who has frequently played gangsters, would play Confucius was met with scepticism – analogous perhaps to Sylvester Stallone being cast as Shakespeare. His performance was nonetheless one of the best things about the film, which *The Guardian* characterized as a 'smug biopic'.

Declarations of Harmony

With Confucianism being given such a preeminent position in the public arena, there was an expectation that intellectuals would rally to the support of the cause. Perhaps the most famous person to bolster Confucianism in the mass media is Yu Dan, a professor at Beijing Normal University and celebrity interpreter of ancient philosophy. Yu came to fame as a result of her 2006 TV lectures on *The Analects*, which also became a bestselling book. Translated into English as *Confucius from the Heart: Ancient Wisdom for Today's World*, Yu made the classic text into a self-help guide, a pop version of the Sage, his wisdom made accessible through anecdote and pre-digested life lessons. A blurb on the book cover asked:

> Can the classic sayings of *The Analects* from more than 2500 years ago inspire insights today? Can they still stir up deep feelings in us? Addressing the spiritual perplexities that confront twenty-first-century humanity, Beijing Normal University's Professor Yu

> Dan – with her profound classical learning and her exquisite feminine sensibility – sets out to decode *The Analects* from the perspective of her unique personality...

Not long after Hu Jintao (mis-)quoted the sage, an annual 'World Confucian Conference' was established. The fourth of these was held in late September 2011 to coincide with Confucius's traditional birthdate on the twenty-eighth of that month. The venue was Qufu, Shandong province, where the main Confucius Temple and ancient Kong Family Residence is located. In the previous year, in 2010, the Nishan Forum on World Civilizations was held at nearby Nishan, traditionally regarded as the sage's birthplace. The Nishan Forum is dedicated to the cause of 'dialogue between international cultures', a dialogue in which 'Confucianism' is regarded as somehow being equivalent to 'Chinese culture' and 'Christianity' with 'Western culture'. The keyword in all of these activities was, once again, the Communist Party mantra, 'harmony'. Xu Jialu, the President of the Organizing Committee of the Nishan Forum (and a Vice-chairman of the Standing Committee of the National People's Congress), declared that the themes of the Nishan Forum were 'Harmony with Diversity' and 'the Harmonious World', its slogan 'Harmony, Love, Integrity and Tolerance'. Furthermore, cross-civilizational dialogues would focus on 'social responsibility, credit, tolerance and diversity, and harmonious coexistence.' The Nishan Forum also promulgated a 'Declaration of Harmony', a set of motherhood statements that amounted to a version of Confucianism-lite.

Confucianism has by no means been the only one of China's great philosophical traditions to enjoy an officially approved resurgence. Laozi, the founder of Taoism (Daoism), has yet to be honoured with a statue in Tiananmen Square or a peace prize, but his philosophical legacy, like that of Confucius, has in recent years been recast as an ideological bulwark and global marketing tool.

In October 2011, an International Taoism Forum was held at Hengshan, one of the five sacred Taoist mountains, in Hunan province. With representatives from Taoist organisations and temples throughout mainland China and from overseas (including Taiwan), as well as notable invited foreigners, this conference too released a formal declaration.

The Hengshan Declaration, like that from Confucian Nishan, made a claim that it had relevance for the whole globe, not just China. It promoted Taoist philosophy as a cure for humanity's ills, be they inequality, conflict or environmental degradation. Like its Confucian counterpart, the Hengshan Declaration referred to ideas that while recognizable as Taoist were vulgarized to the point of parodic blandness. The Declaration ended with an admonition to: 'Respect the Tao and honour Virtue for harmonious coexistence.' It was hardly a surprise that the Hengshan and Nishan declarations strike the same note, given contemporary policy imperatives. Xu Jialu, the organizer of the Nishan meeting, was also present at Hengshan. He was interviewed at length on the themes of the forums on the program 'Journey of Civilisation' on national TV.

The 2011 Taoist Forum had been preceded by another in 2007, the International *Tao-te Ching* Forum, held jointly in Hong Kong and Xi'an. During that event the world record for the most people reading aloud simultaneously in one location was broken when 13,839 people recited the Tao-te ching, the famous Taoist classic, en masse in a Hong Kong stadium (this record was broken in May 2011 when when 23,822 people took part in a mass reading event at the Malatya Inönü Stadium, Turkey). The stated goal of the 2007 meeting was to investigate ways of constructing – no surprises here – 'a harmonious society through the Tao.'

The organs of China's party-state have appropriated Confucianism and Taoism in order to reinvigorate a discredited ideology, and a jaded polity, and to create an image of 'civilized China' for local and international consumption. However, such gestures inevitably have consequences far beyond those originally intended. Hu Jintao's appeal to a transcendental Chineseness – an appeal accepted by the man passing by the Confucius

Laozi (老子, also rendered Lao Tzu)

Laozi (literally, 'the Old Master'), the founder of Taoism (or Daoism), is traditionally regarded as having lived in the sixth century BCE. The short text that bears his name is also known as *Daodejing* (*Tao-te Ching* 道德经), or *The Way and its Power.* At barely 5,000 characters, it is written in a terse and frequently ambiguous style that has given rise to a long and varied tradition of commentary and interpretation. Archaeological discoveries from the 1970s onward have shown that the classic version of the text was just one of probably several versions that circulated in the centuries before the Common Era.

Records concerning Laozi date from long after his death and are not consistent. Sima Qian, the author of China's first comprehensive history, *The Records of the Historian* (*Shiji* 史记), which was completed in 91BCE, presents three different and contradictory stories about him.

One famous story places Laozi as Court Archivist in the state of Zhou. At the age of 160 weary of court life he is said to have headed west on the back of a water buffalo. On his journey, the keeper of one of the passes out of the state recognized him and asked him to pass on his wisdom. The result was the *Daodejing*.

Whatever the true story of his life, by the second century CE, Laozi had been transformed into a god, Lord Lao, the Most High One. Zhang Daoling claimed to have received revelations from Lord Lao. Zhang is regarded as the founder of what some scholars refer to as 'Religious Taoism' to distinguish it from 'philosophical Taoism', popular in literati circles throughout Chinese history. The religion flourished in pre-modern China, several dynasties adopted it as their state creed. The imperial family of the Tang dynasty even claimed Laozi as one of their ancestors and included his book in the syllabus for the civil service examinations.

Buddhism entered China from India in the first few centuries of the Common Era. Buddhism and Daoism were in periodic conflict, criticizing and often ridiculing one another, which didn't prevent them from borrowing each other's ideas when it suited. One of the most potent stories the religious Taoists made up claimed that after Laozi had left China on his buffalo, he had ended up in India. Finding the natives there less intellectually able than his own people, he taught them what we might now call a 'dumbed-down' version of his teachings. Indian Buddhism, in this telling, is merely a popularized version of Laozi's wisdom.

In modern times, Laozi's book is widely regarded as an indispensable element of China's philosophical heritage and remains a favourite text of intellectuals who see themselves as non-conformists. The religion of Taoism is one of the five official religions of China's People's Republic. Lord Lao is still worshipped in Taoist temples, where the *Daodejing* is recited like a sutra.

statue who said: 'Confucianism is at the core of Chinese values' – also allows others with different agendas to gain credibility. It provides the space and rationale for clever entrepreneurs to tout themselves and their wares as ancient Chinese wisdom. Such charlatans exploit widespread contemporary ignorance of what 'ancient Chinese wisdom' really was. Their ignorance stems from earlier decades in which the Communist Party promoted cultural nihilism, purges and denunciations of the past and contempt for non-revolutionary education.

Taoism

While today's officially endorsed Taoism buttresses the official ideology of social harmony, in earlier periods it was often a teaching that promoted an inner harmony par excellence – a balance between yin and yang, or between spirit, essence and *qi*. These ideas were not confined to Taoism, but Taoists were amongst their leading proponents. While 'harmony' has only reappeared in the last decade, a renewed focus on self-cultivation (*xiuyang* 修养) – a rediscovery and contemporary recasting of complex ideas that stretch back into China's earliest recorded history – has been in fashion since the 1980s. Usually considered as part of *qigong* practices, self-cultivation re-emerged following the suppression of Falun Gong in 1999, in a more regulated form. In recent years self-cultivation has become big business, a home-grown version of self-help culture that includes gurus, classes, retreats and diets. Adepts and devotees of the practice can become media stars, not to mention a good investment for canny proprietors. A Taoist priest by the name of Li Yi was both.

Taoist master Li Yi featured on the cover of *Southern People Weekly*. The headline reads: 'The Extraordinary Tao of Li Yi: Why Do Jack Ma, Faye Wong, and Zhang Jizhong Acknowledge Him as Their Master?'
Source: *Southern People Weekly*

Li Yi made his first public appearance in 1990, not as a Taoist priest but as a performer in an acrobatic troupe whose members performed uncanny physical feats. Li claimed that he possessed 'extraordinary powers' (*teyi gongneng* 特异功能) – clairvoyance, telekinesis and the power of healing. He even claimed he could hold his breath underwater for two hours. It was a trick that got him onto national TV. In 1993, Li Yi expanded his repertoire opening a massage clinic. In 1998, he acquired control of a run-down Buddhist temple in the Jinyun Mountains outside Chongqing, a city that has featured frequently in this book. He renamed the temple the Palace of Intertwined Dragons and in 2006 Li formally took Taoist holy orders, though he had already been describing himself as a priest for some time. In June 2010, he was named a Vice-president of the National Taoist Association.

Fang Zhouzi 方舟子

Li Yi's fraud was uncovered by China's most famous investigative journalist, Fang Zhouzi. Fang is known as the 'science cop' since much of his media fame has come from exposing academic rather than religious fraud (he studied for a PhD in biochemistry at Michigan State University). He is known for his previous dogged pursuit of Xiao Chuanguo, a Professor of Urology at Wuhan's Huazhong Science and Technology University. In 2005, Xiao's university nominated him to the Chinese Academy of Science, but the Academy rejected this after Fang and his collaborators raised allegations that Xiao's CV was questionable and his academic claims exaggerated. In response, Xiao sued Fang for defamation and published a bitter open letter that began:

> An ugly bride eventually has to show her face to her in-laws. Fang Zhouzi, maybe you can hide for now, but you cannot hide forever. One day you will be brought to justice.

In August 2010, Fang was waylaid and bashed near his home in Beijing. Initially, gangsters were blamed for the assault but it soon came to light that Professor Xiao had hired thugs to beat up the journalist. The media soon dubbed Xiao 'Professor Hammer'. He was gaoled for five and a half months by a local Beijing court in October 2010, not on charges of attempted murder as Fang had suggested but simply for 'causing a disturbance'. Xiao was released from prison in March 2011.

Fang Zhouzi came to public attention again in early 2012 when he claimed that the famous Shanghai blogger Han Han had a ghost writer, claims Han Han vigorously disputed. Fang claims that he and his team have exposed over 700 cases of 'falsification, corruption, and pseudoscience'.

The Palace of Intertwined Dragons was a modern Taoist resort. It featured a version of Taoism updated and tailored for China's *nouveau riche*, a populist version of venerable teachings just as etiolated as the mock-Taoism touted by the Hengshan Declaration. Conveniently located in the cool and picturesque mountains outside the famously sweltering megalopolis, well-heeled urbanites flocked to Li Yi's temple-palace. As one observer noted, the temple provided 'a new version of religious service to society teaching the newly wealthy and accordingly stressed-out class of upscale Chinese businessmen how to relax and keep themselves fit.' It boasted all the features of a contemporary hotel, including a computer room and hot tubs as well as buildings for 'massages, physical treatments, medical diagnoses, herbal prescriptions and exercise.' Both Li Yi and his operation proved to be a resounding popular success. The press reported that over the course of a few years hundreds of thousands of people had attended Master Li's courses and more than 30,000 people had become his disciples.

Li Yi's business also benefited from the patronage of some of China's A-list celebrities. Their number included the singer Faye Wong (who had sung the title song for the film *Confucius*), her husband, the martial arts actor Li Yapeng, the film director Zhang Jizhong and Jack Ma, founder and chairman of Alibaba.com (who would balance his interest in Taoism with his devotion to traditional Party culture – see the following chapter). The media fawningly reported their comings and goings. By 2009, the association of the celebrity couple Faye Wong and Li Yapeng with the Palace of Intertwined Dragons was being excitedly reported in Singapore where the media noted that they had only recently taken part in a nine-day retreat, during which they practised rigorous physical exercise, ate only bland food, listened to lectures on the Tao and spent hours transcribing scriptures, all in strict silence and avoiding physical contact. Li Yi's celebrity reached something of an apogee when, in July 2010, the popular magazine *Southern People Weekly* devoted its cover story to him. The lead read:

> The Extraordinary Tao of Li Yi: Why Do Jack Ma, Faye Wong, and Zhang Jizhong Acknowledge Him as Their Master?

Li also benefited from the assistance of a professional spruiker, a China Central Television presenter by the name of Fan Xinman, who wrote a blog devoted to the doings and sayings of the Master. In 2009, the first tranche of these blog posts was collected into a book called *Are There Immortals in Our Generation?* (Fan Xinman also happened to be the wife of Zhang Jizhong, the film director mentioned above.)

A little over a month later the bubble burst. Another member of the 'Southern' media stable, the influential but controversial magazine *Southern Weekend* exposed Li Yi as a fraud. They revealed his famous special powers to be clever trickery. People rushed to distance themselves from the discredited trickster and his famous disciples issued media denials that they had anything to do with a man now notorious for chicanery, phoney academic affiliations and shady financial dealings. Shortly after the media storm broke, Li Yi left the Jinyun Mountains and Chongqing in disgrace. At the time of writing he has yet to resurface.

Elsewhere in this volume we have discussed the differences between the Chongqing and the Guangzhou models and how they have played into the political, social and cultural life of contemporary China. The 'Li Yi case' is an example of another facet of this broader competition – a media trickster who was closely involved with China's new celebrity culture and self-promotion based in the hyperbolic environment of the boomtown of Chongqing, Li was undone by investigators who published their exposés in the (relatively) liberal media of Guangzhou.

ANXIETIES IN TIBET AND XINJIANG

PROTEST IN TIBET (*Xizang* 西藏)

In the People's Republic, the far western regions of Tibet and Xinjiang are both officially known as 'autonomous regions'. The dominant ethnic groups – Tibetans and Uyghurs – are supposed to enjoy a certain amount of self-governance. But this formal administrative approach, coupled with enormous investment in the local economy and infrastructure, has done little to ease ethnic tensions, nor to allay fears of economic marginalization caused by extensive Han Chinese immigration and worries that educational and religious policies are stifling Tibetan and Uyghur cultures.

On 10 March 2008, a small group of monks in Lhasa organized a street protest to commemorate the forty-ninth anniversary of the Tibetan uprising of 1959, which had led to the Dalai Lama fleeing Tibet for India. These initial peaceful protests were soon quelled but, on 14 March, new protests erupted involving laypeople which quickly turned into a riot that *The Economist* correspondent James Miles described as: 'calculated targeted violence against...ethnic Han Chinese living in Lhasa, but also members of the Muslim Hui minority.' The resulting burning, looting and killing was international news, and the unrest quickly spread to other areas of Tibetan China. According to the Xinhua News Agency, the death toll in Lhasa was eighteen civilians and one police officer, along with some protesters, although the Tibetan government-in-exile claimed that eighty people had lost their lives in the tumult.

While the Chinese government declared that the riots were instigated by the 'Dalai Clique' as part of a strategy to focus international attention on the Tibet question during the Olympic year, other observers noted the ongoing frustration of Tibetans at controls over their religious life, and some argued that this was due to increasing economic marginalization. Outside of China, activists opposing Chinese rule in Tibet organized demonstrations at Chinese embassies and at the Olympic torch rallies that China had organized in France, the US and other countries in the run up to the XXIXth Olympiad to be held in Beijing in August 2008. One particular incident, the snatching of the Olympic Torch from the hands of a Chinese participant in a wheelchair caused particular outrage. A group of young Beijing-based people launched the website AntiCNN.com to track and criticize Western media coverage of China on this and other issues. This site and official Chinese reports of the protests enraged young Chinese Internet users who decried perceived biases in Western press accounts, including the erroneous and misleading use of photos depicting soldiers in Nepal beating rioters. Some Chinese 'patriotic youths' uploaded homemade propaganda videos to the Internet asserting that: 'Tibet is, always was, and always will be part of China.'

By the end of March 2008, Chinese security forces had imposed military rule on Lhasa, with armed paramilitary units stationed at each crossroads in the Tibetan quarter of Lhasa on twenty-four hour duty (the first time since 1990, a situation that continues at the time of writing). In the months (and years) following the riots, strict controls at monasteries were increased (major monasteries were emptied of all monks from other areas; hundreds were held in detention centres for several months; re-education drives were resumed; and, new regulations were brought in to tighten control in monasteries and over Tibetans from outlying areas). Government propaganda emphasized the investments and economic benefits that Beijing's rule was bringing to Tibet. But tensions continued.

On 27 February 2009, a monk in Ngaba county (a Tibetan area in Sichuan province) set himself on fire while shouting slogans calling for Tibetan independence. His was the first of a wave of self-immolations: from mid-March 2009 to June 2012, Tibetan exile groups reported that thirty-seven people, mostly current or former monks and nuns in their early twenties, had set themselves on fire in towns and villages all over the Tibetan plateau, including in the Tibet Autonomous Region, and Qinghai, Gansu and Sichuan provinces. In February 2012, the Dalai Lama blamed the fatal protests on a policy of 'cultural genocide' being carried out in China. Beijing officials accused him or his 'clique' of instigating the self-immolations and called them a form of 'suicide terrorism' and an attempt to 'internationalise the Tibet issue'. In February 2012, the Chinese Premier Wen Jiabao declared that the immolators were 'innocents', signalling a softening of tone, but exiles and their leaders were still accused of encouraging them.

In May 2012, separate meetings between the Dalai Lama and British Prime Minister David Cameron, and Austrian Chancellor Werner Faymann were condemned by the Chinese government with boilerplate rhetoric: such meetings constituted 'interference in China's internal affairs' that 'hurt the feelings of the Chinese people'. In early June 2012, a blanket ban was placed on non-Chinese tourism to the Tibetan Autonomous Region.

TENSIONS IN XINJIANG 新疆

On 5 July 2009, an ethnic riot broke out in Ürümchi (capital city of the Xinjiang Uyghur Autonomous Region) that lasted for several days. Nearly 200 people died, and more than a thousand were injured, most of them Han Chinese. The event that triggered the riots was the death of two Uyghur migrant workers on 26 June at a toy factory in Shaoguan, Guangdong province after a dispute with Han Chinese workers. Han Chinese residents of Ürümchi fought back against the Uyghur rampage by taking to the streets in groups, armed with clubs and knives. Security forces took several days to quell the riots. Hundreds of Uyghurs were arrested, and Internet and long distance telephony in Xinjiang were shut down for more than six months.

The Chinese government blamed Rebiya Kadeer and exile Uyghur groups for instigating the riots. Unlike the Tibetans, the Uyghurs had never had a credible government in exile, or a strong activist force. Until recently, they did not have a charismatic figurehead. Kadeer, a prominent Uyghur businesswoman and former member of the Chinese People's Political Consultative Conference, stepped in to fill that gap. Her business and political career in China ended in 2000 when she was convicted of the crime of 'endangering state security' after she allegedly sent information about events in Xinjiang to exile Uyghur groups. Released in 2005, she went into exile in the United States where she has taken on an increasingly prominent role as an activist for Uyghur causes and an advocate of Uyghur autonomy. Kadeer denied that she had had any part in the riots.

The Chinese government's explanations for ethnic tensions in Xinjiang follow the same template used to explain Tibetan problems: focusing on what they say are machinations of Kadeer and hostile foreign forces that seek to split China. But the 2009 riots also caused discussions in the Chinese media and by academics about China's ethnic policies, and arguments that

China might learn from the 'melting pot' approach of the US, rather than separating minorities into 'autonomous' regions and counties, and offering them privileges such as the right to have more than one child per family. These ideas have been discussed by government officials; the state response has instead been to announce plans to increase investment and infrastructure construction in Xinjiang and the Party secretaries of Ürümchi and Xinjiang were replaced.

However, relations between Uyghurs and the government and Han Chinese residents of Xinjiang remain tense. On 30 and 31 July 2011, two separate knife and bomb attacks in the far western city of Kashgar (*Kashi* 喀什) resulted in at least eight deaths and dozens of injuries; some foreign media reports said thirty-two people had died. Government statements blamed the attacks on Uyghur separatists with Jihadist motives. In February 2012, state media reported that twelve people died after riots broke out near Kashgar. Police said that Uyghurs armed with knives had killed ten people, while two Uyghurs were shot dead by security forces.

7

7 BEHIND THE GREAT FIREWALL

Jeremy Goldkorn

ACCORDING TO the official China Internet Network Information Center (CNNIC), in 2011 the number of Chinese Internet users grew to more than half a billion. It remains, however, a circumscribed and heavily censored space lacking such common global websites as Facebook and services such as Twitter. Some Chinese netizens sarcastically call China's World Wide Web the 'ChInternet' or 'China's vast intranet'.

Despite this, the year 2011 may well have been a watershed. Government officials began reading Internet postings with a care once reserved for picking through editorials in the *People's Daily*. The ability to decipher gnomic utterances in the Party newspaper was once vital to a political career; today, understanding the Internet is arguably even more important for Party and non-Party observers alike for the way it reflects China's restive reality.

A High-speed Crash

Screenshot of a video in which Internet users said they saw a body falling out of a carriage following the Wenzhou train disaster. This was after the authorities had announced a final death toll, and claimed that all bodies had been accounted for.
Source: Youku.com

Yangjuan Quanyang is the online moniker of a student at a Beijing university. She is one of the 250 million people who, in 2011, used Weibo, or microblogs, a Twitter-like service operated by the Internet company Sina. As Gloria Davies has noted in Chapter 5, in the People's Republic of China, Twitter (like Facebook, YouTube, and many other near-universal websites) is inaccessible unless you use a Virtual Private Network (VPN) or other technical tricks to tunnel through the intermeshed system of Internet roadblocks that is generally referred to as the 'Great Firewall of China'.

Yangjuan Quanyang's microblog page is decorated with cute cartoons. Until late July 2011, most of her tweets were about the mundane details of her daily life. On the evening of 23 July, however, she was travelling on one of China's celebrated new high-speed trains, the D3115, speeding between Hangzhou and Fuzhou on the south-east littoral of the country. Just after 8:00pm, the train stalled near Wenzhou, a city famous for its entrepreneurs and the fabulous wealth they have amassed. As passengers sat waiting for an announcement about the delay, the D3115 was rear-ended by another train – the D301 – which was travelling along the same tracks also *en route* to Fuzhou, but from the direction of Beijing. The violent high-speed collision derailed six carriages. The D301 lost four carriages, including two that toppled some forty metres to the ground below from the viaduct on which the crash had occurred.

At 8:47pm, Yangjuan Quanyang tweeted:

> Help! Train D301 is derailed just near South Wenzhou Station. Everywhere you can hear children crying. We can't find the train crew. Please help us!

Yangjuan Quanyang's tweet spread rapidly through the mainland and overseas media; it broke the news of the disaster. While most government journalists and information minders enjoyed their Saturday night as usual, news of the crash lit up the microblogosphere. In the early hours of the following morning, the Ministry of Railways in Beijing released a statement blaming the accident on a lightning strike. At 4:00am on Sunday morning, the state-owned Xinhua News Agency reported that the accident had resulted in thirty-five fatalities, and that all of the dead had been accounted for. But, at 5:00am, a toddler was found alive in one of the carriages. Later that same day, a bystander used a mobile phone to shoot video footage of derailed train carriages being pulled off the viaduct. The video contained a segment that showed what appeared to be a body falling out of one of the carriages. In footage uploaded by another Internet user, a small army of workers was shown burying two of the derailed carriages beneath the high-speed rail viaduct. Not long afterwards, the Ministry of Railways called a press conference and, when asked how the Ministry had found a toddler alive after issuing a statement that there were no more survivors, the official spokesperson Wang Yongping replied: 'It's a miracle!'

Wang was asked if the Ministry was burying the train carriages to cover up evidence related to the fatal crash. He said that he had been told that the ground beneath the viaduct was marshy, and that the authorities had ordered workers to bury the carriages to provide a stable platform for rescue operations. Wang added inexplicably: 'I don't know if you believe it or not, I believe it!' His statement was ridiculed on the Internet as an example of vacuous officialese and the avoidance of responsibility.

Over the next few days, as the Ministry of Railways changed their explanation, now blaming the accident on faulty signalling equipment, confusion reigned. One official even blamed foreign-made equipment for the collision, despite the Ministry's previous proud boast that China's high-speed trains were entirely kitted out with technology developed in China. In the week following the crash, over twenty million tweets about the incident circulated on China's microblogs. Many were highly critical of the Ministry of Railways and its handling of the disaster. For a few days, the front pages of newspapers throughout China featured photos and stories about the accident and its causes. Even the most conservative of the state-owned media weighed in on the debate. Bai Yansong, a popular news anchor at CCTV (China Central Television, the state-owned national network), made highly critical comments about the accident. The *People's Daily*, the official 'mouthpiece of the Chinese Communist Party', even published an editorial declaring that China should not strive for a 'blood-stained GDP'. This was a reference to the rapid development of such things as high-speed rail, which throughout the 2000s had symbolized China's relentless pursuit of GDP growth, often at the expense of the public good.

A collage of front pages of Chinese newspapers the day after the Wenzhou train disaster of July 2011.
Source: Shanghaiist.com

Great Firewall
(GFW; *fanghuo qiang* 防火墙)
The filtering system that blocks mainland Chinese Internet users from some international websites and web pages. Popular global websites restricted by the Great Firewall in 2011 included Facebook, Twitter and YouTube, as well the websites of various dissident groups and activists. Most Chinese Internet users simply write the English letters GFW when referring to the Great Firewall.

Jumping the Wall (*fan qiang* 翻墙)
and Virtual Private Network (VPN)
Using virtual private networks (VPN), proxy servers or other technical tricks to bypass the Great Firewall so as to gain access to blocked websites is called 'jumping the Wall'. A VPN works by encrypting the Internet traffic from a user's computer and sending it to a server hosted abroad. The server connects with the global Internet and then encrypts the traffic again before sending it back to the user's computer in China. Because the data is encrypted as it passes through the Great Firewall, it is not identified as objectionable and so the user can access blocked websites. Proxy servers and a few other technologies can serve the same function.

Former Railways Minister Liu Zhijun standing in front of a high-speed train with then Speaker of the US House of Representatives Nancy Pelosi and member of the House Ed Markey in 2009. Liu was sacked for corruption in January 2011.
Source: Wikimedia Commons

The grievances aired online and in the media that week had been simmering for some time. Earlier in the year, the government had sacked Liu Zhijun, the Minister of Railways for corruption. (Among other crimes and misdemeanours it was reported that he had kept eighteen mistresses.) More importantly, commentators expressed fears that Liu and his juniors had been skimming money from railway budgets by using cheap, inferior materials to build the new rail network, pocketing the difference to fund their lavish lifestyles. In June 2011, high-speed trains on the much-touted line between Beijing and Shanghai had experienced *en route* delays of many hours, leading angry passengers stuck in the trains with no air conditioning to vent their feelings – including via microblog.

'Harmony', the name of all high-speed trains.
Photo: Geremie R Barmé

The welter of complaints and outrage in the mainland media and Internet was, however, short lived. On 29 July, the organs of state responsible for propaganda and the media began clamping down, demanding that media and Internet companies reduce the coverage and criticism of the train accident. Consequently, the Wenzhou train wreck disappeared from the front pages of papers and Internet portals as quickly as it had appeared. For over a month it had been the number one trending topic on microblogs. It vanished completely (or, more accurately, was 'harmonised') from the list of hot topics literally overnight on 30 July. In the following days newspaper editorials appeared duly talking up the high-speed rail project. They declared as in a unified voice that while the Wenzhou accident was unfortunate, it was hardly a sign of a systemic problem.

In tandem with this, a carefully orchestrated campaign was launched in the official media calling for an end to the publication of 'unsubstantiated rumours' in the blogosphere and on the Internet. The Party Secretary of Beijing pointedly visited Sina, the host-owner of China's Weibo microblogs and his remarks on rumour control were widely reported. For its part, Sina sent messages to all of its Weibo users warning them that it would suspend the accounts of anyone guilty of spreading rumours and fomenting trouble. As part of the coordinated campaign, Xinhua New Agency released an article calling for an end to 'poisonous rumours' on the Weibo blogs, employing highly coloured political language that was reminiscent of the Cultural Revolution era (1964-1978) and the 'anti-spiritual pollution' campaign of 1983. Titled 'To Eradicate the Poison of Internet Rumours, There Must be Much Stricter Punishments' the article referred to 'the worthless dregs of Internet rumours', arguing that: 'the Internet is an important vehicle for civilizing and improving society, but Internet rumours are like malignant tumours that harm the Internet and damage society.'

As the discussion was dampened down, the Ministry of Railways publicly issued instructions for high-speed trains to operate at slower speeds than had been originally announced. It was an indication of a lack of confidence in a system that only months earlier had been touted as symbolic of China's unstoppable rise. Although the official death toll from the Wenzhou accident stood (finally) at thirty-nine, Chinese Internet users compiled a shared Google Document with details of killed passengers that indicate an actual death toll of forty-three. In August 2011, *The New York Times* reported this higher number without naming a source.

There had been a brief window of media openness in the week following the crash. But the state's censorship mechanisms kicked into gear quickly not only to silence calls for systemic change, but also in a way to stymie such change itself. People had little confidence that the real cause of the accident would be properly investigated – or that if there was an official investigation that its findings would be truthfully disclosed. Nor did there seem to be much possibility that the authorities would conduct a public investigation into the Ministry of Railways.

High-speed Rail

(*gaojia tielu* 高架铁路, or *gaotie* 高铁)

China's first high-speed rail service, opened in 2004, was the Maglev train connecting Shanghai Pudong International Airport to the outskirts of the city. The Shanghai Maglev employed Japanese and German technology, but soon after Chinese companies began manufacturing everything needed for the construction of high-speed rail networks, from signal systems to seating. There is some debate as to how much of this 'native' technology was sourced via 'unwitting technological transfer'. By the end of 2011, China's high-speed rail network boasted:

- 9,676 kilometres of routes in service;
- an average speed of 200 km/h;
- more than 3,500 kilometres of rail lines with top speeds of 300 km/h; and,
- high-speed routes including Beijing-Shanghai, Shanghai-Hangzhou, Beijing-Tianjin and Guangzhou-Shenzhen.

Building high-speed train lines costs between forty million *yuan* to 200 million *yuan* per kilometre. With such amounts of money involved, it is not surprising that over the years the Ministry of Railways has been plagued by corruption scandals. In early 2011, the Minister of Railways Liu Zhijun was investigated for 'severe violations of discipline' by the Communist Party's Central Commission for Discipline Inspection. He was dismissed from his position on 12 February that year.

The Internet furore and the subsequent government clampdown illustrate the complexity of China's networked reality. There are limits to what can be said online, and the state uses its vast resources of technology and human labour to ensure those limits are enforced. Nonetheless, the media and Internet users continue to shed light on the country's problems and government malfeasances by blogging, tweeting and publishing online and in real time with a freedom that – if often circumscribed – was unthinkable before the advent of the Internet.

The Chinese party-state has been developing and refining its system of control and manipulation of the media and communications for over sixty years. From the earliest days of the People's Republic, all print newspapers and magazines, radio and TV broadcasters, cinemas, and even printing factories were required to apply for and obtain various permits and licences to publish, broadcast or transmit information. Until the 1990s, only government and Party organizations could obtain such permits. But the system adapted itself admirably to the new guided, semi-market economy, allowing permits to operate media companies to be rented and/or purchased as part of a media investment. As 'political errors' can lead to permits being cancelled, private media operators have a strong commercial incentive to toe the line.

The Great Wall has become the most common metaphor for Chinese Internet censorship machinery, first called the Great Firewall of China in a 1997 *Wired* magazine article by Geremie R. Barmé and Sang Ye it is now often shortened to GFW by Chinese Internet users.
Photo: Danwei Media

The Online Masses

In recent years, the government has applied and enhanced both bureaucratic and technical practices that were originally aimed at broadcast and print media to the Internet. It has proven itself to be a formidably efficient manager of the online world.

According to figures released by the official China Internet Network Information Center (CNNIC), as of January 2012 China had 513 million Internet users. This figure represents a massive increase from around nine million in the year 2000. In November 2011, CNNIC reported that 300 million people were using microblog services. At the end of 2011, Sina claimed that there were 250 million active accounts on their microblog or Weibo service alone. At the beginning of 2012, CNNIC statistics showed that of the more than 800 million mobile phone users in China, around 300 million used their phones to get online. That number was increasing rapidly because Internet-enabled 'smart phones' cost as little as 800 *yuan* (at the time of writing, approximately US$125).

Even for people without phones, it was easy to get online anywhere in China thanks to Internet cafés offering a computer and broadband connection for just a few *yuan* per hour. Late 2011 figures released by a state agency (the Ministry of Culture) claimed that, as of late 2009, there were 138,000 Internet cafés with some 135 million customers.

Microblog (*weibo* 微博)

Weibo is the Chinese translation of microblog. These are Twitter-like services, the most popular of which is run by the Internet company Sina at the web address Weibo.com. Although censored and restricted, in 2011 Weibo become the most talked about site of breaking news, caustic political commentary and gossip. New restrictions on microblogs were introduced in March 2012 requiring that users register their real names.

Guided Public Opinion (*yulun daoxiang* 舆论导向) **and the Fifty-cent Gang** (*wumao dang* 五毛党)

Following the crackdown on demonstrators in Beijing on 4 June 1989, the Chinese party-state was critical of some of its own leaders (such as the ousted Party General Secretary Zhao Ziyang) and mass media for 'misguiding' (*wudao* 误导) public opinion. In the Internet age, the expression 'guided public opinion' has come to signify a range of propaganda techniques from egregious Bowdlerization of texts to employing an unofficial army of pro-government Internet commentators who are rumoured to be paid the equivalent of fifty Chinese cents per posting and who are therefore dubbed the 'Fifty-cent Gang' (see also Chapter 5).

That doesn't include the great number of cafés and other places (including airports) that offer free WiFi access. According to CNNIC numbers from November 2011, about twenty-seven percent of Internet users, more than 115 million people, live in rural areas. While the Net used to be dominated by people under the age of thirty, CNNIC says that forty-one percent of Internet users are now older than thirty, and that the average Chinese Internet user spends 19.8 hours per week online.

With such huge numbers of people spending so much time online, how does the government control the Internet? There are two aspects to China's Internet censorship: blocking content from outside the country, and controlling content hosted on servers inside it.

Geremie Barmé and Sang Ye coined the expression the 'Great Firewall of China' in an article published in *Wired* magazine way back in 1997. Although they provided a sardonic view of the future of Internet freedom, North American techno-utopians still believed that: 'The Internet interprets censorship as damage and routes around it.' US President Bill Clinton expressed a similar sentiment in 2000 when he declared: 'There's no question China has been trying to crack down on the Internet – good luck. That's sort of like trying to nail Jello to the wall.' Most observers would now admit that the Jello is just hanging there, festooned with nails.

China's Great Firewall (known also in English as the 'GFW') consists of several components. All of them operate at the nodes or gateways that connect China's Internet to the global network. There are fewer than ten of these. Software at these gateways can block content coming into China in four ways:

- the first and most common form of censorship is to block the web address or the URLs of targeted websites. In 2009, this happened to my own Danwei.org website. (We know that this was a domain name block because our site remained inaccessible from within China even after it was relocated to a different server.) Individual web pages can also be blocked in the same way. For example, although Amazon.

Huawei 华为

Huawei is a Chinese company that manufactures telecommunications and networking equipment, from the infrastructure used by mobile phone operators to the handsets that consumers buy. Ren Zhengfei, an engineer who started his career in the People's Liberation Army (PLA), founded Huawei in 1987. It is now a multibillion-dollar global corporation.

Huawei has often been frustrated in its attempts to expand to Western markets such as the US and Australia. Most governments consider telecommunications to be a sensitive industry and foreign governments have been wary of Ren Zhengfei's military background and possible ongoing connections with China's military and intelligence services as well as a lack of clarity about the role of the Chinese state (if any) in Huawei's management.

com is accessible in China, the pages that promote and sell *The Party*, a book about the Chinese Communist Party's Organisation Department by the journalist Richard McGregor are blocked;

- secondly, IP addresses can also be blocked. An IP address is the unique number that the Internet uses to locate a server. This form of censorship functions in more or less the same way as a domain-name block;
- thirdly, the DNS or Domain Name Server can be redirected, so that when a user tries to call up a website, the filter will redirect the request to a domain name (or URL) that is different from the one the user is trying to access; and,
- finally, there is keyword filtering. The gateway can be instructed to look for web pages that have a high concentration of keywords that the government finds objectionable. In this regard, even if a website is not blocked, an individual page may not load because it features a sufficient number of 'sensitive words' to trigger censorship.

In 2011-2012, there were seven main categories of foreign websites that were blocked in China:

1. Chinese language news outlets that are sometimes critical of the government including the BBC, VOA Chinese, and Hong Kong's *Apple Daily* website;
2. Web pages belonging to organisations that campaign against the Communist Party or that promote Tibetan and Uyghur causes or independence for Taiwan, as well as sites belonging to the banned religious organization Falun Gong;

3. Websites about historical periods or events that are considered sensitive in China, for example the Cultural Revolution, the Great Leap Forward, and the events of 4 June 1989;
4. English and Chinese language blogs and niche websites that follow Chinese current events, for example Danwei.org, ZonaEuropa.com, ChinaGeeks.org, and ChinaDigitalTimes.net (a University of California Berkeley project);
5. Popular social media websites and user generated content websites including YouTube, Facebook and Twitter. The blocking of this type of website started in earnest after the summer of 2009, when the street demonstrations in Iran, sometimes called 'the Facebook Revolution' in international media reports, convinced the Chinese authorities that access to uncensored foreign social media was a danger to 'social stability' in China (see chapters 3 and 5 in this book). The events in Iran were followed by ethnic riots between Muslim Uyghurs and Han Chinese that started in Xinjiang on July 5 of the same year;
6. Pornographic websites; and,
7. Websites that sell or give away services to circumvent the Great Firewall like VPNs and proxy servers.

Aside from these kinds of website, many Google services, from Gmail to Google Documents and even Google searches, do not work properly in China and are subjected to various forms of technical interference. Although the situation changes on a daily basis, it became noticeably worse after Google's much-publicized withdrawal of their search service from Mainland China in early 2010 (discussed in Chapter 5). Paradoxically, and perhaps because it is not yet generating much media coverage, Google's social networking service, Google+, was still accessible at the time of writing.

Online Porn and Games

Although Chinese government spokespeople rarely discuss Internet censorship in detail, the most frequent explanation for the pervasive controls of the Great Firewall is that they are necessary to prevent the masses from being corrupted by 'pornography and violence', as well as for the sake of social stability. Nonetheless, sites offering pornography and violent Internet games such as 'World of Warcraft' are amongst the most popular on the Chinese Internet, perhaps performing the same pacifying function as bread and circuses did for the masses of the Roman Empire. According to a January 2012 report from the China Internet Network Information Center (CNNIC), sixty-three percent of Chinese Internet users or 324 million people regularly play online games.

Because pornography is illegal, there are no statistics available as to how widespread it is. But frequently announced arrests of pornographers attest to its enduring popularity and hint at the considerable sums that can be made by distributing it.

The Great Firewall is constantly being refined and upgraded. One strategy is to interfere with VPNs. A VPN works by encrypting the Internet traffic from a user's computer and sending it to a server hosted abroad. The server connects with the global Internet and then encrypts the traffic again before sending it back to the user's computer in China. Because the data is encrypted as it goes through the Great Firewall, it is not identified as objectionable, allowing the user to gain access to blocked websites. VPNs were once a problem-free tool people could use to straddle the Great Firewall, but from my own experience and anecdotal evidence, in 2011 many VPN services became bug-ridden and difficult to use, probably due to an upgrade of the Great Firewall's software. But the savvy can always set up a VPN or purchase service from a provider.

A programmer and professor named Fang Binxing who is widely known as 'the father of the Great Firewall' gave an interview to the pro-government English-language *Global Times* newspaper in February 2012. In it he revealed: 'I have six VPNs on my home computer. But I only try them to test which side wins: the GFW or the VPN.' (The article containing this quote was later deleted from the *Global Times* website.) However, it is unlikely that the government will completely block the use of VPNs: too many banks and large corporations depend on VPN technology for secure Internet access.

Censorship

Another apparatus, separate from the *cordon sanitaire* that is the Great Firewall, exists to control and censor the Internet within the borders of the People's Republic: censorship. And censorship relies for the most part relies on the tried-and-true style of authoritarian coercion: self-censorship.

This is the way it works:

To start up any kind of website that has its own domain name and server space in China, it is necessary to obtain an ICP or Internet Content Provider licence. Depending on what the website will do – if it involves ecommerce or news, for example – other permits may be required. Many of these permits, including ICPs, are granted by the Ministry of Industry and Information Technology (MIIT), the body that regulates China's telecommunications and Internet. Apart from MIIT, Internet content is subject to regulation by a number of other overlapping state organisations:

- the General Administration of Press and Publications (GAPP), which has oversight over news, print publishing, electronic gaming and electronic magazines;
- the State Administration of Radio, Film and TV (SARFT), which is in charge of film, broadcast media and online video;
- the Ministry of Culture, which among its many other responsibilities also covers online gaming, and sometimes tries to involve itself in such things as the regulation of Internet cafés;
- the State Council Information Office, which is responsible for collating and propagating all kinds of information about China, both for domestic and international consumption;
- the Central Publicity Department of the Communist Party of China (formerly known as the Central Propaganda Department), which has a similar function to the State Council Information Office, but is an organ of the Communist Party, not the government (an often nebulous distinction).

Rumours (*yaoyan* 谣言)

Wags in Beijing have joked for decades that you can't believe a rumour in China until the government denies it. In 2003, mobile phone text messages about SARS (some true and some scandalously false) were how many Chinese people learned about the disease – the official press was silent. In the aftermath of the Wenzhou high-speed train crash in 2011, as online commentary questioned everything from official casualty figures to the role of government corruption in the tragedy, the Internet authorities began clamping down on online 'rumours', described in an editorial in the *People's Daily* as 'poisonous'. The clampdown ramped up following Bo Xilai's removal from his Party positions in March 2012 when rumours circulated online that suspicious troop movements in the Chinese capital could herald a coup.

Cynics describe the campaign against rumours as just censorship by another name. On 16 April 2012, the *People's Daily* published a list of Internet rumours that counted as crimes. The coup rumour was on the list along with spreading fake news about natural disasters, contaminated food, nuclear radiation, acupuncture treatment problems, diseases and tax fraud.

If you have a website, and incur the ire of any of these government departments, they have the power to instruct MIIT to deny your server access to the Internet, shut your company down or, if your offence is deemed suitably serious, detain you on legal charges. So what do you do? You censor yourself! But how do you know what you shouldn't publish? A lot of the time, you don't, and that's part of the genius of the system. Most people are scared of crossing the line, but the government is not always forthright about explaining just where that line is at any given time. As a result, websites tend to err on the side of caution.

On the other hand, the authorities constantly issue instructions, often in great detail, about what is or is not permissible on the Internet. In the case of news websites these instructions outline what type of information must be emphasized or deleted. Any of the organisations just mentioned may issue such instructions, but the Central Publicity Department (mockingly referred to as the Communist Party's 'Ministry of Truth' by the US-based *China Digital Times*, quoting Orwell) is particularly assiduous in this regard. Instructions may be communicated as 'internal' – that is secret – directives, and are often relayed by phone to avoid leaving a paper trail. Major web companies generally assign one or more dedicated people to receive these instructions. The guidance can include orders: to down-play certain news items by removing them from the home page; to delete others altogether; to avoid drawing attention to particular stories; or to not deviate from the authorized version distributed by the official Xinhua News Agency. Instructions are also regularly issued on how media outlets should cover stories that the party-state deems to be of major national or propagandistic significance. For example, the media devoted massive coverage to the lead-up to the ninetieth anniversary celebrations of the founding of the Communist Party on 1 July 2011. In such cases, elaborate guidance is given that may include providing media outlets with officially sanctioned copy, the exact wording for commentaries, acceptable photographic images and centrally formulated slogans and catch phrases. With these mechanisms in place, it is very rare for government officials to have to do anything apart from relay instructions from what are referred to as the 'higher ups' (*shangji* 上级); the owners of websites take care of deleting objectionable content all by themselves.

There are many other types of pressure brought to bear on companies to marshal the domestic Internet in accordance with the requirements of officialdom. One method that the state has frequently used in recent years is to invite companies or their proprietors to volunteer their services to help promote what is called a 'healthy Internet'. Such invitations are a little like an offer from the Godfather: they are best not refused. The volunteers are required to pledge their commitment to upholding the 'correct values' imposed on the Internet by the party-state.

Throughout this volume we have noted that during the years 2009-2011 and up to March 2012, there was a pervasive rise of 'red culture' in China that was directly related to the efforts of the Chongqing Party Secretary Bo Xilai, the man behind the 'Sing Red' campaign. Although this 'red rising' was (perhaps only temporarily) curtailed by Bo's fall in March 2012, for years the new red chorus reverberated throughout the country, including on the domestic Internet. In July 2011, the government organized a meeting in Beijing of Internet company executives to commem-

Han Han 韩寒

Born in 1982, Han Han came to national prominence after the publication of 'Triple Door' (*San chongmen* 三重门), a semi-autobiographical novella about a high-school student that many 'post-Eighties' young people (that is those born after 1980) saw as expressing their own frustrations and desires. Han Han later began driving in professional car races and, in 2006, he started a blog. His caustic takes on contemporary society, government follies, and state media bumblings attract a broad readership. Han Han has also enjoyed a lucrative career as a celebrity endorser of products including clothing, instant coffee and cars.

In late 2011, Han Han published a series of blog posts that came to be known as 'Han's Three Essays' (*Han Han san pian* 韩寒三篇). They were titled 'Talking Revolution' (*Tan geming* 谈革命), 'Discussing Democracy' (*Shuo minzhu* 说民主) and 'Wanting Freedom' (*Yao ziyou* 要自由). The essays sparked considerable discussion, with some commentators speculating that Han Han was playing into the hands of the authorities by arguing that China is currently unsuited to broad-based democracy. The anti-fraud campaigner Fang Zhouzi accused Han Han of having used ghostwriters, leading to a public feud that lasted several months (see also Chapter 6).

Han Han: racing car driver, writer, blogger and heartthrob.
Source: Wikimedia Commons

orate the Party's ninetieth anniversary. At the meeting, Charles Chao (Cao Guowei) and Robin Li (Li Yanhong), the respective CEOs of the microblogging giant Sina and Baidu, sometimes called 'the Google of China', themselves sang a number of 'red songs' that glorify the Communist Party. It was an unedifying spectacle, one in which two of China's richest individuals, who run the country's leading non-government Internet services, literally paid lip service to Communist values at a time of increasing social anomie and acute inequality. This small example illustrates what companies that succeed in the Internet industry under one-party rule need to and will do to survive and prosper.

The state also uses the combined power of its centrally controlled media organizations to attack and reprimand independent websites. All Robin Li's red singing couldn't prevent CCTV from attacking Baidu for alleged unethical advertising sales. CCTV, *People's Daily* and Xinhua have each played a part in the campaign against online 'rumours', that is unauthorized and unsanctioned stories and popular speculation about politics, corruption and a range of other issues. Such state media outlets regularly call for tighter regulation, by which they mean the prohibition of any information that casts the government in a bad light.

For more than a decade, the Internet was one of the few major industries in China not dominated by large state-owned players. Now the authorities are on the march. We have observed throughout this book a phenomenon known as 'the state on the march and private enterprise in retreat', an expression that encapsulates the reassertion of party-state authority in the years following the 2008 Beijing Olympics. In recent times, both Xinhua and *People's Daily* have launched search engines and microblog services of their own. It remains to be seen whether any of these new services will gain real traction with users. If independent companies were left to their own devices the state will find the marketplace competition stiff, but the state has never had to contemplate a level playing field.

A bad air day in Beijing (original colour).
Photo: Danwei Media

Particulate Matter

When information perceived as threatening stability circulates on the Chinese Internet, it can be ruthlessly suppressed using the various mechanisms described above. As Gloria Davies has noted in Chapter 5, attempts by anonymous activists in the spring of 2011 to use the Internet to organize 'Jasmine Movement' protests in Chinese cities were scrubbed from the domestic Internet, while similar webpages and sites hosted abroad were effectively blocked by the Great Firewall. But in the northern autumn of 2011, a different kind of online activism appeared in China that hinted at ways in which the Internet could possibly develop as a platform for public discussion.

A screenshot of the Twitter feed maintained by the US Embassy in Beijing that sends out hourly air quality measurements.
Source: Twitter.com

In October and early November 2011, Beijing residents began complaining online about the grave air pollution in the city. They noted the number of consecutive days of poor air quality on which they could quite literally see with their own eyes, and sometimes even taste, the pollution. They showed that it did not tally with claims by the State Environmental Protection Agency (SEPA) about blue-sky days. Nor did crowd-sourced statistics about pollution-haze days match the numbers released by the government. Previously, the simmering resentment might have found no outlet or redress. However, SEPA is no longer the only body tracking air pollution in the capital. Since 2008, an air quality monitor installed on the roof of the US Embassy had been sending out hourly updates on Twitter (user name: @BeijingAir) on air quality. These readings include the measure of PM2.5, a form of fine particulate matter that is considered to be the most dangerous to human health because the tiny particles can enter the lungs as well as other organs, and even the skin. SEPA's readings did not include PM2.5 measurements.

Although Twitter is blocked by the Great Firewall, a stream of tweets can easily be fed onto another website that is not blocked or to an iPhone application that doesn't require the user to visit the inaccessible domain website at Twitter.com. The year 2011 was one in which iPhones became *de rigeur* for China's status-conscious urbanites; and many iPhone owners in Beijing downloaded apps that provided them with a constant stream of US Embassy pollution readings. One of these was the real-estate magnate and media figure Pan Shiyi, one half of the husband-wife team behind some of the most grand (and grandiose) commercial building projects in the Chinese capital. Even with his untold wealth, Pan realized he was powerless to stave off the threat of Beijing's awful air. So in October and November 2011, he began venting his outrage at the city's air quality online. He declared to his more than eight million microblog followers that the Chinese government should release data for PM2.5 readings. Pan was not alone in this; thousands of other Beijing residents complained about the air via the microblog system and other social media websites and demanded action. In January 2012, in a rare victory for online people power, the official Xinhua News Agency reported that Beijing would start providing PM2.5 data. The air is still foul, but at least people were better informed about how foul it is.

It is obvious from even the cursory survey offered here that China's Great Firewall is not an hermetically sealed system. Within the Firewall, censors of various kinds work tirelessly (but not always effectively) to adapt to the growing ability of Internet users to say what they think. After years of unfulfilled promise, 2011 truly was a watershed year during which the Internet became the most important platform for public contestation in China and the most influential medium for social and cultural change.

PM2.5, Beijing Air and the iPhone

In 2008, the US Embassy in Beijing began posting air quality data from its own sensors on the embassy roof to Twitter. The measurements include a reading known as PM2.5 which refers to air pollution particles under 2.5 micrometres in size, so small that they can go from the lungs to other organs in the body causing a range of health issues, from minor to potentially fatal. Although Twitter was blocked in 2009, the embassy's feed, on Twitter as @BeijingAir, continued to be followed, largely by Great Firewall-hopping expatriates. In 2011, Chinese microblogs began reporting the updates from the Americans. Subsequent media coverage and public discussion resulted in government assurances that China would institute PM2.5 measurements for all cities in the future, reveal government PM2.5 readings for Beijing, and open air quality monitoring stations to the local and international press on certain days.

On 5 June 2012, a Vice-minister of the Ministry of the Environment declared that only the Chinese government was authorized to monitor and publish air quality information. Data from 'other sources' was deemed not to be standardized or rigorous enough. The Vice-minister called on foreign embassies in the Chinese capital to stop reporting on the air quality. To do so, it was claimed, contravened the Vienna Convention on Diplomatic Relations.

8

8 VOICES FROM THE BLOGOSPHERE I

THE VARIETY and depth of information about China available on blogs and niche websites is extraordinary. The best bloggers offer immediate and well-sourced perspectives on events on the ground; news about China often breaks on their sites first. There are also dozens of sites that translate articles from the Chinese media and postings from the Internet.

This and the following chapter provide a selection of writings from the Internet by Chinese and foreign observers, translations and commentary that offer further reflections on topics discussed elsewhere in this book. All material is reprinted with permission from the original author or website. The punctuation and style of these selections accord the house style of the book, the texts have not otherwise been edited. Sources are given in the online notes for this book.

Political trust, not something to be taken with a grain of salt...

By Yajun
From Jeremiah Jenne's blog
Jottings from the Granite Studio
Published on 18 March 2011

The nuclear crisis in Japan has been a test not only of the resilience of that nation but also for the world. Many foreign residents have grabbed the earliest possible tickets out of the country, while residents in Tokyo and in the damaged north-east part of the country have (for the most part) placed their trust in their government's decisions while they try to rebuild their lives.*

Meanwhile, in China, some people are starting to lose their cool. On Wednesday, messages about radiation arriving in Beijing were widely disseminated and many people took the rumours seriously. I received several long-distance phone calls from my family warning me to be careful.

Yesterday, word spread of people rushing to buy salt and the media was flooded with stories, pictures, and articles about the 'salt rush'. As a result, stores throughout China were sold out and the price of salt in some places went from 1.3 *yuan* per bag to ten *yuan*.

To be honest, I don't get it. I suppose some people believe that consuming iodized salt can protect them from radiation, others are afraid that radioactive ocean water will mean not enough salt for sale in the future. Whatever the reason, the situation was serious enough that the CCTV news broadcast spent fifteen minutes this morning trying to convince people that eating too much salt is bad for your health, that China has an adequate supply to meet market demand, and so for the love of God, please stop panicking.

Some buyers might not even be aware of why they are doing this. There are rumours, and everybody else is doing it, and that's enough of a reason to do it too. It's sad to see people abandon their own judgment and just follow the crowd.

However, I'm also saddened to see a good deal of mockery and criticism online blaming the panic buying on people's 'low *suzhi*' [素质 character, 'quality' of a person, or breeding – *Ed.*] and ignorance. I'm sure nobody wants to fight with other shoppers, wait in a long line, and then pay an inflated price for what used to be a basic commodity, but this small bag of salt is something they can trust, something they can count on. Many people, like my grandparents, who survived the Great Famine of the early 1960s and the Cultural Revolution, are still conditioned by that experience, and they have vivid memories of food and basic supplies running out. When a run on a commodity happens, it's hard for them not to compete with others to be sure they are not left behind.

That said, the salt rush is mainly a symptom of a profound lack of political trust.** In the event of a real radiation crisis, many people simply don't know whether or not the Chinese government would tell the truth. Rather than wait and feel helpless, they listen to rumours and take the actions they believe will protect them and their family.

A good recent example of this lack of political trust is last month's 'Xiangshui incident' in Jiangsu province. On 10 February, during the 2011 Spring Festival, a strong odour covered the whole town at 2:00am. Many local residents believed that an accident at a nearby factory had released toxic fumes. In the middle of the night tens of thousands of panicked people from thirty-eight villages fled their homes. In the end, four people were killed as the result of being trampled in the rush to escape or in traffic accidents as the roads jammed with evacuees. The local government didn't respond until 4:00pm the next afternoon, but even after that people still didn't believe the official response because of several previous accidents and leaks from the plant.

Ultimately, the vapours proved harmless, although nothing official has been said about what caused the odour. Nevertheless, when residents finally returned home, several people were arrested on charges of spreading rumours. Even though this was a false alarm, I have no doubt that if this kind of thing happens again, residents will still choose to flee, because they fear not being able to receive reliable and trustworthy information in time. They don't have the confidence to believe that the government would tell the truth, so panicked flight is the best choice in a bad situation. With the recent radiation scare in China, the Ministry of the Environment did announce that China has not been affected by radiation from Japan, but that did little to slow down the run on salt. In times of crisis, people want to feel like they are doing something to help themselves, even if that something might seem silly or even counterproductive. Worried about 'what might be but can't be helped', people instead focus on those things they do have control over, even if it's something as seemingly trivial as buying a bag (or a case) of salt.

* Though as we're seeing, even the patience of the people in Japan is understandably starting to run short. Given everything that has happened over the past few days, it's still impressive that faith in the government response has last as long as it has.

** I actually wrote my senior thesis at Peking University on the issue of political trust. This is why this subject is so interesting for me.

The Sino-Japanese Relationship: (apologies to Facebook) It's Complicated

By Yajun
From Jeremiah Jenne's blog
Jottings from the Granite Studio
Published on 15 March 2011

Over the last four days, CCTV has had comprehensive coverage of the massive earthquake which struck Japan last week. Despite the ongoing NPC and CPPCC meetings, CCTV still filled more than half of its morning news time with the latest information from Japan.

Chinese leaders and the Ministry of Foreign Affairs expressed China's sympathy to its neighbour immediately after the earthquake, and a Chinese rescue team arrived in the disaster zone over the weekend to assist their Japanese counterparts in the relief and rescue efforts.

It seems that the Chinese government has decided to put historic conflict and recent territorial disputes aside for a time, show its humanity, and return the favour of Japan's help during the Wenchuan earthquake three years ago.

However, China's public opinion doesn't always match the government's magnanimity, and there is a debate, online and off, about how China should react to the news of Japan's disaster. There are those who say Japan got what it deserved and cite the atrocities committed against China in World War II, and saw the earthquake as something to be celebrated, but most people feel that at this moment of great tragedy, we should put history aside and reach out to the Japanese people.

Even though the anti-Japanese opinion often makes the loudest noise online and the best story (as in the demonstrations against Japan in 2005), I am glad to see most people taking a different and more compassionate view. But I am also not surprised that this debate occurs in China today, we have such complicated feelings and opinions regarding Japan.

Sometimes, these opinions are even totally contradictory. Japanese people could be ruthless killers, twisted psychos or extremely polite people who value efficiency, discipline and creativity.

Many Chinese people first learn about Japan from 'patriotic' education in elementary schools. I remember when I was a kid, 'Resist Japan' movies were part of the school curriculum. In those black and white movies produced thirty or forty years ago, Japanese soldiers were always described as short, cunning and ruthless people. They were not portrayed as human, but as aliens or killing machines.

Chapters and chapters of history textbooks provide detailed information about the pain and disastrous consequences that Japanese invasions inflicted on the Chinese people. Museums display exhibits showing how Japanese troops used Chinese civilians for grotesque and cruel bio-medical 'research'.

Despite the official line, there is a range of opinions among Chinese, some of which break down along geographic lines. The grandparents of my colleague from Changchun, part of 'Manchukuo' during the war, think Japanese soldiers were much better and more disciplined than KMT soldiers. When Changchun was occupied by Japan, ordinary people felt that life was orderly and safe, but after the war, KMT soldiers brought looting and corruption. Contrast this with Nanjing, where many people had their family members brutally killed or raped during the infamous Nanjing Massacre. In places like this, old hatreds run deep.

It is hard for many foreigners to understand why China's resentment towards Japan is still so strong after seven decades. If one compares the Sino-Japanese relationship today with, say, Germany and France, it seems that narrow minds are the only explanation for lingering Chinese resentment.

But of course it is more complicated than that. Imagine that a single group of people is held up for public scorn and criticism, with museums and the media displaying images of cruelty and evidence of evil, and now imagine these are the only images you have of this group for most of your life. Sadly, this is fertile ground for hatred to spread.

The lack of comprehensive and open information fuels the resentment. For example, the Chinese public always hears about Japan's Prime Minister's visit to the Yasukuni Shrine, but Japan's apologies to the Chinese people are never reported in China. Most news coverage focuses on the flood of Japanese products into China, but no one mentioned that Japan has provided more foreign aid to China than any other country.

Fortunately, times are changing. Young people of my generation grow up with Japanese fashion, music, soap operas, and cartoons. *Tokyo Love Story* showed us how romantic Japanese people are. It inspired fantasies for an entire generation. Tokyo is also a Mecca of fashion for many young people.

With such a large number of ordinary Chinese using the Internet, more and more young Chinese rely on their own critical thinking and information that they find online, rather than rigid patriotic doctrine, to shape their opinion towards Japan. For example, after this earthquake, many online articles applauded how calm and well-organized Japanese people are and compared the solid Japanese buildings with the shabby schools in Sichuan.

The anti-Japanese mood in China is not going to disappear soon, but I believe that in the near future we will see more and more rational thinking about the Sino-Japan relationship.

Two-year-old female child ran over by car, eighteen passers-by ignore her

By Fauna
From chinaSMACK
Published on 16 October 2011

Synopsis: On the afternoon of 13 October around 5:30pm, a car accident occurred at the Guangfo Hardware Market in Huangqi of Foshan. A van hit a two-year-old little girl and then fled. No passers-by reached out to help and then another car ran over her. Over the span of seven minutes, a total of seventeen people passing by failed to extend a hand or call the police, up until the nineteenth person, a garbage scavenger *ayi* [older woman], who lifted her up after discovering her but the little girl in her arms was like a noodle, immediately collapsing back onto the ground. The trash scavenger *ayi* called for help, and the little girl's mother, who was in the vicinity, immediately rushed over and rushed her to the hospital.

The news report video [about the incident and available online] has been viewed nearly 700k times on popular Chinese video-sharing website Youku since it was uploaded seventeen hours ago and currently has over 6,200 comments spanning 210 pages. This story is also spreading on China's popular microblogging service Sina Weibo in addition to receiving a lot of views and comments on China's major Internet news portals and communities.

In addition to showing the little girl, Yueyue, being run over twice and many of the bystanders who didn't stop to help her, it also shows that Yueyue is currently in the hospital in critical condition. Police have already found the second driver but have yet to find the first driver as they were unable to read the first van's licence plate and are calling upon witnesses for help. Yueyue's parents are also shown.

Guo Meimei Red Cross Controversy Pissing Off Chinese Netizens

By Fauna
From chinaSMACK
Published on 29 June 2011

Perhaps the most popular controversy on the Chinese Internet over the past week has been about a twenty-year-old Chinese girl named Guo Meimei, her wealth, and how her wealth may have come from corruption in the Red Cross Society of China. Many incredible twists and turns have occurred in this ongoing controversy that has confused many, so below is a translation of a Chinese reporter's effort to explain how this story has developed so far, as well as the latest updates involving Chinese netizens petitioning the Australian Embassy to deny Guo Meimei a visa to prevent her from fleeing China.

From ifeng:
This morning, when Guo Meimei appeared at the Beijing Capital International Airport and was besieged by over ten media reporters, the 'Guo Meimei showing off wealth' Internet controversy reached a climax in the real offline world.

Since 21 June, when Guo Meimei first was exposed on microblogs for showing off her wealth, until yesterday when she posted three apologetic microblog posts in succession, just how did a twenty-year-old young girl come to be besieged by netizens? And why is it that the statements of the relevant government organs and companies are unable to get the trust of netizens?

This reporter, while putting together the path this incident took as it spread on the Internet, discovered that over seven days, she made one lie after another, and we believe that her lies will definitely be exposed.

1. Incident begins (21 June, evening)
21 June evening, a netizen discovered the Sina Weibo verified user 'Guo Meimei Baby' [郭美美baby] really liked to show off her wealth, and even

identified herself as the 'Business General Manager of Red Cross Society'. Within two hours, her microblog was shared over a thousand times.

Guo Meimei: The Red Cross Commerce that I am at and the Red Cross Society of China have a partnership; Red Cross Commerce is a commercial business and is of a different nature from the Red Cross Association.

Red Cross Society of China: No response.

2. Human Flesh Search (21 June, evening onward)

Parties involved: Red Cross Society of China, Sina Weibo.

21 June evening onward, netizens began a 'massive human flesh search'.

Netizens discovered Guo Meimei's Netease photo album and her information on the 58.com automotive sales website. She has had plastic surgery before, previously rented in Shenzhen and Beijing, dressed and decorated her room very ordinarily, and was using a domestic clamshell mobile phone [not foreign name brand like Apple, Samsung, or Nokia].

Yet in less than two years, she's moved into a large villa, is driving a luxury sports car, and has suddenly become rich.

Guo Meimei:

2008: Renting, using a domestic mobile phone, selling cars.

2011: Upgraded to a sports car and villa [detached single-family home].

Red Cross Society of China: No 'Red Cross Commerce', no 'Business General Manager' position, and no employee by the name of 'Guo Meimei'.

Sina Weibo: Guo Meimei's identity/profession was initially verified as an actress and later personally applied to have her profession changed to 'Business General Manager of Red Cross Society'. Sina's existing verification procedures are not strict.

3. Getting to the bottom of the matter (22 June, noon onward)
Parties involved: Red Cross Society of China, Shenzhen Tian Lue Group, Red Cross Society of China Business Systems.

A netizen 'uncovered' Guo Meimei as a car model under the Shenzhen Tian Lue Group banner, has close relations with the group's upper level management, and even came to know Red Cross Society of China Vice-president Guo Changjiang through the Tian Lue Group.

24 June evening, the Red Cross Society of China, Red Cross Society of China Business Systems, and Tian Lue Holding Group issued statements regarding the 'Guo Meimei Incident'.

Statements:
Red Cross Society of China: Vice-president Guo Changjiang has no contact with Tian Lue Group's Chairman of the Board Qiu Zhenliang. We have already reported this matter to the public security organ, and have decided to launch legal proceedings.

Red Cross Society of China Business Systems: We have never authorized Tian Lue Group to conduct any fund-raising activities, much less divided/embezzled money from donations.

Shenzhen Tian Lue Group: No relationship with Guo Meimei.

4. More developments (22 June, afternoon onward)
The Guo Meimei Showing Off Wealth Incident continued to develop, with the content of her latest microblog update having already been reposted/shared over 100,000 times.

On the Tianya website, a picture began circulating that detailed the relationships in the Guo Meimei Incident, with Guo Meimei at the center, and the Red Cross Society, Red Cross Business Systems, Tian Lue Group and others arranged around her.

The people and organizations/companies involved in the Guo Meimei Incident: Guo Changjiang, Guo Dengfeng, Red Cross Society of China, Red Cross Society of China Business Systems, Tian Lue Group.

5. Ridicule and jeering (25 June)
On the afternoon of the twenty-sixth, Guo Meimei once again posted a statement on her microblog, continuing to distance herself from having a connection to the Red Cross Society.

However, she did not respond to what netizens cared about which is the issue of her sudden wealth, and the style/tone of her speech was completely different from before, resulting in wide-ranging scepticism and suspicion.

6. Apology (26 June, afternoon)
'Guo Meimei Baby' posted the following microblog messages in succession:

> I have already received severe criticism and condemnation from family and friends! These past few days, I have been reflecting on the harm and headaches I have caused everyone with my thoughtless behaviour and hope netizens will stop creating a fuss. I have decided to use even more time to reflect upon myself and educate myself!

'Guo Meimei Baby' said:

> I ignorantly claimed that I was a 'Business General Manager for Red Cross Society' on Sina Weibo, and for the damage to the reputation of the Red Cross Society of China and the public misunderstandings that my ignorant behaviour has caused, I deeply apologize! I have never worked at the Red Cross Society, and this identity was something I completely fabricated.

7. Follow-up (26 June, evening)
Locations: Houxiandai Cheng [a residential community in Beijing], Beijing Capital International Airport.
26 June, around eight o'clock in the evening, netizens 'uncovered' that Guo Meimei's mother is currently moving at Houxiandai Cheng. At around ten o'clock at night, a netizen posted on their microblog that Guo Meimei is on a flight returning to Beijing, and publicized the flight number, arrival time, seat number, etc.

This morning at 1:30am, Guo Meimei appeared wearing a black T-shirt and red shorts, a cap worn low over her face, and a website journalist following her asking questions, but she didn't provide many responses and left immediately after getting in a taxi.

Guo Meimei: Australia is not your safe harbour.

Regarding further developments in the 'Guo Meimei Baby' incident, yesterday while she was flying from Shenzhen to Beijing, there were netizens constantly broadcasting her itinerary on their microblogs. Upon arriving at Beijing, this girl calmly and with a low profile got in a taxi and left. However, according to netizens at the scene and media reports, someone was on the telephone with her throughout it all, instructing her on how to act/what to do. And not long after her person left, two new postings appeared on her microblog, ridiculing netizens and expressing that in two days, she will leave China for Australia. Sina Weibo netizen @三爷笑人生 made a screenshot of these microblog messages, and several minutes later, these microblog postings were deleted, but netizen @三爷笑人生 already saved the evidence.

Her first message: Coming to the end, next week running off to Australia with Mommy, leaving this lousy place, hahaha.

Her second message: Can't handle it anymore...

Given that this girl is the main character involved in the Red Cross Society's corruption case, if she leaves the country, it will interfere with determining the illegal origins of the Maserati luxury car, dozens of LV bags, the luxury villa, etc, and the whereabouts of the people's donations will become a mystery. Sina Weibo netizen 三爷笑人生 issued a call online to collect signatures on the Internet and call the Australian Embassy in China, requesting that the Australian government suspend the visas for Guo Meimei and her mother. Amongst them, netizens 无弦无歌 and 中山首里 have already called the embassy asking the Australian government to suspend the visas for Guo Meimei and her mother and received a response from the Australian Embassy personnel saying they are already aware of the Internet incident and will relay the message to their superiors. The Australian Embassy telephone is: 010-51404111.

After netizen 三爷笑人生 posted his call, he received enthusiastic responses from netizens, with the number of microblog reposts breaking the thousands, with innumerable netizens calling the Australian embassy's telephone, asking the Australian government to suspend Guo Meimei and her mother's visas. At the same time, the signature collection campaign initiated by 三爷笑人生 has already broken into the thousands. Some netizens have worried whether or not this Weibo microblog account belongs to Guo Meimei, but according to netizens in the know, this Weibo account is Guo Meimei's secondary account; and it was because not many people know of this account that she dared to reveal that she was leaving the country and mock netizens. The reason why netizens are so angry with this incident is due to not knowing where the money the public donates goes and with the suspects involved being able to escape [with their ill-gotten gains] and live happily without consequences.

The Story of W&L: China's Great Internet Divide

By Kai Lukoff
From TechRice
Published on 7 June 2011

Here's an introductory quote from The Story of W&L, a tale of China's great Internet divide:

'China does not have one so-called "national Internet", instead there's a great divide. It encompasses the elite with ThinkPad laptops and also the grassroots with MTK *shanzhai* [山寨 fake or 'rip-off' – *Ed.*] mobile phones. Our elites are on a par with America, while our grassroots are on a par with Vietnam. This is the story of W&L, two representatives of China's great Internet divide.'

The original post (Chinese-language) was written in July 2010 by Simon Shen 申音 and sent to me by TechRice reader Tim Wang (thanks Tim!). The English-language translation and all errors therein are my own. See the end of this article for speculation as to the identities of W&L: 'W' is suspected to be based on Wang Xing (founder of Xiaonei/Renren (Facebook clone), Fanfou (Twitter clone), and Meituan (Groupon clone) and 'L' on Li Xingping (founder of web directory site: Hao123).

The Story of W&L

I have two friends.

L's company is in Shanghai, but he's running it from Guangdong (southern China) most of the time. He graduated from a lesser-known university in southern China, where he studied literature years ago. My friend L makes mobile games. I've seen him use many different mobiles, but the most expensive was no more than 1,000 *yuan*. Rather than concepts of Web 2.0 or mobile Internet, he follows the tens of thousands of migrant workers and the 'ant people' (marginally employed university graduates) on the outskirts of cities.

How does he follow them? He drinks beers with them over midnight snacks from street vendors, spends the night at Internet cafes in the Foxconn factory district, and chats with the convenience store owners who got their BMWs by selling to them.

W is from Beijing's Zhongguancun district (the 'Silicon Valley' of China). From early on he was a brainy talent with shining eyes, with stellar grades in maths and science, outstanding critical thinking, equally fluent in English and Chinese. He graduated from a famous university in Beijing, after which he went directly to a famous American university for a Masters, and then returned home to start a company. I've always thought he's the Chinese edition of a Silicon Valley geek. He's always the first with the latest technology, like iPad. Inside of China he's still on Facebook, Twitter, Groupon, and Foursquare. What's the future of the Internet you ask? W's websites are the future of the Internet.

W enjoys more applause and fame than L. But the regret is, while he's made many sites that investors think are super cool, he's never made big money.

The reasons are the following: maybe his company is early, but it's soon encircled by a crowd of copycats; maybe funds aren't enough, so he's annihilated by a strong, well-funded competitor; or maybe he touches on a high-voltage wire and is shut down by an Internet regulatory body.

L's business generates real revenues everyday, he can already play golf, but he has no desire to tell strangers about the money he's making. No one would believe him anyway, how could he make several hundred thousand *yuan* a month?

This all comes from workers making not even 2,000 *yuan* who use 300 *yuan* to buy a Shanzhai mobile phone. They play the games by L's company, contributing a few hundred *yuan* in ARPU (average revenue per user) value. In other words, they happily turn over a tenth of their salary to L.

I sometimes fail to understand – W's customers are all in Beijing and Shanghai, elites with the highest discretionary income. Why are they willing to pay for the most expensive mobile phone, switch to the newest laptop, eat at the finest restaurants, but online they want everything to be free?

My circle agrees only W's doings are widely watched. He has the eyes of his industry peers, the media, marketers, word of mouth, and his site's traffic is almost a steady upward slope. But the weird thing is, after not long his momentum suddenly stops, his heart starts to beat like that of an older man.

I also asked L, and only a handful of his grassroots users own a computer or have a 3G connection. So how could this happen? L smiled and said, Internet cafés are not the most effective channel. Next to the factory districts there are convenience stores, where the workers assemble after work. The boss supplies a computer installed with all the mobile games, MP3s, movies, and an old-style karaoke songbook. There's no need to go online, with a USB cable workers can download what they wish. Even more convenient, there's a pushcart set up that can wheel this equipment to the workers' dormitories.

One time over a meal with L, he asked me: 'Who is suitable as a spokesman for our game targeted at 450,000 Foxconn factory workers?' I guessed Jay Chou (a famous Taiwanese pop star), but L shook his head, he's for city folk. So I guessed Chris Li [春哥 – a highly popular winner of a talent show a number of years ago], but also incorrect, she's only for students and young married women. Annoyed, I guessed Feng Jiao [当红的凤娇 – the star of a reality dating show], but that guess was also rejected. The correct answer is Phoenix Legend [凤凰传奇 – a singing duo that came to fame through reality shows that are popular in western parts of China], with hundreds of songs as evidence. And I felt jealous of L's knowledge that far outstripped my own. I'm lucky I never suggested Han Han! [韩寒 – racecar driver, blogger and maverick.]

In the past, W earnestly believed technology could change society, but now he knows you can even stay away from the government, but the government will still inquire about you. L was once angry, but now he's practical. A good businessman knows how to read the news. He closely follows official personnel changes, the crackdown on pornography, and even participated in a few 'friendship association' labor meetings, though his aim was to promote his games.

Upon the string of suicides at Foxconn, he solemnly told me: 'this is our fault.' I was startled. He said these youth jumping off buildings are the customers who feed me. Usually the mobile phone is the only entertainment for these workers, their only connection to the outside world. It's our responsibility to give these workers happier lives.

All my investor friends have high praise for W, but all more comfortable investing in L. Because in their hearts they know: in China, you target elites to make noise, but you target the grassroots to make money. Are not Tencent and Baidu perfect examples?

A Shanghai comedian [Zhou Libo 周立波] says: 'I drink coffee, but Northerners eat garlic. Coffee is an imported product, very Western, but garlic is good for the body. This year garlic producers are earning a lot of money, but I haven't heard of coffee makers making money. Is not China's Internet the same?' [Note: The stereotype is that Chinese Southerners fancy themselves as more civilized, sophisticated than Northerners. More W than L.]

I suddenly thought if W and L switched places, would the result be the same? Would they understand each other's markets? But then I realized that's improbable.

W seeks an 'elegant, American-style Internet'. American's information revolution started in the 1960s, and those 1950-1990 are all of the digital generation. There's no big Internet divide, their business and lives, work and entertainment, cannot be separated from the Internet. That's why Mark Zuckerberg, and Steve Jobs of the 1950s, Jeff Bezos of the 1960s, and Larry Page of the 1970s all compete with each other. America's societal structure is like an olive [*sic* – *Ed.*], there's not so much inequality, regional differences, rural-urban divide, so one can say America has a 'national Internet'.

We once thought Chinese society was like a pyramid, but it's now becoming a nail. Between W and L, one is at the tip of the nail, while the other is far away at the head of the nail. China does not have one so-called 'national Internet', instead there's a great divide. It encompasses the elite with ThinkPad laptops and also the grassroots with MTK Shanzhai mobile phones. Our elites are on a par with America, while our grassroots are on a par with Vietnam.

In reality, China's 'digital generation' exists in the north and a few big cities, in the tens of millions of twenty to forty year-old middle class citizens. The remaining hundreds of millions use only QQ. If the Internet can't change this status quo, can it provide a societal and economic revolution?

I believe L sees the essence of China's Internet. The insatiable desires of the elites, a limited group being chased by far too many entrepreneurs. On the other hand, there's a huge number of 'digital peasants' who have no way to use the Internet to change their fate, no way to access the Internet and improve their lives, they can only get drunk on cheap entertainment. L's business suits China's condition.

I've always believed there'll finally be a day when W can make something that represents the future of the Internet, make Americans sit on their butts and look up to China and learn. But will his trials today wreck his willpower?

According to the philosopher Plato's theory of the cave, everyone is born into his own cave, we only see a reflection of real life cast by the sun's shadows. But everyone believes the shadows in their cave are the real world, because we've never seen anything else. But the real world is outside of the cave, in the sun.

The elite readers of this blog must admit, there's a huge group (labourers, recent grads, about 300 million), who live in a completely different world. If you can follow this group, you'll have more opportunities. But in all likelihood, we'll never emerge from our own caves.

Identities of W&L

There's much speculation as to the identities of W&L. Many believe W refers to Wang Xing 王兴, the founder of Xiaonei (early Facebook clone, sold to Oak Pacific and renamed Renren), Fanfou (early Twitter clone, shut down by government after Tibet riots in 2009) and Meituan (Groupon clone). With Meituan, one of China's largest group-buying sites, Wang Xing should finally make his bank.

L is speculated to be Li Xingping 李兴平, founder of Hao123.com, an Internet directory used by many Chinese, especially those new to the Internet, as their homepage and a list of the most popular sites on the Chinese Internet. Sites can pay to be featured in the listings and thereby attract significant traffic. Hao123 was sold to Baidu in 2004.

Wang Xing's profile strikes me as a better fit for W than Li Xingping is for L. But the author, Simon Shen, ultimately says: 'There's no need to make this a guessing game. These are no more than two representatives, with elements from others as well.'

When Rape is Not Rape

By C. Custer
From ChinaGeeks
Published on 13 July 2011

Today I read one of the most disgusting headlines I've seen in my life. I think this whole story speaks for itself, so here you have it.

Translation:
Female teacher raped by government official, police say it's not rape because he was wearing a condom.

Recently, the topic 'official implicated in the rape of a teacher' has been appearing on forums and has attracted a lot of attention. The person who made the post was the Huajue City Middle School English teacher, twenty-six-year-old Zhou Qin. She says that on 17 May 2011, the school principal ordered her to accompany eight [government] leaders for drinks. After she was drunk, she was raped by the city rural land resources manager, Wang Zhonggui. What's even more shocking is that according to what's being said on the net, when Zhou Qin reported this to her local police station, the police said: 'If he wore a condom, it's not rape.'

Over the past two days, a reporter for the morning edition [presumably of the Southeastern News Net, where this was originally published] investigated.

Investigation Summary
The article is lengthy and, being at work at the moment, I don't have the time to translate it in full. However, here are the main points that are made in the article, according to the reporter's research.

That morning, the school had been holding a special government event, of which Zhou Qin was one of the hosts. After this, the teachers all retired to the government cafeteria to eat with the leaders. The teachers were all originally eating in a separate room, but the principal ordered Zhou specifically to go to the officials' table and toast each of the eight men in succession, and she was also ordered to toast several other people including police officials who were also at the event.

Zhou Qin says that she was ordered to toast the officials repeatedly, around fifteen or sixteen times (generally speaking, each 'toast' would be equivalent to around a shot of *baijiu* [strong grain alcohol – *Ed.*], although there's no mention of how big the glasses were.)

Zhou says that this actually happens regularly, the principal often orders her to drink with important guests during official functions.

A police official at the event said he did remember the principal yelling at Zhou Qin to drink with the officials, but that he could not recall precisely how much she had had to drink.

Because she was drunk, it seems Zhou Qin was put into a car with Wang Zhonggui, who she had never met before that day. She, or perhaps someone else [the article isn't totally clear on this] asked that he take her home, as she was stumbling. But when she got to the car, she realized that she didn't really know him, and that her home was less than 1km from the government cafeteria, and she began to refuse the ride. Wang insisted on offering a ride, and after a few more refusals, she took it, reasoning that as a teacher it would be best for her to be driven, as if she walked some students might see her drunk.

But Wang drove her towards the Land Management offices, the opposite direction of her home. They picked up a co-worker of hers on the way, and when they got there, Wang invited them to his office. Her co-worker agreed, so Zhou followed.

In Wang's office, there was a lower-level employee who Zhou knew personally, so she felt safe. But as soon as that person left, Wang locked the door, and began to molest Zhou. Zhou struggled, but was quite drunk and unable to put up much of a fight. She began to feel threatened, and said she had to go to the bathroom (Wang's office has a private bathroom reserved for his use). Once there, she locked herself in.

But after she had been missing a while, Wang came pounding on the door. She stalled, saying she would be better soon, using the time to throw up several times and try to sober herself up. However, the booze got the better of her, and she passed out.

She awoke around 6:00pm to find herself lying on Wang Zhonggui's bed (his office also has a private bedroom, ostensibly for naps). She was alone, and completely nude. She vaguely recalled being dragged, and Wang squirting her mouth with something that seemed like water – later she would realize he must have climbed in through his bathroom's window and unlocked the door from the inside.

She realized that she had been raped and, hearing people downstairs but not wanting anyone to know about it, she quickly put on her clothes and climbed out the window for a quiet escape.

When she got home, she locked herself in her room and refused to speak or come out. Her mother recognized that this was very odd, and asked her what was wrong. After numerous attempts, Zhou finally told her: 'I was raped.'

Together, the two decided they should tell the police, and Zhou charged her boyfriend with going to the police station to report the crime. The police investigated Wang's office-bedroom on 19 May, finding (among other things) a used condom. They told the reporter: 'This is proof that Wang Zhonggui and Zhou Qin had intercourse.'

However, the investigation remains unresolved, as the procuratorate maintains there is insufficient evidence, and have asked the police to provide evidence in addition to the used condom, other chemical evidence, and circumstantial evidence such as a broken window lock that matches Zhou's story.

Zhou says that on the eighteenth, when she was first putting the story down formally at the police station, the person guiding her told her that: 'If he was wearing a condom, it's not rape.' Zhou recalled that this person was none other than Zhong Xiancong, one of the men she had been ordered to toast the day of the rape.

Zhou says that Zhong also told her: 'This is all something you did to yourself, and you don't want to make it public now. Think of your reputation. I will keep it secret for you.' The reporter tracked Zhong down at the police station yesterday, and he said that he had told Zhou that there wasn't much evidence of rape, and that additionally with a used condom rape would be very difficult to confirm. 'That's why I advised her to settle privately,' he said.

Many other people have also advised Zhou Qin to settle the case privately.

The reporter got Wang Zhonggui's phone number from the police and has called him repeatedly for comment, but no one is answering his phone.

UPDATE: As one would expect, this and other news stories are drawing more attention to this case and many are discussing it on Weibo. To find relevant messages, try searching for terms like '毕节阿市' or '教师被强奸'.

UPDATE 2: This story seems to be accelerating fast on Weibo, where it's now being RTed by dozens of people every minute.

Chinese Government: 'Internet Rumours Are Like Drugs... Attack Creators And Spreaders... Head-On'

By Bill Bishop
From DigiCha
Published on 4 December 2011

It looks like the campaign to squash Internet rumours, especially on microblogs (aka Weibo), has kicked into high gear.

In the last week there have been multiple articles in official Chinese media about the importance of the proper handling of microblogs and the dangers of Internet rumours. The coordinated propaganda effort appears to have started with a signed article in the 28 November issue of the *People's Daily* by Wang Chen, head of the State Internet Information Office and a deputy minister of the Central Propaganda Department: 'Actively Carry Out Microblog Public Opinion Guidance Work' (*Jiji kaizhan weiboke yulun yindao gongzuo* 积极开展微博客舆论引导工作).

Wang Chen references the 'Decision' of October's Sixth Plenum of the Seventeenth Communist Party Congress in his opening paragraph. Party members at all levels will likely be studying this article and implementing, or at least making a show of implementing, his suggestions.

Also on 28 November, *People's Daily* Online published an article entitled 'Internet Rumours Are Drugs, Please Resist And Stay Far Away From Them' (*Wangluo yaoyan shi dupin qing zijue dizhi he yuanli* 网给谣言是毒品 请自觉抵制和远离) while Xinhua Online ran the first of a series of commentaries on the subject titled 'Internet Rumours Are Like Drugs' (*Wangluo yaoyan ru 'dupin'* 网络谣言如'毒品').

On 28 November, Xinhua Online published the second in the series – 'Please Do Not Let Internet Rumours Poison Our Kind Hearts' (*Qiemo rang wangluo yaoyan duhai women shanliangde xin* 切莫让网络谣言毒害我们善良的心) and on the thirtieth carried the third – 'Use A "Combination Punch" To Cut The Internet Rumour Propagation Chain' (*Rang 'zuhequan' zheduan wangluo yaoyande chuanbolian* 让'组合拳'斩断网络谣言的传播链).

On 1 December, *People's Daily* Online ran 'Attack Creators And Spreaders Of Internet Rumours Head-On' (*Dui wangluo zaoyao chuanbozhe jiu ying dang 'yingtoutongji'* 对网络造谣传谣者就应当'迎头痛击'). The article states that 'Internet rumours are "societal drugs"...which are no less harmful to society than Internet pornography, gambling or drugs.'

That 1 December article admits that the rapid spread of Internet rumours is partly due to a credibility deficit of the government and its officials. It also states that 'some foreign forces, who always want to play the role of "saviour"...are using the Internet to disseminate rumours to smear the image of officials, to attack leaders of the Chinese Communist Party, use distortions to illustrate that China's current political regime is lacking in legitimacy and stability.'

The language in these articles has echoes of campaigns and crackdowns from an earlier era. The comparisons to drugs and drug dealing, sometimes a capital offence in China, may be a sign of an impending harsh crackdown on those who spread Internet rumours. The backdrop is concern about social stability, especially in the worsening economic environment, and increasing conservatism in the run-up to the leadership change at the 2012 Eighteenth Party Congress. This week also saw a much publicized talk by top security official Zhou Yongkang.

Government pressure is increasing on the leading Chinese Internet companies, especially Sina for its Weibo, and Tencent, both for its Weibo and for QQ, the leading real-time messaging platform in China. Investors should be wary.

FROM VICTORY TO VICTORY

SEDUCED BY THE WEST

For too long a corpus of Western media theory and its conceptualisation of journalism have been popular among certain individuals in China. Some media figures constantly refer to the West, its 'freedom of expression' and the 'Fourth Estate' as though they were some gold standard. To them giving prominence to the achievements of national development is 'hypocritical news'; reporting on the dark underbelly or talking about social anomie, however, are 'socially responsible'. In reality these people are revealing their ignorance of the Western media approach.

In a dual-party or multi-party system, as in the West, media groups have their own political agendas which aid and abet their political masters. They report negative news and attack each other, their bag of tricks including rumour-mongering and the sullying of opponent's reputations. Our unique national conditions [*guoqing* 国情] differ from those of the West. If we were to introduce such skullduggery to China it could all too easily undermine and divide the social consensus and it would be disadvantageous to the creation of a stable and harmonious social environment.

What Chinese society needs is a responsible and modulated media that truly protects the fundamental interests of the state, the nation and the people. We do not need a media that, under the cover of 'objective reporting', constantly finds fault. It is only right and proper that our media participate in building and supporting China's search for wealth, power and development. We require a media that enthusiastically encourages society to develop in a positive way and that can nurture an uplifting, energized and optimistic information environment.... Media should take a creative stance in helping resolve conflict, breach differences and forge consensus. It should not pursue its own interests to egg people on to greater excesses nor incite the public.

...A correctly guided media creates good fortune for our Party and for our people; an arrant media direction will be destructive of both the Party and of our people.... Our political system determines that China's media will sing in tune with the keynote determined by the Party. This is in accord with the realities of a country of 1.3 billion people. The reality is that for China to develop social stability must be maintained; and a media environment must be created that benefits the overall stable situation. This then is the true responsibility of China's media; it is also in the basic interests of the people's of China.

– from 'Media Enthusiasm for Negative Reporting is the Result of Western Seduction', *Beijing Daily*, 19 May 2012.

The following is *a list of the achievements of the People's Republic of China and the Communist Party from 2009 to 2012. This information is drawn from annual Government Work Reports (available at www.gov.cn) and the Xinhua News Agency. Direct quotes are taken from the English versions of Government Work Reports.*

2008

- The Summer Olympic Games were successfully held in Beijing with China topping the gold medal count.
- China's economy maintained steady growth despite the global financial crisis. Gross Domestic Product (GDP) topped thirty trillion *yuan*, an increase of nine percent over the previous year, while overall price rises were held in check.
- Grain output rose for the fifth consecutive year and totalled 528.5 million tonnes, a record high.
- In September, the Shenzhou-7 spacecraft was launched, sending three astronauts into space, one of whom completed China's first space walk.
- Reform and opening up were 'further deepened'. New breakthroughs were made 'in reforms in key areas and crucial links, such as the fiscal, taxation, financial and pricing systems and administration'.
- More than eleven million new urban residents entered the workforce. Urban per capita annual disposable income reached 15,781 *yuan*, an increase of more than eight percent, while rural per capita net income reached 4,761 *yuan*, an increase of eight percent.
- Great victories were won in the fight against massive natural disasters: rescue and recovery operations during the Sichuan earthquake were successful.

2009

- On 1 October, a 'grand celebration of the sixtieth anniversary of the founding of New China' was held. The 2009 Government Work Report notes: '[T]he outstanding achievements we made in that time have greatly boosted the confidence and pride of the people, strengthened the cohesiveness of the Chinese nation, and raised China's international standing and influence.'

- A four trillion *yuan* stimulus package helped 'ensure a steady growth rate for China, which remain[ed] one of the least-hit major economies amid the financial crisis.'

- GDP reached 33.5 trillion *yuan*, an increase of more than eight percent over the previous year.

- Grain production was 530.82 million tonnes, a new record and an increase for the sixth consecutive year.

- More than eleven million urban jobs were created. The per capita disposable income of urban residents was 17,175 *yuan*, and the net per capita income of rural residents was 5,153 *yuan*, up more than eight and nine percent respectively from the previous year.

- In 2009, China's higher learning institutions had 29.79 million students, with a gross enrolment rate of 24.2 percent, equalling the world average level.

2010

- The 2010 Shanghai Expo was successfully held, attracting more than seventy million visitors.

- In October, the Chang'e-2 lunar probe was lifted into space by a Long March-3 carrier rocket.

- The 2010 Asian Games were successfully held in Guangzhou.

- GDP grew at an average annual rate of more than eleven percent to reach more than thirty-nine trillion *yuan*.

- New record highs were set for grain production, which reached more than 5.46 trillion tonnes. The per capita net income of farmers continued to grow rapidly and reached 5,919 *yuan*.

- 7,356 large and medium-sized reservoirs and key small reservoirs were reinforced, ensuring the safety of drinking water for 215 million rural residents.

- New power generating units with a capacity of 445 million kW were brought on line, including hydro power plants with 96.01 million kW capacity and nuclear power plants with 3.84 million kW capacity. More than 25.29 million hectares of land were re-afforested. Sulphur dioxide emissions were cut by 14.29%.

- Foreign exchange reserves soared to US$2.85 trillion as of the end of 2010, up twelve times from US$212.2 billion in 2001.

- China's overseas direct investment flow increased by an average of forty percent annually from 2001 to 2010, when it amounted to US$68.8 billion.

- China surpassed the United States in the annual volume of car production and sales in 2009; in 2010 auto sales reached 18.06 million units, while output rose to 18.26 million units.

2011

- The Beijing-Shanghai high-speed rail link opened to the public.

- China became the world's second largest economy, with GDP expanding to 40.12 trillion *yuan*.

- The unmanned Shenzhou-8 spacecraft was launched in November, returning safely to earth after completing China's first space docking with the target module Tiangong-1, which was launched in September.

- China's GDP reached 47.2 trillion yuan, an increase of 9.2 percent over the previous year.

- China's grain output reached a record high of 571.21 million tonnes.

- A total of 12.21 million new urban jobs was created. The per capita disposable income of urban residents and the per capita net income of rural residents rose in real terms by more than eight and more than eleven percent respectively.

- The government continued to renovate dilapidated houses in rural areas, ensured the safety of potable water for more than sixty million additional rural residents, delivered electricity to 600,000 people in areas that had no power supply, and 'further improved rural working and living conditions'.

- The government implemented the 'second phase of the project to protect virgin forests and raised related subsidies' and planted more than six million hectares of trees.

- Preferential policies were implemented 'to promote the leapfrog development of Tibet and Xinjiang'.

- China's urbanization level exceeded fifty percent, marking a historic change in the country's social structure.

- Reconstruction of earthquake-hit areas around Wenchuan, Sichuan province, was completed; major progress in disaster relief and reconstruction in Yushu, Qinghai; Zhugqu, Gansu; and Yingjiang, Yunnan was achieved.

- The government 'fully attained the goals of making nine-year compulsory education universally available and basically eliminating illiteracy among young and middle-aged adults'. The children of rural migrant workers were 'generally granted access to compulsory education in cities where they live'.

- The government 'vigorously strengthened development of the cultural sector', increasing financial support for cultural programs that benefit the people. 'Major progress was made' in protecting cultural relics and in protecting China's intangible cultural heritage.

- Coverage of basic medical insurance was extended to 1.3 billion urban and rural residents. The government implemented a 'national system for basic drugs in all community-level medical and health care institutions run by the government, and basic drugs became safer and more affordable.'

THE REASONS FOR CHINA'S 'GLORIOUS DECADE'

People's Daily Online
4 July 2012

The past ten years has been the result of the relentless and comprehensive development of what is called the 'Glorious Decade' in China. China had effectively deal with the public health crisis known as SARS, swiftly responded to the tragic Wenchuan earthquake, completed amongst some of the world's largest reconstruction tasks, successfully hosted the 2008 Beijing Olympic and Paralympics' Games, Shanghai World Expo and Guangzhou Asian Games. It has successfully dealt with the international financial crisis, and accomplished the main tasks of the Tenth Five-Year Plan and the Eleventh Five-Year Plan.

In ten years, China's status on the world stage has undergone historic changes: An annual average 11.5 percent of high economic growth, with an economic aggregate ranked first at sixth quickly jumping to second highest in the world; an annual average of

18.8 percent of growth in export and import of trade jumping from fifth to second highest in the world; an annual average of 23.5 percent in the growth of R&D expenditures, with total R&D spending also jumping from fifth to second highest in the world.

Never before has China received so much attention from the world, and the world, until now has never been more in need of China. So what is the cause behind China's brilliance and shining success?

From the perspective of the characteristics and conditions of the political development, the political superiority from the socialist system in China means a strong Central Politburo Standing Committee, which is the key condition for the correct decision-making and successful development. The Standing Committee is comprised of nine members, representing eight leading institutions, such as the Party, State and Army, forming a 'collective presidential systems' with Chinese characteristics.

The most important feature of this type of system can be summed up with one word: 'collective'. Everything is referred to as 'collective members' rather than the 'individual member', representing a 'collective body' rather than an 'individual', the 'collective wisdom' as opposed to 'personal wisdom' and finally 'collective decision-making' instead of 'personal decisions'. This is reflected in the five parallel running mechanisms; collective shift succession, collective division of labor, collective learning, collective research and collective decision-making.

The 'collective presidential system' is far superior to a 'personal presidential system' in terms of the interaction between the information sharing structure that enables fully information sharing and the decision-making structure that is fully democratic, therefore it is more democratic, more coordinative and more efficient. This explains why China not only maintained the best macroeconomic indicators, but also rapidly narrowed the GDP gap with the US in the financial crisis. In addition, China played the most significant and active role in the global response since the credit crunch.

In terms of development theories and strategies, the CCP Central Committee innovated the 'people-orientated' scientific concept of development, which is the latest theoretical achievement of the Party with regards to the laws of construction of socialism, social development and the understanding of the Party's governance. It has become the ideological 'soul' for the 'Giant in the East' to further advance. Over the last ten years, China has accelerated its development in the scientific development field, and excelled in its impact and transformation over economic developments. All this in turn allows for comprehensive, well-coordinated and sustainable development in the form of the world's first green development plan, the Twelfth Five-Year Plan.

Finally, from the perspective of creative power, there are 1.3 billion people each creating the miracles of true heroes, whom all share the same core values for development. China is home to some of the world's most diligent and also most intelligent people, packed with robustness and with unlimited potential to give. With 1.3 billion people all learning together, innovating together; we shall build common prosperity and we can achieve a great rejuvenation for the Chinese nation.

These are the fundamental reasons for China's continued success.

9

VOICES FROM THE BLOGOSPHERE II

THIS CHAPTER continues our selection of writings from the Chinese Internet by local writers and foreign observers that engage with some of the topics discussed in this book. All material is reprinted with permission from the original author, editor or website.

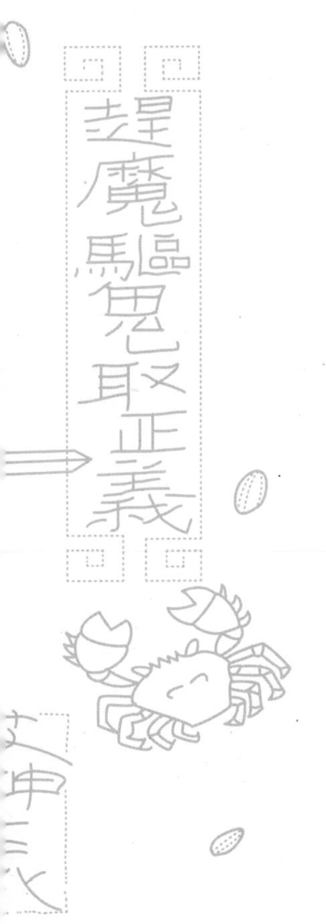

Reading Culture in the *People's Daily*

By David Bandurski
From China Media Project
Published on 2 December 2011

Unpacking China's latest policies on cultural reform, which emerged from October's Sixth Plenum of the Seventeenth Central Committee of the Chinese Communist Party, will be a process of many months. The October 'Notice' on cultural reform is not so much a coherent program of cultural development as a mess of politics, ideology and commercial interests. And the Party's own attempts to explain what these changes mean lead only to more befuddlement.

Take, for example, today's edition of the Party's official *People's Daily*. While articles on cultural reform are scattered throughout the paper, page seven offers a series of pieces with the stated goal of 'exploring methods of transition and development for the cultural industries'.

The first piece in the series, 'Breaking Through Deep Issues in the Development of Culture Industries', comes from the Hebei Province Research Centre for the Theoretical System of Socialism with Chinese Characteristics. Here is the centre's introduction:

> In a modern society, culture and the economy grow together into one with each passing day. Owing to various regional, industry and administrative lines, our country's cultural industries have not only suffered the limitation of their own development, but the support of and drive for economic and social development in a larger sense has not been fully brought into play [as a result]. Therefore, various regions and industries should, in the forming and implementation of cultural reform and development planning, set their eyes on cooperative development, united development, breaking through…[the situation] of the backwardness of cultural development relative to the economic development.

Readers hoping for specifics are rewarded instead with more generalities. The article says that achieving cross-regional and cross-industry cultural industry development requires 'the strengthening of top-level design, innovating the systems and mechanisms for cultural construction'.

The objectives broadly defined in this article seem valid enough. China must move toward greater innovation. Indeed. China must transition from a 'made in China' model to a 'created in China' model. Sure.

> While there are many reasons for the emergence of '*shanzai* [imitation or rip-off – *Ed.*] culture', on one level it can illustrate the loss of impetus for innovation and creation in the cultural industries. At the moment, our culture industries lag behind the overall economy and society in terms of innovation and creativity, and this has restrained the development of the culture industries as well as economic and social development. Fostering the impulse for creativity and innovation has become... a strategic focus and urgent task in the cultural and also social and economic development. Realizing the leap from 'made in China' and 'assembled in China' to 'created in China' and 'brand China' requires a salient emphasis on innovation consciousness [创新意识] and creative thinking [创造思维], making innovation and creativity the leading and driving forces of cultural industry development. [This means] strengthening the protection of intellectual property and creating a social environment that respects knowledge, respects talent, respect work and respects innovation. [This means] strengthening the position of creativity and innovation in the cultural service value chain, raising the quality and effectiveness of acts of innovation and creativity.

But how do you drive home a 'salient emphasis on innovation consciousness and creative thinking' and nurture 'the impulse for creativity and innovation' without relaxing the political and ideological environment in which people create in the first place? This, as I've stressed before, is the fundamental blindspot of China's cultural reforms.

How do you create 'a social environment that respects knowledge' and innovation when the fundamental law on culture is the Party's, the demand that culture 'follow the correct political orientation' as spelled out in the October 'Decision' on cultural reforms?

The paragraph above also talks about the 'quality and effectiveness' of innovation and creativity. But what are the metrics for quality and effectiveness? Who decides what is quality and what is effective? Who gets to allocate resources on that basis?

The second article in the series begins with an assessment of the need for more cultural production on the basis of broader trends in economic growth:

> In step with our country's economic development and rising household incomes, the spiritual [or 'non-material' = 'cultural'] consumer demand of the people has steadily expanded, and this has promoted the emergence of cultural and creative industries. In the past few years, the cultural and creative industries in our country have developed rapidly, and the scope of development has expanded from several large cities like Beijing and Shanghai to principal cities throughout the country.

How will China now meet this rising demand? The article states confidently that 'many major cities have placed great priority on cultural innovation and industry development, and have gained clear results.'

The city of Shanghai has raised the concept of 'innovation industrialized and industry innovated'; the city of Nanjing has raised [the idea of] 'making it such that every person's creativity is encouraged, that every good creation has the opportunity to be marketed (市场化) and industrialized (产业化), and that every creator receives effective institutional support and favourable policy support'; the city of Guangzhou has raised [the concept of] 'grabbing hold of the animation industry just [as it has] the automotive industry'; the city of Shenzhen has talked about building 'the capital of innovative design, etcetera.

So the Party everywhere is talking about innovation. That's no surprise, of course. They have little choice given that innovation has become the pre-eminent Party buzzword. And what about action? The article goes on to mention other specific measures, such as a pilot project offering tax reductions for cultural enterprises in Beijing, investment in the building of 'cultural industry accumulation areas' (产业聚集区) – culture industry parks, that is – and working with banks to encourage loans to 'cultural innovation enterprises' (文化创意企业).

I may seem to some to be belabouring this point, but there is an ongoing tension here between the 'material' of hoped-for culture and the 'spirit' of innovation. 'Cultural industry accumulation areas' and loans for 'cultural innovation enterprises' are all well and good. But the assumption seems to be that people will be innovating simply because these loans and parks exist. And there is that nagging question about the 'social environment' for innovation alluded to in the first article in the *People's Daily* series. Can you talk about innovation without talking about freedom? Whether you can or not, China is doing just that.

Nor can the discussion of cultural development escape the ideological conditioned response of defining Chinese cultural creation in opposition to the West – and thereby unnecessarily restricting its meaning and twisting its purpose. Who is going to decide whether innovations are sufficiently 'Chinese'?

A third article on page seven of the *People's Daily* urges that policy making on cultural development take into account the uniqueness of the Chinese condition:

> The writer believes that every country's cultural industries have their own soil on which they live and their own conditions that give them full scope. Departing from definite historical conditions and social environments, the development modes of cultural industries must change. Therefore, in setting down policies for the cultural industries, while the advanced experiences of developed Western nations should be adopted, we cannot apply or mechanically copy development modes...

So innovation is great, but China has to make sure that whatever innovation it gets is Chinese enough.

This prerogative of 'Chineseness' leads us to another of the bewildering contradictions in this push for cultural reform. As I said at the outset, this policy is a mess. So perhaps it shouldn't surprise us that the top-down push to create innovative culture that is quintessentially Chinese also maintains as its 'guiding principle' the political tenets of a nineteenth-century German philosopher.

An article in the *People's Daily* series addressing the 'need to thoroughly leverage the capacity of [China's] excellent traditional culture' offers the following proviso for cultural industry development:

> [We must] adhere to the correct development direction. In bringing traditional culture into [overall] cultural industry development, we must adhere to Marxism as the guiding principle, keeping to the tenets of serving the people and serving socialism . . .

Digital Rants from Ai Weiwei

Ai Weiwei (born 1954, son of a famous pro-Party poet, Ai Qing) is an artist and provocateur who first rose to prominence as a member of 'The Stars', an avant-garde Beijing art group formed in 1978. He went to the United States in 1981 and lived in New York until 1993. He returned to Beijing where he became a fixture of the art scene.

In 2008, the collapse of shoddily constructed schools in the May 12 Wenchuan Earthquake in Sichuan prompted Ai to begin a series of performances, events and art works that drew attention to government corruption and malfeasance. He became increasingly outspoken in the media and on the Internet, notably using Twitter.

On 3 April 2011, Ai was detained at Beijing Capital Airport before a flight, and held incommunicado by security forces until 22 June. Following his release he was charged with tax offences, charges which embroiled him well into 2012. He remained an outspoken critic of the Chinese authorities and an international cultural celebrity.

Following his release from detention, Ai Weiwei was for a while all but silenced. On 24 June 2011, the US-based *China Digital Times* website noted the blanket censorship of his name, and related names, on the mainland Chinese Internet. 'A very long list of keywords is currently banned on Sina Weibo's search function', it reported. Among those banned keywords were: 艾未未 (Ai Weiwei), 艾未 (Ai Wei), 未未 (Wei Wei), 艾 (Ai), 未 (Wei), 未来 (Future [similar to Weiwei]), 艾胖子 (Fatty Ai), 胖子 (Fatty) and 月半子 (Moon Half Son).'

The following material is reproduced with the permission of Lee Ambrozy, editor of *Ai Weiwei's Blog: Writings, Interviews, and Digital Rants, 2006-2009*, Cambridge, Mass.: MIT Press, 2011.

An Account of an Arrest Foretold

On 20 November 2009, Weiwei posted a blog that appears in the English version of his rants under the title 'I Really Can't Believe It'. We record it here first since, given the circumstances of his April 2011 disappearance and his sudden resurfacing in late June the same year, it seems particularly prescient:

Yesterday the Ministry of Public Security sent someone who spent the entire afternoon at the Bank of China investigating my account information. Their reason for the investigation was that I was involved in 'fraud'. What are they trying to do?

The Ministry of Public Security investigated very thoroughly, for more than three hours. Such actions prove they have no moral or ethical bottom line. I'm not surprised at all. When I heard that I was involved in 'fraud', I laughed – at least they are sharing their honour with me.

My mother and sister both received inquiring calls from the bureau. At first they were worried and thought that anything could happen, but I don't see things that way. I believe that no matter what happens, nothing can prevent the historical process by which society demands freedom and democracy.

This afternoon we had a family meeting, where I gave my family an account of my 'work', expressed my views and point of view, and analyzed the situation. Everyone understands that I've already considered the worst of what might happen, and they all feel much more secure.

What can they do to me? Nothing more than to banish, kidnap, or imprison me. Perhaps they could fabricate my disappearance into thin air, but they don't have any creativity or imagination, and they lack both joy and the ability to fly. This kind of political organization is pitiful.

Bury those children, give them kidney stones, and act like it's nothing, exercise violence near and far, but don't dare to face the facts... and this is how you make it in this world I really can't believe it.

2006

The Longest Road

One painful truth of today is that, as we import new technologies or lifestyles from other nations, we are helpless to import the corresponding mental awareness of the strength of justice. We are unable to import souls.

Modern Chinese cultural history is one that scorns the value of the individual, it is instead a history of suppressing humanity and spirituality. Intellectuals are invariably attacked from all directions by powerful Western culture represented by aggression and by decaying cognitive structures represented by Chinese feudalistic influences. All of which have placed our intellectuals in an embarrassing predicament.

Over the past one hundred years, virtually all reform efforts have begun with submission to Western culture, and all conclude with compromising native traditions. Simple emulations and resistance have amounted to a central characteristic in China's modern cultural development.

Doubtless, the tides of history are pulling this archaic ship ever nearer to the banks of democracy, as communication, identification, understanding, and tolerance have begun to supplant methods of coercion and exclusion. ...

[Written in November 1997 and posted on 23 February 2006]

Hurt Feelings

Invoking the emotions of more than a billion people to make a point makes it seem as if there exists an apparatus that can measure the feelings of more than a billion people. In my understanding, feelings aren't that easy to hurt, and I don't believe that the universal feelings of a nation are selective, that they can only be hurt at some specific time or place. In fact, the Chinese people have weathered many great storms, and their feelings have proven rather resilient. How deep is the wound, once an injury has an opportunity to heal itself? Why are these feelings only revealed when they are hurt? Once such a situation touches upon the masses, the dubious facts multiply to excess.

[10 April 2006]

The People

This mysterious culture that birthed Confucianism and Taoism, adopted Buddhism, and likewise has faith in a system for realizing socialist ideals; this cultural tradition with the most comprehensive and systematic ethical code, yet the most materialistic, desire-driven reality; this society overloaded with dogmatic political theory but likewise inundated by laissez-faire practice; this plot of land is energy and injury, it bears possibilities and impossibilities, opportunity and danger, surprise, excitement, frustration and despair.
[Written on 16 December 2004, posted on 10 January 2006]

2008

Rule of Law

For a moment, forget the struggle between tyranny and civil rights; forget the extravagant dreams of referendums or citizen votes. We should struggle for and protect those most basic, miniscule bits of power that we truly cannot cast aside: freedom of speech and rule of law. Return basic rights to the people, endow society with basic dignity, and only then can we have confidence and take responsibility, and thus face our collective difficulties. Only rule of law can make the game equal, and only when it is equal can people's participation possibly be extraordinary.

Bullshit is Free

Will China have a bright tomorrow? If so, where will it come from? What kind of people will pay what kind of price for it? That is the question that we must ask ourselves.

Relying on individuals to pay the price is taking stock in a notion of history created by heroes. There is no lack of courageous individuals in China's history, yet courageous people are in short supply. Everyone else is either an experienced and astute onlooker or an ignorant person rejoicing in the calamity of others.

People. There are many people, but they have not taken shape as a collective People, for there are no shared sentiments, no common will, or shared values and necessary human sympathy. A human sense of righteousness is lacking. This is generally why some people are always avoiding 'universal values', and undermining the seeds of free democracy. Touching upon the shared and inseparable parts of humanity, this concept doesn't exist in China. Once warriors are apprehended, all of their efforts come to a halt on the honorary lists of various overseas human rights organizations, and they will sooner or later be completely forgotten in their own nation. But that's a bit exaggerated – their fellow countrymen will never even know of their efforts. That sounds more like the truth.
[Written following the detention of Liu Xiaobo, a key organizer of Charter 08]

Simulating Domestic Introspection

Meddling with blogs and censoring comments is just a universal reminder of who the blog host really is on this patch of land. Although the government is not liberal or decent, it can't be criticized. The lack of freedom of expression and the absence of public debate are old habits; it's just that this makes blogging a little less interesting.

Peace is flourishing, and aside from relying on pens and the barrels of their guns, all dictators can do is make the common people's lives a little less joyful, every day just a little less, every time just a little less. The erosion and disintegration of freedom, dignity, equality, transparency and openness has encroached upon the innocent human nature of people and their free will, corroded our innate convictions, courage and rights. All dictators are short on humour and are obsessive-compulsively sterile.
[30 December 2008]

2009

Bullshit Tax

The pre-1947 KMT was, among other things, lambasted for its petty-fogging miscellaneous fees and taxes. On 1 February 2009, Ai suggested a series of new taxes. He suggested a 'post-harmonious discord fee' along with numerous other categories to allow the state to circumvent under the cloak of law all manner of unregulated behaviour, and to make a profit at the same time. One of the new charges the artist suggested was the 'Observing Flag Raising in Tiananmen Square Fee':

Large numbers of out-of-town floating populations gather in Tiananmen Square to watch the flag-raising ceremony. Their numbers exceed the proscribed amount for unlawful gatherings, and these ceremonies could potentially evolve into a mob scene of unscientific cults. A fee for entrance onto Tiananmen Square is proposed.
[1 February 2009]

My Regards to Your Mother

What kind of plaything is the media? To call them whores would degrade sex workers. To call them beasts of burden would humiliate the animal kingdom. They are only the most disappointing, most uninteresting, most lowly race of people, the most ignorant human beings belonging to the species....
[27 February 2009]

Day of True National Revitalization

You persistently delete, so I'll just repost. Words can be deleted, but the facts won't be deleted along with them. This process will be repeated for a long time, until the day arrives when we evolve, and facts and truth are no longer important to everyday life, so we can forget as we please.

It's not difficult to see that the main similarity in the endless disasters occurring on this plot of land takes the concealing of facts as an important component. The distortion and concealing of basic facts – what happened, how it happened, and why it happened – has become the most sincere, most

valuable, and most productive effort this race has ever put forth. The truth is always terrible, unfit for presentation, unspeakable, and difficult for the people to handle, just speaking the truth would be 'subversion of the state'. Concealing and lying are the foundation ensuring our society's survival. On the day that truth manifests itself, the sky will brighten; that would be true liberation.
[13 April 2009]

I'm Ready

'Be careful! Are you ready?'

I'm ready. Or rather, there's nothing to get ready for. One person. That is everything that I have, it is all that someone might possibly gain and everything that I can devote. I will not hesitate in the time of need, and I won't be vague.

If there were something to be nostalgic about, that would be the wonders that life brings. These wonders are the same for each and every one of us, a game where everyone is equal, and the illusions and freedom that come with it. I see any manner of threats on any human right as a threat on human dignity and rationality, a threat to life's potential. I want to learn how to confront.

Relax, I learn fast, and I won't let you down. Not long ago, the collective deaths of those children who forfeited their lives helped me to realize the meaning of individual life and society.

Reject cynicism, reject cooperation, reject fear, and reject tea drinking, there is nothing to discuss. It's the same old saying, don't come looking for me again. I won't cooperate. If you must come, bring your instruments of torture with you.
[28 May 2009]

The Global Times and Ai Weiwei

By Richard
From The Peking Duck
Published on 13 April 2011

Nine days ago, Hu Xijin, the editor in chief of *The Global Times*, assembled all of the Chinese staff into the paper's large conference room and shut the door. As is nearly always the case with such meetings, the expats, known as 'foreign experts', were not permitted inside.

Hu had a direct and simple order for his shock troops staff: they were to go to their desks and seek out any Chinese comment threads, any discussions on Chinese BBS's and portals and blogs – any discussion on the Internet at all – about the detention of Ai Weiwei and counter them with the Party line, as expressed so clearly and ominously in a recent *Global Times* editorial, namely that Ai Weiwei is a self-appointed maverick who deserves to be detained, and who is being used by hostile Western powers to embarrass, hurt and destabilize China. This was not a request, it was a direct order. It was compulsory.

This tells us quite clearly how determined the Party is to get its message out about Ai Weiwei, even if it's in gross violation of journalist ethics, if not downright sleazy. It adds a whole new dimension to the concept of the Fifty-cent Gang.

I've avoided Ai Weiwei, mainly because I'm on vacation and my Internet connections have been remarkably dodgy, which I attribute to Ai Weiwei, or at least to what he stands for. The Communist Party has to stifle voices of dissent when it feels vulnerable, and the Internet is always the first place they clamp down. I'm sitting in a hotel in Nanjing and will try to make this a brief post, although I am brimming with thoughts on the topic.

The Global Times showed its truest and most sinister colours with a now infamous editorial warning that Ai Weiwei was about to hit a 'red line,' and if/ when he does he is asking for trouble. This was a not-so-veiled threat to all Chinese activists. The Communist Party is on the march, my friends. They're kicking butt and taking names, and they're coming for you.

> It is reckless collusion against China's basic political framework and ignorance of China's judicial sovereignty to exaggerate a specific case in China and attack China with fierce comments before finding out the truth. The West's behaviour aims at disrupting the attention of Chinese society and attempts to modify the value system of the Chinese people.
>
> Ai Weiwei likes to do something 'others dare not do'. He has been close to the 'red line' of Chinese law. Objectively speaking, Chinese society does not have much experience in dealing with such persons. However, as long as Ai Weiwei continuously marches forward, he will inevitably touch the 'red line' one day.
>
> The West ignored the complexity of China's ruling judicial environment and the characteristics of Ai Weiwei's individual behaviour. They simply described it as China's 'human rights suppression'. 'Human rights' have really become the paint of Western politicians and the media, with which they are wiping off the facts in this world.

This is disturbing on so many levels I don't think I need to drill down. It speaks for itself. It's nauseating. Instead, I'd like to talk about a meeting I had with a senior editor of *The Global Times* just forty-eight hours ago. She is urbane, sophisticated, educated, talented and a truly wonderful person. She also epitomizes the archetype of the sophisticated, urbane, educated Chinese who insists on toeing the Party line at all costs. I believe – I know – that this is completely sincere. But it's also quite frustrating. 'Getting through' to such a person, especially when it's a good friend you admire, is infinitely frustrating when they seem to put up seamless, airtight mental barriers that you simply cannot break through.

I paraphrase, but with accuracy:

> Why doesn't the West see that we do things our way in China? We have 1.3 billion people, all those mouths to feed and to protect through a harmonious society. You don't have this situation. You are developed and your populations are small. Human rights doesn't mean to the West what it means in China. Most Chinese support Ai Weiwei's detention. They support Liu Xiaobo's detention. He is a criminal trying to impose Western-style government on a society that doesn't want it. Why won't the West understand how humiliating it was to award the Nobel Prize to someone we put in gaol, a man who is a criminal to the Chinese? How should we feel? How should we react?

This led to a very long conversation – over an hour – in which I explained that if only China would actually engage in a dialogue about these issues with the outside world instead of sabre-rattling and always sounding like a misunderstood and petulant child, maybe then China would advance its cause and help people outside China understand what China is really all about, how human rights are seen through Chinese eyes.

I specifically pointed to the Ai Weiwei editorial:

> Don't you realize the entire expat community here in Beijing and many others around the world are buzzing about this editorial, shocked at its belligerence, its snide and strident tone, its implied threats and its undercurrent of violence? Maybe, as you keep saying, the West truly doesn't understand China. Well, you are focusing now on soft power. *The Global Times* itself is actually an outgrowth of China's thirst for soft power, for global reputation and respect. And look at how you're failing. You are driving away foreign talent and making China look worse, not better – in precise contradiction to the paper's stated goals. If your media and leaders could articulate China's point of view as clearly and calmly as you just did in this

> conversation maybe then China could get somewhere in fostering understanding. But railing against Ai Weiwei at the top of your lungs – a man seen as an artist and a celebrity – is exactly what you should not be doing. Why not throw the West a bone and let him go, declare an amnesty and then explain why he was detained in the first place.

This evoked quite a response.

> Let Ai Weiwei go? But Richard, how can we do that? How can China admit to the world it is being defeated, it is bowing to international pressure and not doing what is right for China? How can we humiliate ourselves like that?

I said it's been done before (look at North Korea surrendering reporter 'spies' after Bill Clinton paid them a visit). In an instant, it would force a new dimension to the issue, and show China was willing to be less hysterical. And I said China appears hysterical, becoming increasingly strident, and that nothing demonstrates this more clearly than the direction *The Global Times* is taking.

This was, as I said, a long, polite and serious discussion. I never experienced anything quite like it before, because despite the mental barriers I referred, to, she genuinely wanted to hear my opinion and to learn how the West sees China, and I think she actually 'got' that *The Global Times*, even if they're right, is scaring people away and damaging its own cause with readers who are not Chinese. She actually said she wanted to discuss my argument with her superiors. (And no, I am not so vain or arrogant or naive as to believe my little talk will change the shape of Chinese journalism.)

All of this said, the detention of Ai Weiwei and many other activists who have the misfortune of being nameless and faceless to us is unpardonable, and self-defeating. I know, they were sending a message to the people of China, not to Americans 10,000 miles away. But again, they say they want soft power, they say they want to be a global super power, they say they want fair treatment in the media. Well, sorry, but you can't have it both ways. You can't repress with one hand and paint a picture of a happy harmonious rules-following society with the other. Detaining Ai Weiwei was the worst thing you could have done, trumped only by your idiocy in attacking him in savage, ugly, deranged editorials.

Go out and do your thing, *Global Times*' Fifty-cent Gang members. While a lot of people will be fooled, enough will see through the propaganda. I admire the young aspiring journalists I worked with there two years ago. If any of you are reading this (which is not very likely), I urge you to think for yourselves, and understand that while journalists have several roles, astro-turfing message boards isn't one of them.

I am delighted to read that *The Global Times* editorial has sparked 'scorn and ridicule' among much of China's Twitterati and social media users. I am glad to make my small contribution to this much-deserved scorn and ridicule.

Update: *The Global Times* and Ai Weiwei

Published on 13 April 2011

Five full days after my post on Ai Weiwei and *The Global Times* was published, I received an email from someone relatively high up at the paper telling me that my description of the meeting with Mr Hu and the staff as depicted in the post was categorically untrue. I'm putting this post up because I want the newspaper's response to be on the record.

I can say definitively that the lower portion of the post, in which I describe my conversation with *The Global Times* editor, is true because I was there having the conversation. I cannot say definitively that the episode involving Mr Hu is true, as I wasn't there, obviously. But I can say that I heard about it from sources I trust like brothers/sisters. I was told that throughout the day, after the meeting, the office was buzzing about Mr Hu's announcement.

That said, it is still hearsay. A former journalist, I used trusted sources and thought long and hard about putting up the post to begin with. I wasn't there. Maybe the meeting was perceived differently by different attendees. Maybe the story I heard was exaggerated, or maybe it was totally accurate. I definitely believe that the story, or at least the gist of it, is true, but I also have to offer the other side of the story.

In spite of my frustrations with the direction *The Global Times* has taken, underscored by the recent Ai Weiwei editorials, I still have great respect for many who work there, and good memories of our working together. The higher-level person who contacted me and insisted the story is false is one of those people I deeply respect.

So there's both sides. I wanted to put it all on the table and let readers know how the paper responded.

As I said, it was five full days before the paper contacted me. The entry was translated into Chinese the very day it posted and got a fair amount of distribution. If it were categorically false I wish they had contacted me on day one, when they first read it.

Apologies for a long and possibly ambiguous post. I hope it's clear why I felt I had to write it.

A Last Word: The Derailed Country

By Han Han

While many commentators have analyzed the 2011 Wenzhou high-speed train disaster, the Shanghai-based bon-vivant *essayist Han Han offered a powerful meditation on the tragedy in the form of an online essay. It was translated by Matt Schrader (with minor modification by Geremie R. Barmé) and originally published by Charles Custer at ChinaGeeks on 28 July 2011 and in* China Heritage Quarterly *Issue 27 (September 2011).*

You ask, why are they acting like a bunch of lunatics? They think they're the picture of restraint.

You ask, why can't they tell black from white, fact from fiction? They think they're straight shooters, telling it like it is.

You ask, why are they running interference for murders? They think they've thrown their friends under the bus. And they're ashamed.

You ask, why all the cover-ups? They think they're letting it all hang out.

You ask, why are they so irretrievably corrupt? They think they're hardworking and plain living.

You ask, why are they so infuriatingly arrogant? They think they're the picture of humility.

You feel like you're the victim. So do they.

They think: 'During the Qing dynasty, no one had TV. Now everyone has a TV. Progress!' They think: 'We're building you all this stuff, what do you care what happens in the process? Why should you care who it's really for, so long as you get to use it? The train from Shanghai to Beijing used to take a whole day. Now you're there in five hours (as long as there's no lightning strike). Why aren't you grateful? What's with all the questions?'

'Every now and then, there's an accident. The top leaders all show how worried they are. We make someone available to answer journalists' questions. First we say we'll give the victims 170,000 *yuan* apiece. Then we say we'll give them 500,000. We fire a buddy of ours. We've done all that, and you still want to nitpick? How could you all be so close-minded? You're not thinking of the big picture! Why do you want us to apologize when we haven't done anything wrong? It's the price of development.

'Taking care of the bodies of the dead quickly is just the way we do things. The earlier you sign the confidential document agreeing to cremate your loved one's body, the more money you get; the later you sign it, the less you receive. Our pals in the other departments – the ones who knock down all the houses – taught us that one. Burying the train car was a boneheaded move, true, but the folks upstairs told us to do it. That's how they think: if there's something that could give you trouble, just bury it. Anyway, the real mistake was trying to dig such a huge hole in broad daylight, and not talking it over with the Propaganda Department beforehand, and not getting a handle on all the photographers at the site. We were busy, ok?

'If there's anything we've learned from all this, it's that when you need to bury something, make sure you think about how big it is, and make sure you keep the whole thing quiet. We underestimated all that.'

They think that, on the whole, it was a textbook rescue operation – well planned, promptly executed, and properly managed. It's a shame public opinion got a little out of hand, but they think: 'That part's not our responsibility. We don't do public opinion.'

They think: 'Look at the big picture: We successfully held the Olympics, we did away with the agricultural tax, and you guys still won't cut us a break. You're always glomming on to these piddling little details. No can-do spirit. We could be more authoritarian than North Korea. We could make this place poorer than the Sudan. We could be more evil than the Khmer Rouge. Our army's bigger than any of theirs, but we don't do any of that. And, not only are you not grateful, you want us to apologize! As if we've done something wrong!'

Society has people of means, and those without. There's people with power, and those that have none. And yet everyone thinks they're a victim. In a country where everyone's the victim, where the classes have started to decouple from one another, where it's every man for himself, in this huge country whose constituent parts slide forward on inertia alone – in this country, if there's no further reform, even tiny decouplings make the derailings hard to put right.

The country's not moving forward because a lot of them judge themselves as if Stalin and Mao were still alive. So they'll always feel like the victim. They'll always feel like they're the enlightened ones, the impartial ones, the merciful ones, the humble ones, the put-upon ones. They think the technological drumbeat of historical progress is a dream of their own making. The more you criticize him, the more he longs for autocracy. The more you piss him off [*gao mao* 搞毛], the more he's nostalgic for Mao.

A friend in the state apparatus told me: 'You're all too greedy. Forty years ago, writers like you would've been shot. So you tell me, have things got better, or have they got worse?'

I said, 'No, you're all too greedy. Ninety years ago, that kind of thinking would have gotten you laughed out of the room. So you tell me: after all that, have things got better, or have they got worse?'

10

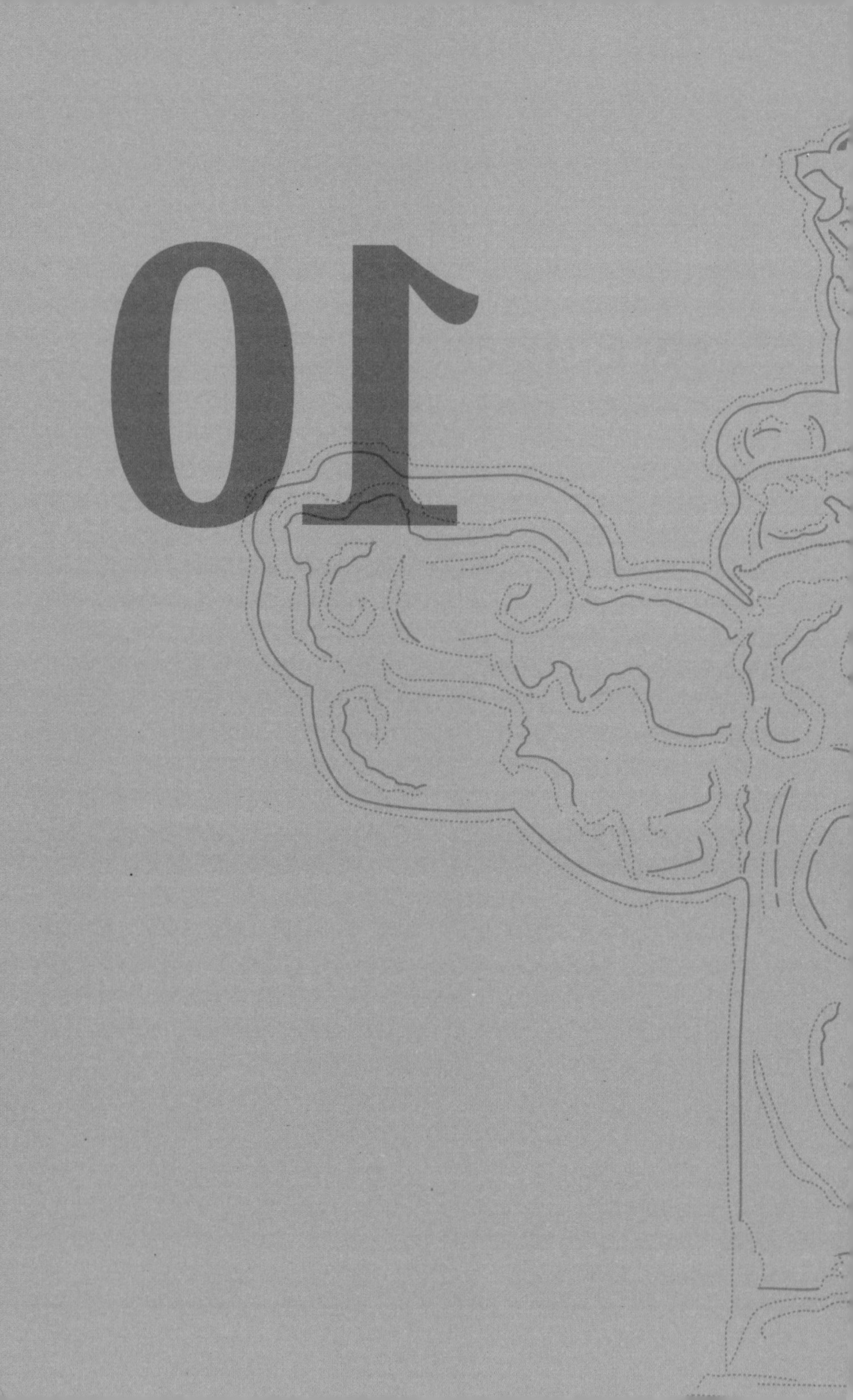

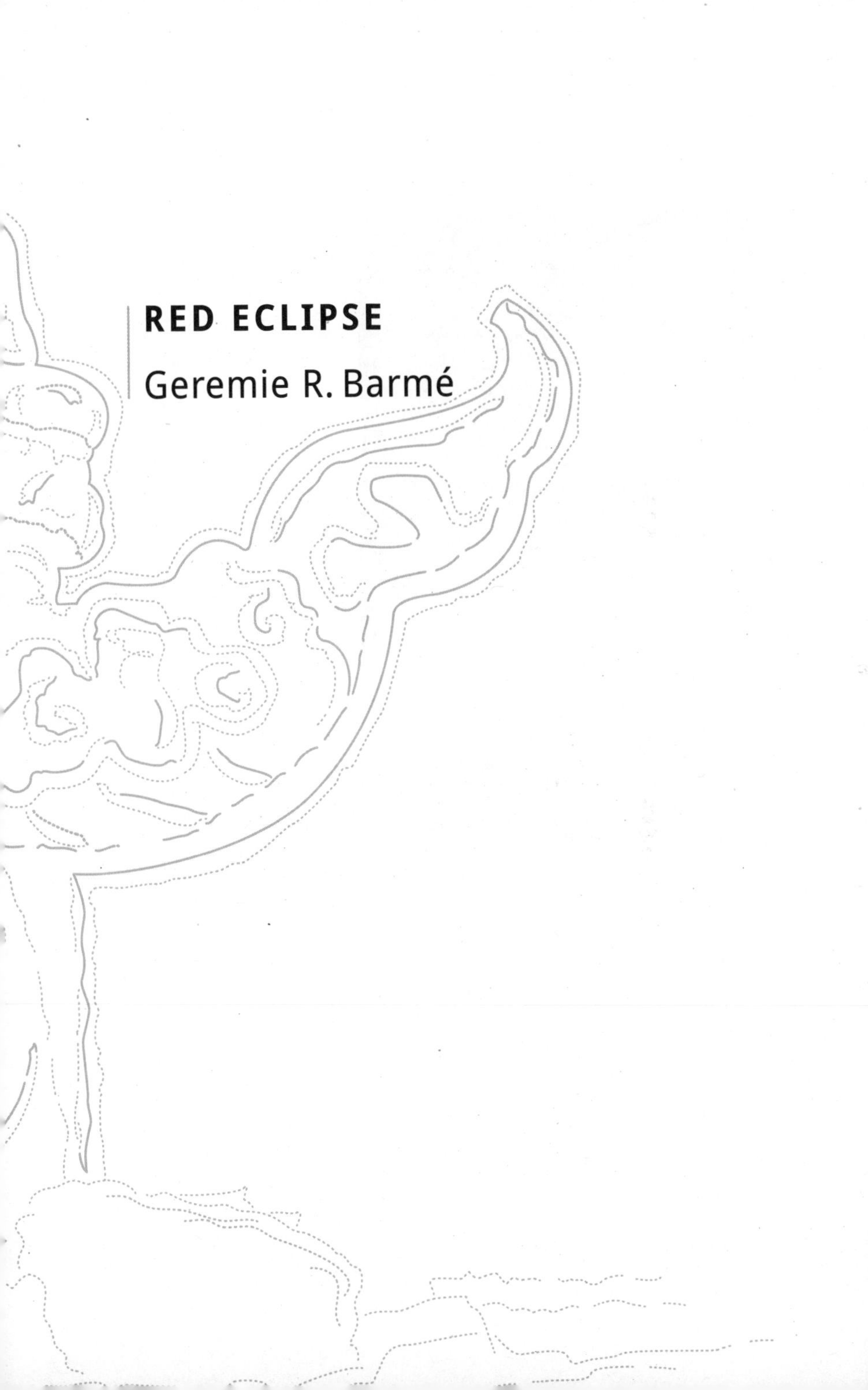

RED ECLIPSE

Geremie R. Barmé

Film poster for the 2009 film made as a homage to the party-state on the occasion of the sixtieth anniversary of the founding of the People's Republic of China.
Source: *The Founding of the Republic*, poster

'The China Story' as told by the Chinese authorities is a grand romantic narrative of struggle, progress and socialist transformation. It is a glowing history of how the Party has brought about the 'great renaissance of the Chinese nation'. On the occasion of the celebration of the sixtieth anniversary of the People's Republic in 2009, China's President Hu Jintao repeatedly cited this phrase, first used by Party General Secretary Jiang Zemin a decade ago. Hu reprised it when marking the centenary of the 1911 Xinhai Revolution on 9 October 2011.

The state-ordained China Story begins with the decline in power, economic might and unity of the Chinese world from the eighteenth century. It then moves through the century of humiliation (roughly 1840-1949) at the hands of Western and Japanese imperial powers and culminates in the birth of a New China and the two acts of 'liberation' (1949 under Mao and 1978 under Deng Xiaoping). It is a story of national revolution, renewal and vigour that, crucially, cleaves to Mao Zedong's leadership, career, thought and politics.

This univocal, uni-linear story denies the complex of what would be better described as 'China's Stories' as well as the myriad nature of China's modern history. In the past the Chinese party-state asserted itself as the sole authority on what was happening on the ground in China. If some individuals or groups claimed that official version was at variance with their own experiences, the authorities would dismiss such cavils as partial, biased, ill-informed views that pandered to anti-government forces and 'anti-China' interests. According to one formula, the party-state could 'see far ahead from its privileged viewpoint' (*gaozhan yuanzhu* 高瞻远瞩): informed as it was by a Marxist-Leninist worldview and perspective on long-term historical trends and in-depth local knowledge, its view alone represented Chinese reality as well as the direction in which the country was moving.

人民日报
RENMIN RIBAO

胡锦涛致电祝贺金正恩出任朝鲜劳动党第一书记

胡锦涛会见梁振英
强调中央全力支持香港特别行政区行政长官和特区政府依法施政
习近平等参加会见

自觉维护改革发展稳定的良好局面

各地党员干部群众表示
衷心拥护党中央的正确决定

吴邦国主持召开人大常委会第八十次委员长会议
决定人大常委会第二十六次会议24日举行

重庆干部群众坚决拥护中央决定
全力维护政治社会大局稳定

稳中求进，央企发挥中坚作用

天津滨海新区
深化改革勇为先

Front page of *People's Daily* on 12 April 2012 featuring an article urging readers to 'Conscientiously maintain the good situation of reform, development and stability'. The article also states that the broad masses of Chinese cadres and people strongly support the Central Committee of the Chinese Communist Party's decision to investigate Bo Xilai.
Source: *People's Daily*

重慶商報
印度射"烈火"惊扰全亚洲

纳税50强是重庆经济发展的脊梁骨
黄奇帆出席全市纳税50强表彰大会并讲话

房交会首日成交747套
高层建面均价5878元

966965
QQ 800002320

张学友今晚奥体开唱
奥体周边路段交通管制

借力新能源
重庆抢滩一线车城？

戴"色盲眼镜"过驾考体检，危险

力帆新帅有"三宝"：细致 铁腕 口碑好

银行卡在手竟遭复制
百万巨款不翼而飞

韩判我船长30年徒刑
中方表示不接受

The front page of *The Chongqing Economic Times* 20 April 2012: in a turn away from the formerly robust Red Campaign the paper's headline praised major companies in Chongqing that through the taxes have proved that they are 'the backbone of Chongqing's economic development'.
Source: *Chongqing Economic Times*

Dissidents argued against this mainstream view. But until the adve
of the Internet, their opinions didn't travel far beyond their own circl
and a few engaged outside observers. While they might be published
a sensation-hungry media (Hong Kong, Taiwan, or international) the
ability to reach wider audiences was limited by a strictly controlled m
dia and publishing industry at home. The rise of the Internet, blogs an
more recently, microblogs, has democratized information (as well
misinformation), which can circulate in new ways that both challen
the Chinese state and our understanding of this vast, complex and eve
changing country. The China Story is now more accessible, nuanced, d
tailed – and out of control – than ever before.

The China Story, as presented in this volume, is that of a former
underground political party that recast itself, first as a revolutiona
national leadership in the late 1940s and then as a legitimate gover
ment in power (*zhizhengdang* 执政党) some three decades ago. For a
the paraphernalia of state power, to this day its internal protocols an
behaviour recall its long history as a covert, highly secretive and fa
tion-ridden organisation. Even under Mao, some commentators calle
China a 'mafia-state'.

This aspect of the party-state was thrown into sharp relief in Fe
ruary 2012 when the former Deputy Mayor of Chongqing, Wang Liju
a man previously famed for having led the attack on that city's ow
'mafias', was ordered to undergo an extended period of what was euph
mistically termed 'therapeutic rest' (*xiujiashi zhiliao* 休假式治疗) follow
ing his appearance at, and subsequent disappearance from, the US Co
sulate in Chengdu, Sichuan province. (Soon after, 'treatment' came t
include detention and investigation.) Then, on 15 March, his erstwhi
boss and local Party leader, Bo Xilai, was dismissed from his variou
positions and put under investigation himself.

Corruption and Privilege

Although recent commentators have claimed that China has become increasingly corrupt in the last decade, and indeed a 'mafia-state' has developed, critics of one-party rule made similar charges from before the founding of the People's Republic in 1949. In the early 1940s, the writer Wang Shiwei famously criticized Party leaders at the Communist base of Yan'an for their special privileges, grades of food, clothing and accommodation. He was denounced as a Troskyite and eventually beheaded.

After the founding of New China, an elaborate system of 'privileged supply' (*teshu gongying* 特殊供应, or *tegong* 特供 for short) was introduced from the Soviet Union. A network of restricted-access shops and farms was created to cater to the needs of the Party nomenclatura, a vast body of Party functionaries, bureaucrats and their families divided into twenty-four grades. Cars and telephones were among the special privileges limited to the fortunate few. Mao Zedong and other leaders enjoyed these along with (for the time) luxurious villas located at the most scenic places in the country. The central party-state leaders themselves ruled from a former imperial pleasure ground in the centre of Beijing, Zhongnanhai, the 'Lake Palaces'.

When Mao called on intellectuals and others to help the Party 'rectify its work style' in light of criticisms of party rule in the Eastern Bloc in 1956, many spoke out against the secretive privileges and power of Communist Party cadres. In 1966, when Red Guard rebels were allowed to attack the Party they identified privilege, corruption and abuse of power as the greatest enemies of the revolution. Again, at the end of the Cultural Revolution, when there was a period of relatively free criticism of the Party, privilege and corruption were identified as the greatest threat. In 1989, during a nation-wide protest movement, some protesters released a detailed account of the connection between Party bureaucrats, their children and new business ventures that had sprung up during the early stages of reform. One of the Party leaders directly blamed for the corrupt nexus between Party power, private enterprise and global capital was Zhao Ziyang, later ousted as Party General Secretary.

China's Party leaders echo Mao Zedong's old refrain that corruption can lead to the collapse of the Party and the nation when they bewail the rampant corruption of recent years. In the 2012 attacks on Bo Xilai and his wife, Gu Kailai, a system of cronyism and corruption endemic in the Chinese one-party state, has been protected while the couple were made an object of national vilification.

Party leaders and their families, be they in Beijing or in the provinces, continue to enjoy food produced at special organic farms, dedicated water supplies, luxurious accommodation, clubs and villas and a range of other perks. As in other areas of its activities, the Party is unaccountable. None of its self-allocated privileges are open to public scrutiny and budgetary allocations are a carefully guarded state secret.

In the 2009 film 'The Founding of a Republic' (*Jianguo Daye* 建国大业) produced to celebrate to sixtieth anniversary of the founding of the People's Republic, Chiang Kai-shek says: 'If we fight corruption, we'll destroy the party; if we don't fight corruption, we'll destroy the nation' (*fan fubai jiu wangdang, bu fan fubai jiu wangguo* 反腐败就亡党；不反腐败就亡国). The party he was referring to was the Nationalist Party not the Communists, but many viewers of the film posted comments online saying that the words were perfectly applicable to contemporary China.

Officially, at least, the party-state authorities 'oppose corruption and espouse frugality' (*fanfu changlian* 反腐倡廉).

A Two-track Story

Since the end of the Cultural Revolution, approximately once every decade cataclysmic events in China have led to a clash of views about the country and its rapid transformation. In 1979, the closing down of the Xidan Democracy Wall, where people had aired complaints against the Party and the Chinese government (including those who, like the electrician Wei Jingsheng, warned that to be a modern nation China need democracy), marked the beginning of the bifurcated or 'two-track' understanding of contemporary China. Ever since, even as the country's remarkable economic growth has been hailed locally and internationally, the country's persistent and often draconian one-party rule has elicited constant critique.

The nationwide protest movement of 1989 and its violent suppression on 4 June entrenched this two-track understanding of China. The Chinese authorities' version of the story is that demonstrators in dozens of cities were witless tools in the machinations of plotters and schemers, themselves serving US-led international efforts to undermine the Communist Party, weaken China and thwart its re-emergence as a major global power. Others call it a pro-democracy movement that was brutally suppressed by an armed dictatorship.

It is not only the Chinese party-state, but average Chinese and patriots of all persuasions, however, who are prone to attack 'the West' for its ignorance of Chinese reality in that case and others. The constant flow of negative stories about mainland China in the non-mainland Chinese press in Hong Kong and Taiwan is harder for the party-state to dismiss. Harder still is it to deny the lived realities and self-told stories of people who can increasingly speak out for themselves and have their voices heard in no small part thanks to the Internet.

Two other notable manifestations of the two-track story of China occurred in 1999. The first happened on 25 April when thousands of practitioners of the Falun Gong religious sect surrounded Zhongnanhai, the seat of the Chinese party-state. This was followed later in the year by repression of the sect and resulting international disquiet about religious freedom and human rights abuses. The second happened on 7 May, when NATO forces bombed – mistakenly it was claimed – the Chinese Embassy in Belgrade, killing three Chinese journalists. And then there was March 2008, when protests and a riot in Lhasa led to an uprising throughout Tibetan China. This was another moment when mainstream international media reporting in particular clashed with China's official account of reality.

More recently, in February-March 2012, speculation and rumour about the fall of Bo Xilai were rife. The Chinese authorities resorted to their default mode of high dudgeon to aver that Western accounts of Bo's fall alleging unprecedented levels of corruption, nepotism and Party cronyism, lacked objectivity. But the speculation was hardly limited to 'the West'. The ambient political hysteria and rumour-sharing sparked by ructions in China's political life is the by-product of the secretive Chinese party-state itself and are also common in China. The opaque Chinese political system and its censorious vigilantism with regard to the guardianship of The China Story are facing unique challenges from the People's Republic's new-found prosperity, global role and international heft.

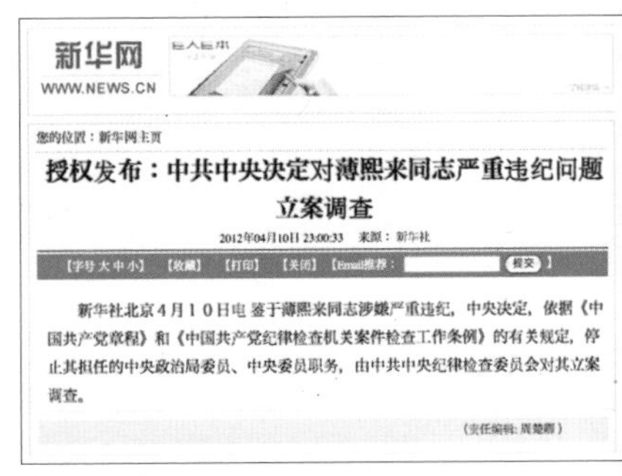
新华网
WWW.NEWS.CN

您的位置：新华网主页

授权发布：中共中央决定对薄熙来同志严重违纪问题立案调查

2012年04月10日 23:00:33　来源：新华社

【字号 大 中 小】【收藏】【打印】【关闭】【Email推荐：　提交】

新华社北京4月10日电 鉴于薄熙来同志涉嫌严重违纪，中央决定，依据《中国共产党章程》和《中国共产党纪律检查机关案件检查工作条例》的有关规定，停止其担任的中央政治局委员、中央委员职务，由中共中央纪律检查委员会对其立案调查。

（责任编辑：[illegible]）

Screenshot of the terse Xinhua News Agency announcement of the Party's investigation into Bo Xilai, 10 April 2012.
Source: Xinhua

Writing in June 2012, the activist artist Ai Weiwei, a man who has featured in the pages of this Yearbook, saw in the fate of three very different public figures, a shared condition:

> Reflect on Bo Xilai's case, [the blind lawyer] Chen Guangcheng's and mine. We are three very different examples: you can be a high Party members or a humble fighter for rights or a recongnised artist. The situations are completely different but well have one thing in common: none of us has been dealt with through fair trials and open discussion. China has not established the rule of law, and if there is a power above the law there is no justice.

A Cyclical History

'Go Among the Masses; Eschew Empty Talk', in Mao Zedong's hand.
A modern-day sculpture at the original headquarters of the Xinhua News Agency and *Liberation Daily* on Qingliang Shan 清凉山, Yan'an, Shaanxi province.
Photo: Geremie R. Barmé

Critics of the Communist Party-centric China Story often decry it as being politically bankrupt. Many countries and their governments strive to create a unifying narrative that transcends quotidian realities related merely to economics, wealth creation and financial markets. China is no different. Now that country has achieved many of the formal goals of a revolutionary century and China has become a strong and relatively wealthy nation, Chinese from all walks of life have increasingly questioned the rationale for the continuation of the one-party state. They question its ability to oversee a restive nation encompassing divergent needs and interests. Maintaining the status quo while pursuing economic and social transformation by the old methods of police force and political coercion is a fraught, and hugely costly, exercise, as we have noted throughout this volume.

On 4 July 1945, Mao Zedong asked the educator and progressive political activist Huang Yanpei (1878-1965) what he had made of his visit to the wartime Communist base at Yan'an in Shaanxi province. Huang lauded the collective, hard-working spirit evident among the Communists and their supporters. But he expressed his doubts about whether the wartime frugality and solidarity could last. He predicted that the revolutionary ardour of the Communists could well wane if they ended up in control of China, and wondered out loud whether the endemic political limitations and blemishes of earlier Chinese regimes would return to haunt the new one, despite the best efforts of its committed idealists. Would autocracy, cavalier political behaviour, nepotism and corruption once more come to rule over China? Huang said he could see no way out of the 'vicious cycle' of dynastic rise and collapse, though he certainly hoped that Mao and his followers would be able to break free of the wheel of history.

In response, Mao declared unequivocally:

> We have found a new path; we can break free of the cycle. The path is called democracy. As long as the people have oversight of the government then government will not slacken in its efforts. When everyone takes responsibility there will be no danger that things will return to how they were even if the leader has gone.

Following the 4 June 1989 suppression of a protest movement that had been characterized by inchoate demands for democracy and greater freedom, Mao's remarks on breaking free of the vicious cycle of the past were dutifully recalled by pro-Party mass media historians. During Chinese Lunar New Year celebrations in February 2011, a group calling itself the Fellowship of the Children of Yan'an recalled Mao's 1945 declaration that the Communists would lead China away from the tradition of autocracy and the cyclical history of the past. At what had become an annual gathering, the Fellowship warned that the party-state faced a momentous task, that of realizing the promise of Yan'an made some seventy years earlier. At their meeting they canvassed a document in which they called for major structural changes including the implementation of substantive democratic reform within the Communist Party.

The former Communist Party revolutionary base, Yan'an, Shaanxi province.
Photo: Geremie R. Barmé

The Children of Yan'an believed that they were well within their rights to offer their policy advice to the Party, an organization which many of their parents had contributed to building both before and after 1949. The members of the Children of Yan'an were predominantly descendants of men and women who had lived and worked in the Yan'an Communist Base in Shaanxi from the 1930s to the 1940s, as well as the progeny of the Party who were born and educated in Yan'an. Their outspokenness was a sign that China had entered a new era of ideological uncertainty, social anomie and open political contestation reminiscent of that which had lead to the chaos and suppression of 1989.

Hu Muying, daughter of Hu Qiaomu, a Party wordsmith par excellence and Mao Zedong's one-time secretary (Deng Xiaoping called him 'The First Pen of the Communist Party') has led the group since 2002. In 2008, the Fellowship expanded its membership to include others without any direct link to the old Communist base. Henceforth, the Children of Yan'an would include anyone who wanted to collaborate under its banner and support its vision: 'to inherit the revolutionary tradition, glorify the Yan'an spirit, build camaraderie with the children of the revolution, sing the praises of the national ethos and to work in various capacities for the old revolutionary areas, ethnic regions, the nation's frontiers and impoverished areas.'

Yan'an 延安

Yan'an is a once-isolated town in the barren mountains of northern Shaanxi province. Celebrated as the 'cradle of the revolution', it was the last station on the Long March, becoming the Communist Party and Red Army's base from 1936 to 1948. Many of the policies and systems that the Chinese government employs to this day were first articulated by Mao and established at Yan'an. Much early Communist iconography relates to Yan'an, where the leadership, soldiers and camp followers, including some prominent urban intellectuals, film stars and foreign fellow travellers like Edgar Snow and Agnes Smedley, lived and worked in the cave dwellings common to the locality in an atmosphere of austere but sociable egalitarianism.

In 1984, some of the children of Communist Party members who were born or grew up there set up an organization that now calls itself 'Children of Yan'an'. The group is dedicated to realizing the ideals that their parents devoted themselves to in the heyday of the revolution.

The Children of Yan'an

At the 2011 Lunar New Year meeting, Hu Muying declared:

> The new explorations made possible by Reform and the Open Door policies [inaugurated in 1978] have, over the past three decades, resulted in remarkable economic results. At the same time, ideological confusion has reigned and the country has been awash in intellectual currents that negate Mao Zedong Thought and Socialism. Corruption and the disparity between the wealthy and the poor are of increasingly serious concern; latent social contradictions are becoming more extreme.
>
> We are absolutely not 'Princelings', nor are we 'Second-generation Bureaucrats'. We are the Red Successors, the Revolutionary Progeny, and as such we cannot but be concerned about the fate of our Party, our Nation and our People. We can no longer ignore the present crisis of the Party.

Hu went on to say that through the activities of study groups, lecture series and symposiums the Children of Yan'an had formulated a document that, following broad-based consultation, would be presented for the consideration of the authorities in the lead up to the Communist Party's late-2012 Eighteenth Party Congress. She said:

> We cannot be satisfied merely with reminiscences nor can we wallow in nostalgia for the glories of the sufferings of our parents' generation. We must carry on in their heroic spirit, contemplate and forge ahead by asking ever-new questions that respond to the new situations with which we are confronted. We must attempt to address these questions and contribute to the healthy growth of our Party and help prevent our People once more from eating the bitterness of the capitalist past.

In essence, the document drafted by the Children of Yan'an and publicized by them in the lead up to the politically momentous 2012 Party Congress, called for a revival of the legacy of the revolutionary past and for the recognition of a left-wing faction within the Communist Party itself.

Since 2008, the Party has expended considerable energy on silencing or sidelining liberal ideologies in China. The sentencing of the writer Liu Xiaobo, later Nobel laureate, on Christmas Day 2009 and the detention of the artist Ai Weiwei in April 2011 are the two highest-profile examples of these efforts. As the contributors to this volume have noted, it has also expended considerable energy in containing civil unrest, NGO activism, Internet agitation and a range of demands from dissenting thinkers advocating western-style democratic reform (in particular during 2011 as a result of the Arab Spring). So it is significant that those inside the Party who still identify with its Maoist leftist heritage were also actively agitating for reform and for a kind of internal Communist Party 'democratization', even if this particular version of populist democracy within an autocratic one-party schemata may appear to be less than attractive.

Also noteworthy, if not unsettling, was the fact that among the key speeches and documents produced by the Children of Yan'an in recent years there has been scant importance placed on China's burgeoning global influence, its enmeshment with the international economic order or awareness of regional concerns about the country's rapid military build-up and the impact of its intermittent bellicosity.

The Red Chorus

'The Place Where Red Songs First Resounded'.
A poster celebrating the location where the song 'Without the Communist Party, There Would Be No New China' was written at Xiayun Ling 霞云岭, Hebei province.
Photo: Geremie R. Barmé

The Children of Yan'an declared that China's new political talent could be found among the masses, in particular among the enthusiastic Party faithful. They claimed, for instance, that the 'Sing Red' campaign of Chongqing that was subsequently encouraged by the Party nationwide, had led to the discovery of the kind of enthusiastic younger Party stalwarts who would ensure the continuation of the Communist enterprise long into the future. In the 1960s, Mao Zedong had warned that after his demise people would inevitably 'wave the red flag to oppose the red flag'. Now it would appear that the Children of Yan'an were using their very own red flag to oppose the red flag of economic reform that, since 1978, had itself been employed to oppose the red flag of Maoism.

Red culture has formed the audio-visual backdrop to mainland Chinese history since the 1950s, and to some extent since the Japanese War period of the 1930s and 40s. After the end of the Cultural Revolution, it was reduced to little more than a disco-fication of Revolutionary Model Operas until after the 1989 protest movement. Following the suppression of that nationwide mass uprising against one-party rule and media control, the Communist Party used police force, indoctrination, re-education and cultural 'soft power' to reassert its authority, reviving Red Culture in the process. For a period, the momentum for further economic and social change of the 1980s was lost. Then, with his inspection Tour of the South in 1992, Deng Xiaoping encouraged further radical change that led to unprecedented opportunities for people to improve their living standards, and the Red Culture movement subsided once more. When, in early 2012, Deng's Tour was recalled, commentators remarked that China again faced a stark choice: to carry out further systemic reforms that would unleash greater creativity and future prosperity, or to maintain the satus quo allowing thereby entrenched interest groups to advance a form of crony capitalism under the umbrella of party-state protection. Others would argue that a hyper-cautious collective leadership served China well, allowing the country to maintain stability and steady growth in a period of global fiscal uncertainty.

As we have noted in this book, in early 2012, the complex negotiations surrounding the power transition of 2012-2013 were thrown into sudden relief when Wang Lijun, until then a key ally of Bo Xilai in his 'Sing Red, Strike Black' campaign from 2009 fell from grace and made an abrupt and mysterious visit to the US Consulate in Chengdu, where he unsuccessfully sought asylum. Wang's fall led to wild speculation about the fate of Bo Xilai

Red Songs

On 20 April 2011, *Guangming Daily* reported that Bo Xilai's Chongqing government had drawn up a list of thirty-six 'Red Songs' that party-state cadres and the masses should learn to sing as part of the 'Sing Red, Strike Black' campaign (see Chapter 3). Not all the songs were ideological in nature – some were merely popular tunes familiar to older people who grew up before Chinese popular music came to be dominated by singers and tunes from Hong Kong and Taiwan. The thirty-six songs on the list were:

1. Moving Towards Rejuvenation 走向复兴
2. Flag Fluttering in the Breeze 迎风飘扬的旗
3. The Most Beautiful Song is for Mother 最美的歌儿唱给妈妈
4. Concerned about the common people 情系老百姓
5. China I sing for you 中国我为你歌唱
6. Nation 国家
7. Water chestnut flowers bloom on the southern lake 南湖菱花开
8. The romance of the red flag 红旗之恋
9. Happy days 喜庆的日子
10. The taste of home 家乡的味道
11. Loving each other devotedly 相亲相爱
12. Love China 爱中华
13. Let's go China! 加油中国
14. A good lad must become a soldier 好男儿就是要当兵
15. I want to go to Yan'an 我要去延安
16. Two sides of the Straits, one family 两岸一家亲
17. On the sunny road 阳光路上
18. Ballad of Lugou 卢沟谣
19. The skies above us 我们的天空
20. Horse wrangler 套马杆
21. Pursuit 追寻
22. So beautiful tonight 今宵如此美丽
23. Spring ballet 春天的芭蕾
24. My sister forever 永远的姐姐
25. Power inside your heart 心中的力量
26. If I were you 假如我是你
27. Drink a toast to love 为爱干杯
28. So good 多好啊
29. Rain in my hometown 故乡探雨
30. You are a hero 你是英雄
31. Long live the motherland! 祖国万岁
32. Red and green 红色绿色
33. That piece of red land 那一片红
34. Nostalgia 圆圆的思念
35. My snowy mountain, my sentry post 我的雪山我的哨卡
36. Worried about home 家的牵挂

This particular list did not include the song 'Without the Communist Party, There Would Be No New China' which was a standard item in Chongqing's 'Sing Red' campaign.

> *Without the Communist Party,*
> *There Would Be No New China*
> 没有共产党就没有新中国
>
> Without the Communist Party, there would be no new China
> Without the Communist Party, there would be no new China
>
> The Communist Party toiled for the nation
> The Communist Party, unified, saved China
> It pointed to the road of people's liberation
> It led China towards the light.
> It fought the War of Resistance for over eight years
> It has improved people's lives
> It built a base behind enemy lines
> It carries the benefits of democracy
> It practises democracy, whose benefits are many
>
> Without the Communist Party, there would be no new China
> Without the Communist Party, there would be no new China

and the role of 'Princelings' in Chinese politics. Some commentators believe that the 'Red Culture' campaign itself would be imperilled by this latest shift in the country's power politics. Yet, while other forms of resistance to the Party's current policies remain effectively outlawed, the red heritage of the Maoist era can provide another means by which to challenge the status quo.

Red Rising

The Children of Yan'an concluded their February 2011 plea for Party reform by referring back to Mao Zedong's July 1945 exchange with Huang Yanpei in Yan'an. They reminded their readers of Mao's belief that the Party had identified the final solution to China's historical trap:

> We have found a new path; we can break free of the cycle. The path is called democracy. As long as the people have oversight of the government then government will not slacken in its efforts.

In no uncertain terms the Children of Yan'an now declared:

> We are calling on the whole Party to take a substantive step in this direction.

Not only had the Children of Yan'an formulated a manifesto and begun agitating for political reform, for in their pursuit of a Maoist-style 'mass line' they reportedly made tentative contacts with grass-roots organizations and petitioner groups in and outside Beijing. For left-leaning figures in contemporary China to engage in such pragmatic, and non-hierarchical, politics was highly significant, and alarming for the authorities.

In the wake of the events of February-March 2012, the Children of Yan'an gradually fell silent. Even before Bo Xilai's March ouster, when they had met again to welcome in the Year of the Dragon at Chinese New

Year in February 2012, they refrained from making further calls for internal Party reform, although in private some of their members expressed despair about the fate of the Party and the future of the nation.

Even in power, Mao Zedong frequently spoke about the dangers of bourgeois restoration and revisionism. He declared a number of times that he would have to go back into the mountains to lead a guerrilla war against the power-holders, indeed that rebellion was justified. In contemporary China heated discussions about the legacy of revolutionary politics continue in the cloistered security of academic forums; but Mao's guerrilla spirit of rebellion, the active involvement with a politics of agitation, action and danger, are part of a red legacy that seem long forgotten. Restive farmers and workers may cloak themselves in the language of defunct revolution, but the evidence suggests that their metaphorical landscape is a complex mixture of traditional cultural tropes and an awareness of modern rights.

Creative Industries and the Party's October 2011 Decision on Culture

In 2001, a book by the creative industries specialist John Howkins appeared under the title *The Creative Economy: How People Make Money From Ideas*, that same year the Department of Culture, Media and Sport in the United Kingdom produced a document called 'Creative Industries Mapping Document'. Together they assured the place of 'creative industries' in the minds and hearts of urban planners and bureaucrats across the globe.

Over the past decade as the Chinese government has pursued a combination of state directed economic reform and neo-liberal social experimentation it has absorbed ideas such as those related to 'creative industries'. In the process of urban planning and renewal, for instance, since 2004 it has developed 'creative cultural zones' (*wenhua chuangyi chanyequ* 文化创意产业区) and official documents emphasize the importance, and economic value, of the creative economy. Together they form part of a strategy to make uplifting anodyne socialist culture and entertainment part of China's very own 'cultural industries' (*wenhua chanye* 文化产业).

In October 2011, the Seventeenth Central Committee of the Chinese Communist Party concluded its Sixth Plenary Session at which it adopted a new set of guidelines for improving the nation's cultural soft power and promoting Chinese culture. A major document on cultural issues was issued for detailed study and implementation throughout the nation and Hu Jintao's keynote speech on the subject was widely reproduced. In that speech he emphasized the need for China to become a cultural superpower and to ensure the regulation of the cultural industry. He also pledged to redouble efforts to promote the 'healthy and positive development' of the country's Internet culture.

Red Eclipse

One of the most abiding legacies of Red Culture is the paradigm of the Cold War. Cold War attitudes and rhetoric are easily applied to the tensions between the People's Republic of China and its neighbours as well as other nations with which it finds itself in conflict. The use of such rhetoric by the party-state and those in its thrall (from state think tank apparatchiki and a swarm of left-leaning academics to semi-independent media writers) of course encourages a response from the other side in any given stoush.

Since 2009, rhetorical clashes of this kind, some quite aggressive, have revolved around such topics as climate change, US arms sales to Taiwan, the valuation of the Renminbi, Internet freedom, territorial disputes in the South China Sea, Sino-Australian relations, as well as ongoing disturbances in Tibet and Xinjiang. In regard to these issues – and here we are concerned with Chinese rhetoric, not the substantive matters involving different national and economic interests – the default position of the Chinese party-state remains that of the early Maoist days when conspiracy theories, class struggle and overblown rhetoric formed the backdrop to any official stance. This is not to underplay the importance of real and ongoing clashes of national interests, worldviews, or political and economic systems, but simply to make the point that the way in which the party-state responds is very much dictated by the official parameters of The China Story.

Many questions remain as yet unanswered. Have revolutionary politics and ideology lost their traction in The China Story as the fall of Bo Xilai and the eclipse of red culture might indicate? Has the neo-liberal turn of Chinese statist politics in the decades of reform reshaped The China Story around a concocted and self-interested 'Chinese race', in which the main narrative is that of a nationalistic rise to superpower on the world stage? Or, do the various red legacies that date from China's Republican era (be they communist, socialist or social-democratic) still contribute something to the ways in which thinking Chinese, in and out of power, contemplate that country's future direction? Can a left-leaning legacy distinguish itself from a failed Maoism or Red Culture as entertainment? Or is Maoism and

Sun Yat-sen (Sun Zhongshan, 1866-1925), the 'father of the Republic of China', who is recognized as a progressive revolutionary leader on both sides of the Taiwan Straits. This statue is located at the entrance to Zhongshan Park immediately to the west of Tiananmen Gate, Beijing.
Photo: Geremie R. Barmé

its panoply of language and practices the only viable source of resistance to the continuing spectre of Western imperialism? How do the discourses of universalism, as well as of economic and human rights fit into The China Story today?

This book has attempted to account for some aspects of The China Story over recent years. It is inevitably a limited and narrowly focused effort. We hope this first *China Story Yearbook* does, nonetheless, make accessible to a broad and engaged public some of the key issues, ideas and people important in China today.

For the Children of Yan'an and those of a more general leftist persuasion – those who were intellectually or sympathetically retro-Maoist or neo-Marxist, the red rising of recent years seemed to offer a glimmer of hope, a chance to recapture some of the lost ethos of China's socialist possibility. Despite their objections to party-state policies that helped enrich the few, there was within this disparate group a broad endorsement of state power. The strong state, or what we call throughout this volume the party-state (*dangguo* 党国) was seen as being the essential guarantor of Chinese unity and economic strength.

We have noted the concern expressed by economists and journalists, thinkers and web activists that the social and economic transformation of China has, in recent times, been bedeviled by an increasingly assertive state and the vested interests represented by a nexus of party-state-business concerns. This situation is summed up in the expression 'the state has advanced while the individual has been in retreat' (*guo jin min tui* 国进民退).

Xu Jilin, a prominent Shanghai-based intellectual historian, has called this version of Chinese cultural-politics a form of 'statism' (*guojiazhuyi* 国家主义). He has noted its previous, malevolent incarnations in twentieth century Europe, and warned that behind the vaunted 'China Model' lurks an unaccountable form of authoritarianism. Gloria Davies, a contributor to the present volume, has noted that: 'In his robust critique of statism… Xu Jilin has argued that because it privileges an ideal scenario of responsible governance, statism is constitutively skewed toward legitimizing authoritarian rule. As a consequence little consideration is given to protecting individual rights and freedom of speech and association as guaranteed in the Chinese constitution.'

Among a myriad of dilemmas facing China in its post-transition age, it is that of the polity itself that remains contested. At the same time, the contemporary unitary party-state of the People's Republic of China confronts the liberal market democracies of the world with the reality of a resilient state, a liberalized guided economy and a form of harsh paternalism. It is this particular Chinese 'national situation' (*guoqing* 国情) and what it means domestically, regionally and on a global scale that will be the focus of *China Story Yearbook 2013*, the title of which is: *Civilising China*.

CHRONOLOGY

The following outline chronology covers some of the key events touched on in this book.

2007

January: China fires a missile at its own (obsolete) satellite and obliterates it, causing fears of a military build-up in space.

April: China seeks to contain global concern over contaminated food exports. On 23 April, following the discovery of melamine in animal feed from China, US food regulators are given permission by the Chinese authorities to investigate Chinese suppliers of pet food ingredients.

August: one and a half million Chinese-manufactured toys sold under US-owned brands are recalled in the US after excessive quantities of lead were discovered. In September, there is another recall of toys in the US market.

June: the term 'collective stroll' enters the Chinese vocabulary. It describes a slogan-free public protest against a planned chemical factory that would produce paraxylene (often called PX) and emit pollution near a residential zone in Xiamen, Fujian province. Collective strolls are organized online and via mobile phone messages.

17 June: the Chinese media begin to report on the Shanxi brick kiln slave scandal, in which parents of around four hundred children forced to work in inhumane conditions in a brick factory were exposed on the Internet. The factory is soon closed and some officials sacked.

21 October: the Communist Party unveils a new leadership lineup for the next five years; Hu Jintao wins a second term as Party and army chief, while four new men join the Politburo Standing Committee: Shanghai Party chief Xi Jinping, Liaoning province head Li Keqiang, as well as He Guoqiang and Zhou Yongkang.

24 October: China launches its first lunar probe the Chang'e from Xichang space centre in southern Sichuan province.

2008

14 March: the largest protests against Chinese rule in Tibet since 1959 escalate into riots with the violence spreading to 'Tibetan China', including parts of neighbouring Gansu province and an outlying area of Sichuan province.

March-April: creation of the website www.anti-CNN.com by a young, Beijing-based technology entrepreneur, Rao Jin. The website denounces Western media reports of the uprising in Tibet (in particular those by CNN) and becomes the online face of a rise of populist support amongst young people for the Chinese government. One of the events that boosted support for Anti-CNN occurred during the Olympic Torch Relay in Paris on 7 April, when Tibetan independence protesters tried to grab the Olympic torch from a Chinese paralympic athlete in a wheelchair. The Chinese leadership responds by fuelling a pro-China anti-

Western propaganda push and takes over direct management of the upcoming Beijing Olympics.

9 April: Australian Prime Minister Kevin Rudd delivers a speech at Peking University in which he defines Australia's relationship with China as one of a true and frank friendship (that of a *zhengyou* 诤友) that 'offers unflinching advice and counsels restraint'. Chinese media discuss the speech – and its use of the word *zhengyou* – with interest.

12 May: an earthquake measuring 7.9 to 8 on the Richter scale devastates Wenchuan county, Sichuan province. The death toll surpasses 80,000. The disaster prompts a nationwide charitable movement including cash donations and volunteer rescue efforts.

16 July: the first report of the 'poisoned-milk scandal' appear in the media when infant formula produced by Sanlu is found to contain melamine, an industrial additive that has the effect of artificially raising a reading of the milk's level of protein. The deadly chemical is soon found in the products of other major dairy manufacturers. By November, the number of infants and young children affected by drinking contaminated milk reaches some 300,000 and there are more than 50,000 babies sickened and four confirmed dead. The scandal is hushed up by Sanlu executives and government officials and only goes public after the Beijing Olympic Games are over, with the first government acknowledgement of the scandal on 22 September.

8 August: the Opening Ceremony of the XXIXth Olympiad begins in Beijing at 8:08pm. The Beijing Olympics, widely deemed a success, costs US$44 billion.

27 September: a Chinese astronaut takes China's first space walk

15 September: Lehman Brothers files for bankruptcy, setting off a global financial crisis.

November: China announces a US$586 billion economic stimulus package.

8 December: the pro-democracy dissident Liu Xiaobo is detained for his role in drafting Charter 08. Initially signed by 300 people, the document calls for an end to one-party rule, the introduction of substantive democracy and full human rights for Chinese citizens. On 25 December 2009, Liu is sentenced to eleven years in prison.

2009

January: an anonymous Internet user uploads a spoof posting of 'Ten Legendary Beasts of Baidu' to the Wikipedia-like *Baidu Baike Encyclopaedia*. One of the beasts is the Grass Mud Horse (*caonima* 草泥马), a play on the words *cào nǐ mā* 肏你妈, literally 'fuck your mother'. The Grass Mud Horse – a creature with the appearance of an Alpaca – is said to roam the Mahler Gobi Desert (*malege bi* 妈了个逼 – that is 'curse your mother's cunt') and its existence is supposed to be endangered by ravenous River Crabs (*hexie* 河蟹), creatures whose name is a pun on the word 'harmonize' (*hexie* 和谐), a term that in Chinese Internet slang means to censor or delete unacceptable online content.

13 January: during a visit to Beijing Zbigniew Brzezinski proposes the creation of a 'Group of Two' (G2) to facilitate talks between the US and China on global issues.

8 March: five Chinese vessels perform aggressive maneuvers against a US surveillance ship – the USNS *Impeccable* – in the South China Sea, marking the start of China's growing assertion of what it regards as its regional territorial rights.

30 March: China's State Administration of Radio, Film and Television (SARFT), which controls media content, issues a list of thirty-one new regulations under the heading 'Concerning the Tightening of Management Over Internet Audio-visual Content'. Aimed at blocking online spoofs such as Grass Mud Horse, this list is an extension of similar regulations first introduced in 2006. The 2006 regulations coincided with the media publicity surrounding video blogger Hu Ge's 'Murder by *mantou*', a satirical take on the veteran filmmaker Chen Kaige's martial arts epic, *The Promise*. Hu Ge's video enjoyed even greater publicity when the infuriated Chen threatened legal action.

June: in Chongqing, Party Secretary Bo Xilai launches his 'Sing Red, Strike Black' campaign. The campaign gains momentum over the following weeks and months, helping turn Bo into China's leading political celebrity.

This month, China's Ministry of Industry and Information Technology mandates that, starting from 1 July 2009, all personal computers sold on the mainland must have content-control software pre-installed, known as the Green Dam Youth Escort. Following a negative reception from Chinese Internet users, on 30 June the mandatory installation of Green Dam is delayed indefinitely.

5 July: ethnic violence in China's western autonomous region of Xinjiang kills around 200 people and injures 1,700. The government blames the violence on exiled Uyghur leader Rebiya Kadeer, a charge she denies. Following the riots, the authorities shut down Internet access and long-distance telephony in Xinjiang for over six months.

30 July: China expresses 'strong dissatisfaction' over Australia's granting of a visa to the Uyghur human rights advocate Rebiya Kadeer to attend the Melbourne International Film Festival. This and other issues lead to then Australian ambassador to the People's Republic Geoff Raby dubbing 2009 the *annus horribilis* of the Australia-China relationship.

1 October: a grand National Day Parade is held on Beijing's Tiananmen Square to celebrate the sixtieth anniversary of the founding of the People's Republic of China. The parade includes a vast array of military hardware and around 10,000 soldiers.

18 December: at the 2009 Copenhagen talks on climate change, China's strident criticism of historical Western behaviour with regard to the environment and assertion of its own interests over those of the globe attract international media attention and spark new tensions in China's relations with developed nations. Nevertheless, following the summit, US President Obama announces that the US, China and other nations have signed a non-binding treaty setting a mitigation target to limit global warming to no more than two degrees Celsius.

2010

8 January: Chongqing's judiciary sentences the Beijing-based lawyer Li Zhuang to thirty months in gaol for allegedly encouraging his client, Chongqing crime boss Gong Gangmo, to perjure himself. The charges against Li were known to be false, leading other prominent Chinese lawyers to publicize their colleague's plight.

12 January: Google, claiming that China-based hackers have interfered with the Gmail accounts of dissidents, announces it will no longer censor search results on its mainland-based portal Google.cn and that its China operations may be closed down. Eventually in March, Google closes its offices in Beijing, and re-routes mainland Chinese users to its Hong Kong site.

21-24 January: US Secretary of State Hillary Clinton's support for Google's anti-censorship stance leads to an angry rebuttal from the *People's Daily*.

30 January: following the US government's decision to sell *Black Hawk* helicopters and PAC-3 missiles to Taiwan, China announces suspension of military exchanges with the US along with other retaliatory measures.

19 February: US President Barack Obama meets with the Dalai Lama; China expresses formal disapproval.

March-April: China angers South Korea and worries the international community by its refusal to criticize North Korea's sinking of the South Korean Navy corvette *Cheonan* on 26 March.

29 March: a Shanghai court sentences Australian national and executive of mining giant Rio Tinto, Stern Hu, to ten years in gaol for bribery and the theft of commercial secrets. Three other defendants also received prison sentences.

13 April: hundreds of people are killed when a 7.1 magnitude earthquake strikes China's north-western Qinghai province with the epicentre near the Tibetan region of Yulshul (Yushu).

May: an ethnic Mongolian herder named Merger is run over and killed on 10 May while trying to stop a convoy of coal trucks from driving through grazing pastures. His death sparks a major riot in Inner Mongolia.

1 May – 31 October 2010: with the theme 'Better City – Better Life', Shanghai stages Expo 2010, attracting the largest-ever number of participating countries and a record seventy-three million visitors.

8 July: the head of Chongqing's Bureau of Justice and former Deputy Police Chief, Wen Qiang, accused of having accepted bribes in excess of one hundred million *yuan*, is executed by lethal injection as part of Chongqing's 'Strike Black' campaign.

29 August: Fang Zhouzi, 'the science cop', China's most famous academic fraud-buster, is attacked and wounded near his home in Beijing. The two assailants had been hired by Xiao Chuanguo, a Professor of Urology at Wuhan's Huazhong Science and Technology University, whom Fang had exposed as an academic fraud. (In October 2010, Xiao is charged with 'causing a disturbance' and sentenced to a gaol term of five and a-half months.)

7 **September:** a Chinese fishing trawler collides with a Japanese Coast Guard vessel in disputed waters, exacerbating diplomatic tensions between China and Japan. The captain is eventually released by Japan on 24 September and he returns to China in a blaze of publicity.

14 September: the celebrity Taoist priest, Li Yi, a TV personality claiming extraordinary powers, is exposed as a fraud. Media stars among his some 30,000 disciples scramble to dissociate themselves from him.

1 October: twenty-three Communist Party elders publish an open letter online demanding the abolition of the 'invisible black hand' of censorship and respect for freedoms granted in the 1982 constitution of China.

8 October: Liu Xiaobo is awarded the 2010 Nobel Peace Prize, leading the Chinese government to unleash a media campaign denouncing the award, the Nobel Committee, Liu's supporters in the West and the country of Norway.

16 October: the twenty-two-year-old drunk driver Li Qiming hits two female university students, killing one and injuring the other. When confronted by security guards, he allegedly yells: 'Charge me if you dare. My dad is Li Gang!' The meme 'My dad is Li Gang!' goes viral on the Internet. On 30 January 2011, Li is sentenced to six years in gaol.

20 October: a traffic accident turns into a homicide when twenty-one-year-old driver and music student Yao Jiaxin purposely kills a woman he had just injured in an accident to prevent her from reporting his licence plate number to the police. Yao is later sentenced to death and executed on 7 June 2011.

9 December: a private group, with tacit official support, establishes the Confucius Peace Prize in retaliation for Liu Xiaobo being awarded the Nobel laureate. The first Confucius Peace Prize is awarded to Lien Chan, former Vice-president of the Republic of China on Taiwan. (In March 2005, Lien, as Chairman of the Nationalist Party in Taiwan, visits the mainland as part of the so-called Pan-Blue visits, which are hailed at the time as the highest level of exchange between the Communists and the Nationalists since 1945.) Lien's office declines the prize, however, noting that he has never heard of the award.

10 December: Liu Xiaobo receives the Nobel Peace Prize *in absentia*. The award ceremony in Oslo is boycotted by China and eighteen other countries: Afghanistan, Colombia, Cuba, Egypt, Iran, Iraq, Kazakhstan, Morocco, Pakistan, the Philippines, Russia, Saudi Arabia, Serbia, Sudan, Tunisia, Ukraine, Venezuela and Vietnam. Liu's wife, Liu Xia, and other members of his family are prevented from travelling to Oslo to accept the prize on his behalf. Liu Xia is placed under house arrest in October after informing her husband of his award.

2011

January: Ma Ying-jeou, President of the Republic of China in Taiwan, hails the coming of a new golden age. He proposes that the Taiwan-based government espouse 'Cultural China, Political Survival' (*wenhua Zhonghua, zhengzhi pian'an* 文化中华，政治偏安).

11 January: a 9.5-metre bronze statue of Confucius is installed outside the National Museum of China on Tiananmen Square. A *People's Daily* poll released a week later indicates that sixty-two percent of some 820,000 respondents disapprove of the statue. (On 21 April the statue is removed without notice or explanation.)

13 February: China overtakes Japan as the world's second-largest economy.

17 February: online dissidents (apparently based outside China), inspired by the Arab Spring, call for weekly pro-democracy 'Jasmine' rallies in China. The Chinese government responds with an immediate and harsh crackdown on rights activists and lawyers that continues for several months. No demonstrations take place.

25 February: China's Railways Minister, Liu Zhijun, is dismissed on corruption charges.

5 March: Beijing announces an annual budget for 'stability maintenance' of 624.4 billion *yuan*, generating heated debate on the Chinese Internet.

14 March: the Twelfth Five-year Plan is approved by the National People's Congress. The plan, covering the period 2011-2015, explicitly aims at addressing rising inequality and creating an environment for more sustainable growth, as well as encouraging the growth of the country's domestic consumer market.

3 April: prominent artist and provocateur Ai Weiwei is intercepted by police at Beijing Capital Airport as he is about to board a plane for Hong Kong. He is detained without charge for nearly three months. On his release, he is forbidden from travelling and accused of tax evasion.

4 May: the Mayor of New York, Michael Bloomberg, officially launches Ai Weiwei's outdoor installation, 'Circle of Animals/Zodiac Heads', at Central Park's Grand Army Plaza. Ai, still under detention in China, is represented in New York by several cultural figures from New York who read quotations from his interviews and blog posts.

30 June: Henry Kissinger, visiting Chongqing to meet with executives from some 500 US companies based there, takes part in one of Bo Xilai's 'Sing Red' mass rallies. He heaps praise on the achievements of Chongqing.

During July: Bo Xilai, Party Secretary of Chongqing and Wang Yang, Party Secretary of Guangdong, present opposing views about the best way forward for China. Whereas Bo calls for 'the realisation of common prosperity', Wang claims that economic growth is more important, stating that 'division of the cake is not a priority right now. The priority is to make the cake bigger.' Their differences are publicized in the print media and online as 'the cake debate'.

16 July: US President Obama meets with the Dalai Lama again, eliciting strong disapproval from the Chinese government. Photos circulate online of the Dalai Lama leaving the White House through the back door, walking past rubbish bins.

23 July: the collision of two high-speed trains in Wenzhou, Zhejiang province becomes the most talked-about topic in China via micro-blogging. Complaints and criticism of the government's handling of the tragedy, which resulted in thirty-five deaths, circulate freely for several days before censors shut it down.

27 July: China and South Korea hold their first 'strategic defence dialogue'. China pledges to deepen bilateral military exchanges and cooperation.

10 August: China launches its first aircraft carrier on a test voyage. The ship is a refitted former Soviet carrier, the *Varyag*, which China purchased from the Ukraine in 1998.

14 August: in what is described as a 'white collar demonstration', tens of thousands of protesters join a march against the building of a chemical plant in Dalian in Liaoning province. The plant had been designed to produce paraxylene or PX.

10 October: anniversary of the centenary of the Wuchang Uprising and the Xinhai Revolution that saw the end of dynastic rule. Chinese President Hu Jintao uses the term 'revival' (*fuxing* 复兴) twenty-three times in his commemorative speech, made the previous evening in the Great Hall of the People on Tiananmen Square.

21 October: a two-year-old girl named Yueyue dies in a hospital in Foshan, Guangdong province, after being run over by two vans and ignored by eighteen passers-by. The entire incident, caught on a surveillance camera, goes viral on the Chinese Internet and incites a vigorous debate on the state of Chinese morality.

17 November: US President Barack Obama and Australian Prime Minister Julia Gillard formally announce an enhancement of US-Australia defence cooperation through the accommodation and rotation of US marines in Darwin and the greater use of RAAF bases in the Northern Territory for US aircraft.

19 November: At the sixth meeting of the ASEAN-led East Asia Summit in Bali, Chinese Premier Wen Jiabao meets with seventeen Asian leaders to discuss the South China Sea and broader related questions of maritime security.

December: A local protest against corrupt officials who had seized and illegally sold land in Wukan, Guangdong province, grows into one of the country's largest mass incidents. Following the death on 10 December of a leader of the outcry, Xue Jinbo, in police custody the protest escalates. The provincial government intervenes and allows village leaders to represent themselves in local government.

2012

3-4 February: Premier Wen Jiabao visits Guangdong province, re-enacting Deng Xiaoping's famous Tour of the South of February 1992. He reprises and endorses Deng's 1992 pronouncements on the need for continued reform.

6 February: Wang Lijun, former police chief of Chongqing, seeks refuge in the US Consulate in Chengdu, Sichuan province. It is not granted, and Wang emerges from the Consulate only to be whisked off into what is officially called 'vacation-style therapy'. This series of events marks the beginning of the end of Bo Xilai.

26 February: The World Bank presents China with a report, entitled *China 2030*, on the state of the Chinese economy. It offers a stark choice: transition to a freer commercial system or face economic decline. Some leftists and neo-Maoists denounce the report as the work of spies and traitors.

5 March: on the fiftieth anniversary of the death of Lei Feng, a legendary PLA soldier devoted to selfless service to the people, a propaganda campaign is launched to encourage people to 'learn from Lei Feng'. The campaign is met with scorn and derision on the Chinese Internet.

15 March: Chongqing Party Secretary Bo Xilai is dismissed from all official positions and put under official investigation. On 10 April, it is announced that Bo's wife, Gu Kailai, is under investigation for the death of an English business associate, Neil Heywood.

3 April: to mark the year since his detention at Beijing Capital Airport, Ai Weiwei installs webcams in his compound in a mocking gesture of self-surveillance. His broadcasts on weiweicam.com are banned by the authorities within days.

6 April: the neo-Maoist website Utopia is shut down for 'maintenance' after the site's sister bookshop is visited by the authorities. In the subsequent weeks, Utopia contributors circulate messages of support for Bo Xilai on microblogs. In early May, an open letter purporting to be from Utopia is sent to the media and websites outside of China. The letter calls the Bo and Wang affairs the 'most significant case of political injustice since Opening and Reform began [in 1978]'.

22 April: the blind lawyer-activist Chen Guangcheng escapes house arrest in Shandong and seeks refuge in the US Embassy in Beijing. On 2 May, Chen leaves the US Embassy to undergo medical treatment amid great controversy. On 19 May, Chen, his wife, and their two children leave Beijing, arriving the same day in New York City.

May: the *Guide to Surviving in China* (*Zhongguo jiusheng shouce* 中国救生手册), a Chinese-language iPhone app devoted to food safety issues and alerts, is released.

To commemorate the seventieth anniversary of Mao Zedong's landmark 1942 'Yan'an Talks on Literature and Art', the Ministry of Culture announces a month of celebrations.

Mao's 'Yan'an Talks' still inform China's official cultural policy. A leading state publishing house produces a version of the text written out by some of the country's most prominent authors.

12 May: the seven-part TV series *A Bite of China* (*Shejianshangde Zhongguo* 舌尖上的中国) on the country's culinary traditions is released by CCTV to rapturous national acclaim.

15 May: when meeting with Chinese leaders in Beijing, the Australian Foreign Minister, Bob Carr, is told that there is considerable official displeasure about US-Australia defence cooperation. It is decried as a Cold War-era strategic move. Carr is also told that Chinese-Australians who were originally citizens of the People's Republic are treated as Chinese citizens when accused of breaking the law.

17 May: veteran Party members address a letter to President Hu Jintao calling for the dismissal of the Politburo Standing Committee member Zhou Yongkang, who they claim is a supporter of Bo Xilai.

24 May: in response to widespread commentary and disgust with high-level corruption, including officials smuggling large sums of money out of the country (often followed by their children), the Communist Party's Central Disciplinary Inspection Commission announces that it will institute provincial 'flight-prevention co-ordinating mechanisms' and boost 'passport management'.

29 May: the chief executive of the online security firm Kaspersky Lab, Eugene Kaspersky, warns that the US and Australia face increasing cyber-threats from China, warning that most cyber-attacks 'come from China and most criminal malware is written in Chinese'.

16 June: China's first female astronaut, Liu Yang, is launched into orbit aboard the Shenzhou-9 spacecraft. On the Chinese Internet, she is compared to another Chinese woman, Feng Jianmei, who was forced to abort her seven-month old fetus in early June after she failed to pay a 40,000 *yuan* fine; widely reproduced photos of her lying next to the dead fetus cause outrage.

29 June: Bloomberg publishes a report on the complex skein of financial dealings, business connections and properties of relatives of Vice-president Xi Jinping.

1 July: the new Chief Executive of Hong Kong, Leung Chun-ying (C.Y. Leung), makes his inaugural speech in Standard Chinese, and not Cantonese, the majority language of the former British crown colony. The Chinese President Hu Jintao is in an audience assembled also to celebrate the fifteenth anniversary of 'the handover' of Hong Kong to Chinese control on 30 June 1997.

PEOPLE AND PERSONALITIES

The following is a list of people who feature in the pages of this book, listed alphabetically.

Ai Weiwei 艾未未 (b.1957): internationally acclaimed artist and outspoken political activist whose disappearance in March 2011 led to an international uproar. Although subsequently released he was accused of various crimes and kept under continuing house surveillance. In June 2012, he was released from bail conditions although prevented from travelling overseas as a range of nebulous charges against him remained pending. He continued to criticise the authorities.

Ross Babbage (b.1949): strategic policy analyst promoting greater Australian military defence preparedness in the Asia Pacific.

Bo Xilai 薄熙来 (b.1949): former Communist Party Secretary of Chongqing and advocate of economic redistribution in the 'cake debate'. Author of the 'Sing Red, Strike Black' campaign Bo was stripped of his posts in March 2012 and put under investigation on suspicion of breaking Party discipline and state law; his wife Gu Kailai was detained over the death of an English businessman, Neil Heywood.

Cai Fang 蔡昉 (b.1956): economic demographer and scholar-analyst of demographic transition who has forecast an end to surplus labour in China.

Charles Chao 曹国伟 (b.1965): CEO of Sina, who together with the CEO of Baidu sang 'red songs' at a commemorative event for the ninetieth anniversary of the founding of the Chinese Communist Party in Beijing in 2011.

Chen Guangbiao 陈光标 (b.1969): President of Jiangsu Huangpu Recycling Resources Company best known for his philanthropic activities, including donations to low income families in Taiwan; Chen's charitable activities have been questioned, with some Internet commentators alleging fraud.

Chen Guangcheng 陈光诚 (b.1979): blind civil rights activist who escaped from house arrest in Linyi, Shandong province to the US Embassy in Beijing. In late May 2012, Chen was allowed to leave China to study law in New York.

Dalai Lama (b.1935): spiritual leader of Tibetan Buddhism, secular head of the Tibetan political administration in exile and a figure regarded by the Chinese party-state as a dangerous 'splittist' whose activities threaten the territorial integrity of the People's Republic.

Deng Xiaoping 邓小平 (1904-1997): past General-Secretary of the Chinese Communist Party and the main author of China's policy of an 'open door' to the outside world and economic reform.

Fang Binxing 方滨兴 (b.1960): computer programmer and professor who developed the Great Firewall of China.

Fang Zhouzi 方舟子 (b.1967): the pseudonym of Fang Shimin, a writer frequently called the 'science cop' for his exposure of academic fraud, known in 2011 for a high profile dispute with the Shanghai-based writer Han Han.

Gao Zhisheng 高智晟 (b.1966): human rights lawyer under police surveillance for defending members of religious groups. An open critic of the Communist Party, imprisoned in Xinjiang.

Gu Kailai 谷开来 (b.1958, aka Bo-Gu Horus Kailai): successful attorney and wife of Bo Xilai. In early 2012, Gu was put under investigation in relation to the suspicious death of the English businessman Neil Heywood in Chongqing.

Guo Meimei 郭美美/郭美玲 (b.1991): a twenty-year-old woman who gained celebrity by flaunting extreme wealth online while claiming to work for the Red Cross Society of China.

Han Han 韩寒 (b.1982): celebrity blogger, best-selling author and race car driver named person of the year by several Chinese media organizations.

He Guangping 何广平 (b.1954): Deputy Director of the Public Security Bureau of Guangdong province.

Hu Xijin 胡锡进 (b.1960): Editor of *The Global Times*, a tabloid under the *People's Daily* that aggressively supports the prevailing Party line.

Hu Jintao 胡锦涛 (b.1942): Communist Youth League leader who as President of the People's Republic of China and General Secretary of the Chinese Communist Party (2003-2012) articulated policies related to 'scientific development' and the 'harmonious society'.

Hu Muying 胡木英 (b.1941): leader of the Children of Yan'an Fellowship, descendants of the founding Party leadership and critics of contemporary conditions under reform.

Huang Qifan 黄奇帆 (b.1952): Mayor and Deputy Party Secretary of Chongqing and former Director of Shanghai's Economic Committee.

Jiang Zemin 江泽民 (b.1926): past President of China and former General Secretary of the Party; previously Party Secretary and Mayor of Shanghai.

Steve Jobs (1955–2011): founder and CEO of Apple, whose death was mourned in China and whose achievements were celebrated by Chinese business people and government officials, including Wen Jiabao.

Rebiya Kadeer (b.1948): businesswoman turned human rights advocate. The figurehead of the Uyghur self-determination movement abroad, she is regarded by the Chinese government as a leading 'splittist'.

Kawamura Takashi 河村たかし (b.1948): Mayor of Nagasaki who, in February 2012, made statements denying the extent of the Nanjing Massacre to a visiting Chinese delegation leading to a suspension of exchanges between Nagasaki and Nanjing.

Henry Kissinger (b.1923): American business consultant, political scientist, former US Secretary of State and policy analyst who negotiated the 1970s rapprochement between the US and China.

Li Gang 李刚 (b.1963): Deputy Police Chief of Baoding, Hebei province whose son Li Qiming 李启铭 (b.1988) flagrantly shouted his name after hitting two girls while driving a car.

Li Keqiang 李克强 (b.1955): member of the Communist Youth League and Politburo member and presumed successor to Wen Jiabao as China's Premier.

Robin Li 李彦宏 (b.1968): CEO of Baidu who together with the CEO of Sina sang 'red songs' at a commemorative event for the ninetieth anniversary of the founding of the Chinese Communist Party in Beijing in 2011.

Li Yi 李一 (b.1969): contemporary Taoist priest and a Vice-president of the National Taoist Association who popularized a Taoist retreat in Chongqing province.

Li Zhuang 李庄 (b.1961): lawyer gaoled for defending individuals charged in Chongqing's 'Strike Black' crime crackdown.

Lien Chan 連戰 (b.1936): former Vice-president of Taiwan and past Chairman of the Nationalist Party and recipient of the Confucius Peace Prize.

Liu Xiaobo 刘晓波 (b.1955): academic, writer, human rights activist and winner of the 2010 Nobel Peace Prize gaoled and sentenced in 2009 for 'subverting state power'. His wife Liu Xia 刘霞, who has not been accused of any crime, is kept in a state of illegal home detention.

Liu Zhijun 刘志军 (b.1953): former Minister of Railways sacked for corruption associated with the construction of China's high-speed rail system.

Liu Zhiqin 刘志勤: Chief of Zurich Bank in Beijing who first proposed the Confucius Peace Prize.

Ma Ying-jeou 馬英九 (b.1950): President of the Republic of China (Taiwan), and the Chairman of the Nationalist Party, elected in 2008 and re-elected in 2012 with the stated aim of improving relations with the mainland. In early 2011, when marking the centennial year of the 1911 Xinhai Revolution that led to the establishment of the Republic of China he proposed that the Taiwan-based Nationalist government espouse 'Cultural China, Political Survival'.

Mao Zedong 毛泽东 (1893-1976): founding member and Chairman of the Chinese Communist Party, first leader of the People's Republic of China in 1949. Mao initiated many policies including those that led to the Great Leap Forward and the Cultural Revolution. His contribution to the nation is officially deemed to have been seventy percent positive and thirty percent negative.

George E. Morrison 莫理循 (1862-1920): Australian-born correspondent in Beijing for *The Times* of London and advisor to the early Republican government. For many years in the Republican period Wangfujing in Beijing was known as 'Morrison Street'. An annual George E. Morrison Lecture on China is held at The Australian National University, Canberra.

Ni Yulan 倪玉兰 (b.1961): Beijing civil rights lawyer under government surveillance for defending individuals and families subject to housing eviction. Sentenced to gaol again in May 2012.

Barack Obama (b.1961): Forty-fourth President of the United States whose administration was said to have performed an 'Asian pivot' in late 2011 by refocusing US military attention to the Pacific and East Asia.

Evan Osnos (b.1976): staff writer and blogger of the American literary magazine *The New Yorker* working in China.

Pan Shiyi 潘石屹 (b.1963): real-estate magnate who initiated a successful microblog campaign to press the Chinese government to release air quality data.

Ran Yunfei 冉云飞 (b.1965): blogger, democracy activist and signatory to Charter 08 living in Chengdu, Sichuan province under house surveillance.

Kevin Rudd 陆克文 (b.1957): former Australian Prime Minister and also former Foreign Minister. He delivered the '*Zhengyou* Speech' at Peking University in April 2008.

Wang Lijun 王立军 (b.1955): former Chongqing chief of public security whose visit to the US consulate in Chendgu in February 2012 prompted an official investigation into the Chongqing leadership and contributed to the fall of the city's Party Secretary Bo Xilai in March 2012.

Wang Yang 汪洋 (b.1955): Communist Party Secretary of Guangdong province and proponent of continuing economic liberalization; provided the guiding metaphor for the 'cake debate'.

Wen Jiabao 温家宝 (b.1942): Premier of China and periodic advocate of political reform. Set to retire from office in 2013.

Wen Qiang 文强 (1956-2010): former head of the Chongqing Bureau of Justice, executed for bribery.

Hugh White (b.1953): policy analyst whose work has focused on constructive engagement between Australia, China and the US.

Wu Hao 伍皓 (b.1970): Deputy Director of the Propaganda Bureau of Yunnan province who put into practice openness in government communication.

Wu Weishan 吴为山 (b.1962): artist and sculptor of the controversial Confucius statue placed outside the National Museum of China on the eastern flank of Tiananmen Square.

Xi Jinping 习近平 (b.1953): Vice-president of the People's Republic of China and Politburo member presumed to succeed Hu Jintao as President of the People's Republic and General Secretary of the Chinese Communist Party during the 2012-2013 power transition.

Xu Jilin 许纪霖 (b.1557): a leading intellectual historian who has written about the dangers of China's aggressive 'statism'.

Yangjuan Quanyang 羊圈圈羊 (b.1992): Internet username of 杨咪, woman student Weibo user who broke the news of the Wenzhou train crash in July 2011.

Yao Jiaxin 药家鑫 (1989-2011): student at the Xi'an Conservatory of Music in Shaanxi province who drove into a pedestrian and then stabbed her to death when he saw she had survived; Yao was executed in June 2011.

Yu Dan 于丹 (b.1965): Beijing-based university professor whose books popularizing classical philosophy turned her into a celebrity author.

Yueyue 小悦悦 (2009-2011): two-year old girl run over by a van in a Foshan market in Guangdong province. Ignored by numerous passers-by she died some days later, prompting national debate.

Zhou Yongkang 周永康 (b.1942): Politburo Standing Committee member and head of the Central Political and Legislative Committee associated with draconian 'stability maintenance' policies.

CONTRIBUTORS

Geremie R. Barmé is an historian, cultural critic, filmmaker, translator and web-journal editor. He works on Chinese cultural and intellectual history from the early modern period (1600s) to the present. From 2006 to 2011, he held an Australian Research Council Federation Fellowship and, in 2010, he became the Founding Director of the Australian Centre on China in the World (CIW) at The Australian National University. He is the editor of the e-journal *China Heritage Quarterly* (www.chinaheritagequarterly.org). His most recent book is *The Forbidden City* (London: Profile Books and Harvard University Press, 2008, reprinted 2012), and he edited *Australia and China: A Joint Report on the Bilateral Relationship*, a collaborative project in English and Chinese by the Australian Centre on China in the World and The China Institutes of Contemporary International Relations, Beijing, published jointly in February 2012 (see: ciw.anu.edu.au/joint_report/).

Carolyn Cartier is an urban geographer and research designer working in social theory and comparative urban change. Her work focuses on the local conditions of urban development and the different ways that people, be they artists, the elderly or government officials, express their concerns about rapid transformations in urban life. She studied geography at the University of California, Berkeley and moved to Australia in 2009. Professor of Human Geography and China Studies in the China Research Centre at the University of Technology, Sydney, she is currently leading a project to understand how China combines multiple territories to form large cities, as well as working on a book about alternative art in the politics of Hong Kong's urban redevelopment. She is an Adjunct Director of the Australian Centre on China in the World.

Gloria Davies is a literary scholar, historian and translator. Her research covers a range of areas: Chinese intellectual and literary history from the 1890s to the present; comparative literature and critical theory; and studies of cultural flows in the digital age. Based at Monash University, she is an Adjunct Director of the Australian Centre on China in the World. Her book on contemporary Chinese thought, *Worrying about China* (Harvard University Press, 2007, reprinted 2009), is currently being translated into Chinese. Her most recent book is on China's most famous modern writer titled *Lu Xun's Revolution* (Harvard University Press, forthcoming 2013). She is currently completing a new book on the language of digital dissent in China. Her recent essays on Chinese ideas of the human and digital dissent appear in the journals *boundary 2* (2009, 2011) and *Social Text* (2011).

Jeremy Goldkorn is a publisher, blogger and entrepreneur based in Beijing. Since 2003, he has published Danwei (now at danwei.com), a daily record of events and news in the Chinese media and Internet. Born in Johannesburg, South Africa, Goldkorn has lived in Beijing since 1995, arriving there after having ridden a bicycle from Islamabad to Kathmandu via Xinjiang and Tibet. He has worked as an editor and publisher with several English and Chinese magazines, and in advertising. He now runs Danwei as a research firm and website full time. Danwei is an affiliate of the Australian Centre on China in the World.

Jane Golley is an economist focused on a range of Chinese transition and development issues. She began her career in the Asia Section of the Australian Commonwealth Treasury before undertaking her MPhil and DPhil in Economics at the University of Oxford. She returned to ANU's School of Economics in 2003, moved to the Crawford School of Economics and Government in 2008, and joined the Australian Centre on China in the World in 2011. She is presently working on various aspects of China's demographic change and economic performance, including rural-urban demographic transitions in economic growth and the economic implications of rising gender imbalances. She is currently the President of the Chinese Economic Society Australia (CESA).

Mark Harrison is a Senior Lecturer in Chinese Studies at the University of Tasmania. From 2002 to 2008, he was a research fellow at the Centre for the Study of Democracy at the University of Westminster in London, UK. He is the author of *Legitimacy, Meaning and Knowledge in the Making of Taiwanese Identity* (New York: Palgrave Macmillan, 2006) and co-editor of *The Margins of Becoming: Culture and Identity in Taiwan* (Wiesbaden: Harrassovitz, 2007) and author of a number of recent chapters and articles on Taiwan and China. He is currently the recipient of a University of Tasmania three-year Rising Star award for his project 'China's Futures'.

Benjamin Penny is Deputy Director of the Australian Centre on China in the World and Chair of the ANU China Institute. He studied at the universities of Sydney, Cambridge, Peking and at ANU. He was the first Executive Officer of the Herbert and Valmae Freilich Foundation, and held research fellowships at the Centre for Cross-Cultural Research and the Division of Pacific and Asian History at ANU. His research interests include religious and spiritual movements in modern and contemporary China, Falun Gong and the *qigong* boom, Medieval Religious Taoism and the history of the religions of the Australian Chinese. He is co-editor of *East Asian History* (www.eastasianhistory.org). His most recent publication is *The Religion of Falun Gong* (Chicago: University of Chicago Press, 2012).

Brendan Taylor is Head of the Strategic and Defence Studies Centre, Australian National University. He is a specialist on Korean Peninsula security issues, great power strategic relations in the Asia-Pacific, economic sanctions, and Asian security architecture. His publications have featured in such leading international journals as *International Affairs, Survival, Asian Security, Review of International Studies* and the *Australian Journal of International Affairs*. He is the author of *Sanctions as Grand Strategy*, which was recently published in the International Institute for Strategic Studies (IISS) Adelphi series, as well as *American Sanctions in the Asia Pacific* (London: Routledge, 2010). He is also the editor of *Australia as an Asia-Pacific Regional Power* (Routledge, 2007).

Luigi Tomba is a political scientist with the Australian Centre on China in the World. His work over the last two decades has focused mainly on social change, class formation and grassroots governance in urban China. His current research projects on neighbourhood politics, urban citizenship and the politics of land conversion focus on the southern region of Guangdong. He holds research grants from both the Australian Research Council and the German Research Foundation. Since 2005, he has been the co-editor of *The China Journal*, the leading international academic journal on contemporary Chinese affairs, now published with the University of Chicago Press, and the support of the Australian Centre on China in the World.

Susan Trevaskes is an Australian Research Council QEII Research Fellow at Griffith University, Australia. She is also an Adjunct Director with the Australian Centre on China in the World and is the Centre's Justice research stream leader. Her research examines political and social issues relating to criminal justice and she has published in both the areas of crime and punishment in China today. Her books include *Courts and Criminal Justice in Contemporary China* (Lexington Press, 2007), *Policing Serious Crime in China* (Routledge, 2010) and *The Death Penalty in Contemporary China* (Palgrave Macmillan, 2012).

INDEX OF INFORMATION WINDOWS

INDEX OF INFORMATION WINDOWS